All School Mathematics
Under One Cover

(A Handbook for Students and Parents)

by David L. Cooper and
Ovsey Dobronevsky

DOBROTECH CORPORATION
EDUCATION

New York

All School Mathematics Under One Cover

Authors: David L. Cooper and Ovsey Dobronevsky
Cover design: Eli Draliuk
Book design: Margarita Tsepenyuk

Published by Dobrotech, Inc.

ISBN 0-9708001-0-X

Printed in the United States
By Mennonite Publishing House
616 Walnut Avenue
Scottdale, PA 15683

CONTENTS

CHAPTER VII: STATISTICS

CHAPTER VIII: PROBABILITY

APPENDIX

Foreword

A lot of schoolchildren want to be good students. They understand that their future success will largely depend on the skills and knowledge that they acquire at school. Their parents are even more aware of this. Whenever possible, they give their children advice, and often provide specific help when needed. Practically all parents have gone through the same sort of school education that their children are experiencing. However, if they have never had the opportunity to apply a particular subject in their daily lives, they may have forgotten the critical information they need in order to assist their child. This is often the case with mathematics, a subject the schoolchild is confronted with every day throughout the school years.

The importance of mathematics in our technological age is hard to overestimate. The study of mathematics develops a child's ability to think logically, cultivates abstract reasoning, provides knowledge that can help to solve many real-life problems, and lays the foundation for learning other critical skills and knowledge.

School mathematics textbooks contain invaluable educational material, but they are often huge (some are more than 900 pages thick), frequently move back and forth between areas of mathematics that are not logically connected, and often build on skills learned in previous years without providing a basic review of those skills. It frequently happens that the schoolchild has difficulty relearning "forgotten" information covered in previous grades. And when the child turns to the parents for help with homework, they may not be able to help with a specific question or even find the information they need somewhere else.

The purpose of this book is to provide a concise, systematically arranged reference that, unlike most school textbooks, covers the essentials of all the major branches of school mathematics from beginning to end, all under one cover. It will help students in all grades to recall important mathematical definitions and formulas, to refresh essential mathematical concepts at any time, to complete their homework assignments, and to prepare for tests. Parents can use it to quickly review what they may have forgotten from their own school years in order to assist their children more effectively.

Each section of the book includes examples that should assist in solving specific problems. Questions that commonly arise are treated in the relevant sections, in language that is less technical than the formal definitions used to develop the topics. The book should be useful for children and parents throughout the school years.

A Word to Parents

Dear Parents:

Fate has determined that, for a significant part of your lives, you will play the role of teacher to your child. You teach him or her how to walk, talk, read, write, behave properly, and many other things. When children reach school age, their lives are divided in two: life in school and life outside of school. A significant portion of the latter is spent on schoolwork: homework, preparing for exams, and the like. The majority of parents take part in the activities of their children outside school. They supervise work on school assignments, help the child to complete homework, and answer questions related to the lessons. In this manner, many parents act as supplementary schoolteachers.

The following are some methodological recommendations, which should be followed when helping school-age children to learn mathematics:

1. The process of learning mathematics should be interesting and convincing to the child. The child should come to realize that knowledge of mathematics would prove helpful in the future. It is a good idea to give examples from your own experience that demonstrate the necessity of mathematics in daily life.
2. The pursuit of learning should be individualized; that is, it is necessary to take into consideration your child's own abilities and character. No schoolteacher will ever know your child's personality like you yourself know it. You should try to assist your child while keeping in mind his or her individual ways of taking in and remembering new information.

3. Every person has several types of memory: visual (based on seeing and remembering an image), aural (based on hearing and recalling a sound-image), motor (memory of motions), and associative (memory stimulated through associations). Observe your own child's preferred methods of memorization and try to make use of them as much as possible in teaching your child. For example, some people learn better if they write down information (visual and motor memory), others if they repeat it out loud (aural and motor memory), et cetera.
4. In order for information to be remembered for a long time, it is usually necessary to review that information numerous times.
5. Mathematics is an abstract science. For that reason, it is best to employ visual aids, analogies, and examples from life whenever possible. In a reference work such as this book, such examples cannot be provided for reasons of space. However, school textbooks are often full of concrete examples and a wealth of visual material.
6. When explaining how various mathematical operations work, emphasize methods of checking the results. This encourages the student to check his or her own work and develop a responsibility for the results obtained.
7. Parental guidance in school activities has two primary aspects: supervision and practical help. While you may not always be able to provide the latter, the former is always your responsibility. To better assist you in providing practical help, each chapter of this book includes a list of questions commonly asked by school children, answered in simple and accessible language.

1 CHAPTER

ARITHMETIC

Arithmetic is the science of numbers. It deals with the simplest properties of numbers and the rules of basic number operations.

1.1 Digits and Whole Numbers

A **digit** is a written sign that represents a number. The fact that our basic number system operates with ten basic digits (0, 1, 2, 3, 4, 5, 6, 7, 8, and 9) is connected with the fact that we have been counting with our fingers since ancient times (note that 'digits' can also mean 'fingers').

Any number which can be used to count a given set of objects (1, 2, 3…) is called a **natural number**. All the natural numbers plus the digit zero (0, 1, 2, 3…) are called **whole numbers**.

If the quantity of objects which must be counted is not larger than nine, then the nine basic digits are sufficient to represent the given quantity (5 apples, 9 boxes, etc.). If the quantity of objects is greater than nine, then a combination of the basic digits is used to represent the quantity. The value of a digit increases by ten each place one moves to the left.

For example: the number 55 consists of two digits, 5 and 5 again. The value of the left digit is ten times more than the value of the right digit; i.e. its value is 50.

Therefore, $55 = 50 + 5$

A number that consists of two digits is called a **two-digit number**. The number 375 (300+70+5) is a **three-digit number**.

1.1.1 The Names of Large Numbers

Each digit in a number has a value based on its place in the number. Notice that commas are used to separate digits into groups of three. This helps make large numbers easier to read.

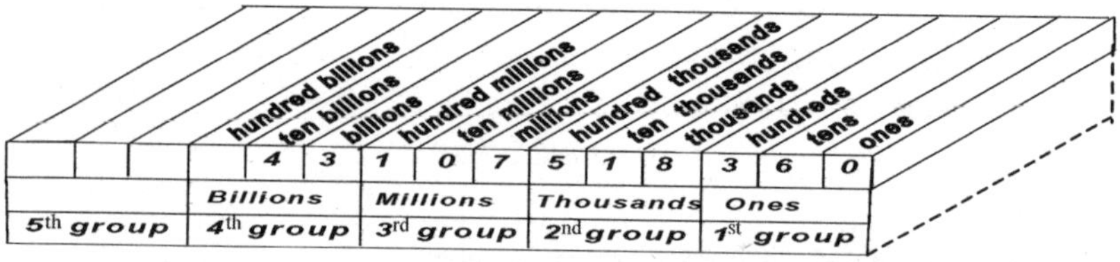

The number shown on the place-value chart is written:
43,107,518,360 and read:
forty-three billion, one hundred seven million, five hundred eighteen thousand, three hundred sixty.

1.1.2 Comparing Whole Numbers

In this operation, the following symbols are used:

Symbol	Example	Read
>	12>9	12 is greater than 9
<	5<7	5 is less than 7
=	3=3	3 equals 3

In order to compare numbers with an equal number of digits, compare the digits farthest to the left. The greater number has the larger digit.

Example: 33,024,117 and 29,912,688:

3 3 0 2 4 1 1 7
2 9 9 1 2 6 8 8

3>2, so 33,024,117 > 29,912,688

This equation is read: thirty-three million, twenty-four thousand, one hundred seventeen is greater than twenty-nine million, nine hundred twelve thousand, six hundred eighty-eight.

When comparing numbers where the leftmost digits are equal, it is necessary to compare the next digits to the right, and so on.

Example: 742,712 and 738,971:

7 **4** 2 7 1 2
7 **3** 8 9 7 1

7=7, but 4>3, so 738,971 < 742,712

This equation is read: Seven hundred thirty-eight thousand, nine hundred seventy-one is less than seven hundred forty-two thousand, seven hundred twelve.

Example: 823,690 and 821,929:

8 2 **3** 6 9 0
8 2 **1** 9 2 9

8=8, and 2=2, but 3>1, so

823,690 > 821,929.

This equation is read: Eight hundred twenty-three thousand, six hundred ninety is greater than eight hundred twenty-one thousand, nine hundred twenty-nine.

In order to compare numbers with an unequal amount of digits, count the digits in each number. The greater number has a greater quantity of digits.

Example: 8,110,016,942 and 988,512,770:

The first number has 10 digits, while the second has only nine. $9<10$

so: $988,512,770 < 8,110,016,942$

This equation is read: Nine hundred eighty-eight million, five hundred twelve thousand, seven hundred seventy is less than eight billion, one hundred ten million, sixteen thousand, nine hundred forty-two.

1.2 Arithmetic Operations with Whole Numbers

1.2.1 Addition

Addition is the operation of adding a number (or numbers) to another number.

The numbers, which are being added are called **items**. The result of addition is called the **sum**. The symbol of addition is **+** (the plus sign).

For example, in the equation 14+15=29, 14 and 15 are the items, and 29 is the sum.

Addition is usually performed in columns.

The process of addition:

Step 1: Add the ones

Step 2: Add the tens

Step 3: Add the hundreds
and so on…

If the sum of the numbers in a column is more than 9, then the extra amount is carried to the next column on the left.

Use the addition table:

1.2.2 The Addition Table

+	0		1		2		3		4		5		6		7		8		9	
	c		c		c		c		c		c		c		c		c		c	
0		0		1		2		3		4		5		6		7		8		9
1		1		2		3		4		5		6		7		8		9	1	0
2		2		3		4		5		6		7		8		9	1	0	1	1
3		3		4		5		6		7		8		9	1	0	1	1	1	2
4		4		5		6		7		8		9	1	0	1	1	1	2	1	3
5		5		6		7		8		9	1	0	1	1	1	2	1	3	1	4
6		6		7		8		9	1	0	1	1	1	2	1	3	1	4	1	5
7		7		8		9	1	0	1	1	1	2	1	3	1	4	1	5	1	6
8		8		9	1	0	1	1	1	2	1	3	1	4	1	5	1	6	1	7
9		9	1	0	1	1	1	2	1	3	1	4	1	5	1	6	1	7	1	8

c = *carried numbers*

Examples:

Solve 12,615 + 12,334 + 7,026

```
carried numbers  →  1   1
                    12,615
                    12,334
                  +  7,026     Add beginning with the ones
                  --------
                    31,975
```

Solve 64,492 + 19,868 + 3,871

```
carried numbers  →  12 21
                    64,492
                    19,868
                  +  3,871
                  --------
                    88,231
```

Solve 9,981 + 11,702 + 99,101

```
carried numbers → 21
                  9,981
                 11,702
              +  99,101
              ---------
                120,784
```

1.2.3 Properties of Addition

- The Commutative Property:

The order of the items does not change the sum.

$$\boxed{7+8=8+7}$$

- The Associative Property:

The way the addends are grouped does not change the sum.

$$\boxed{(2+5)+3=5+(2+3)}$$

- The Identity Property

The sum of any number and 0 equals the first number.

$$\boxed{7+0=7} \text{ and } \boxed{0+7=7}$$

1.3 Subtraction

Subtraction is the operation of reducing a number by another number.

The number which is diminished is called the **minuend**.The other number, the one subtracted, is called the **subtrahend**. The result of subtraction is called the **difference**. The symbol of subtraction is – (the minus sign).

For example, in the equation 26 – 12 = 14: 26 is the minuend, 12 is the subtrahend, and 14 is the difference.

Subtraction is usually performed in columns.

The process of subtraction:

Step 1: Subtract the ones
Step 2: Subtract the tens
Step 3: Subtract the hundreds
and so on…

If in any column the minuend is less than the subtrahend, we "borrow" from the next column to the left.

Examples:

Solve 1,327 – 671

$$\begin{array}{r} 1{,}327 \\ -671 \\ \hline 656 \end{array}$$

(7-1 = 6, write 6; 2<7, so borrow 1 from the next column, 12-7 = 5, write 5; 2<6, so borrow 1 again; 12-6 = 6, write 6)

Solve 18,000 – 9,756

$$\begin{array}{r} 18{,}000 \\ -9{,}756 \\ \hline 8{,}244 \end{array}$$

Solve 20,401 – 12,099

$$\begin{array}{r} 20{,}401 \\ -12{,}099 \\ \hline 8{,}302 \end{array}$$

Solve 17,111 – 16,999

$$\begin{array}{r} 17{,}111 \\ -16{,}999 \\ \hline 112 \end{array}$$

1.4 Multiplication

Multiplication is a form of rapid addition. The operation of multiplication is the same as adding a number to itself several times.

The signs of multiplication are x or · (the point).

$2 \cdot 4 = 8$ is the same as $2 + 2 + 2 + 2 = 8$
$2 \cdot 4 = 8$ is read: two times four equals eight, or two multiplied by four equals eight.

The number 2 is called the **multiplicator**. The number 4 is called the **factor**. The result **eight** is called the **product**. Often all the numbers involved in the multiplication are called **factors**. When multiplying, use the multiplication table.

1.4.1 The Multiplication Table

X	0		1		2		3		4		5		6		7		8		9	
	c		c		c		c		c		c		c		c		c		c	
0		0		0		0		0		0		0		0		0		0		0
1		0		1		2		3		4		5		6		7		8		9
2		0		2		4		6		8	1	0	1	2	1	4	1	6	1	8
3		0		3		6		9	1	2	1	5	1	8	2	1	2	4	2	7
4		0		4		8	1	2	1	6	2	0	2	4	2	8	3	2	3	6
5		0		5	1	0	1	5	2	0	2	5	3	0	3	5	4	0	4	5
6		0		6	1	2	1	8	2	4	3	0	3	6	4	2	4	8	5	4
7		0		7	1	4	2	1	2	8	3	5	4	2	4	9	5	6	6	3
8		0		8	1	6	2	4	3	2	4	0	4	8	5	6	6	4	7	2
9		0		9	1	8	2	7	3	6	4	5	5	4	6	3	7	2	8	1

c = carried number

Examples: Solve 26 x 134

Step 1: Multiply the ones

$$\begin{array}{r} \text{carried numbers} \rightarrow 2 \\ 26 \\ \times\ \underline{134} \\ 104 \end{array}$$

($4 \times 6 = 24$; write 4 and carry the 2; $4 \times 2 = 8$; $8 + 2 = 10$)

Step 2: Multiply the tens

$$\begin{array}{r} \text{carried numbers} \rightarrow 1 \\ 26 \\ \times\ \underline{134} \\ 104 \\ 780 \end{array}$$

Under the 4 write 0, then: ($3 \times 6 = 18$; write 8 and carry the 1; $3 \times 2 = 6$; $6 + 1 = 7$)

Step 3: Multiply the hundreds

$$\begin{array}{r} 26 \\ \underline{\times 134} \\ 104 \\ 780 \\ 2600 \end{array}$$

Under the 8 write 0, then: ($1 \times 6 = 6$; $1 \times 2 = 2$)

Step 4: Add everything together

$$\begin{array}{r} 26 \\ \underline{\times 134} \\ 104 \\ 780 \\ \underline{2{,}600} \\ 3{,}484 \end{array}$$

Result: $26 \times 134 = 3{,}484$

The product is read: Three thousand, four hundred eighty-four.

Example 2: Solve $1{,}256 \times 425$

$$\begin{array}{r} 1{,}256 \\ \times 425 \\ \hline 6{,}280 \\ 25{,}120 \\ +502{,}400 \\ \hline 533{,}800 \end{array}$$

Result: $1{,}256 \times 425 = 533{,}800$

The product is read: five hundred thirty-three thousand, eight hundred.

Example 3: Solve $2{,}001 \times 1{,}010$

$$\begin{array}{r} 2{,}001 \\ \times 1{,}010 \\ \hline 0{,}000 \\ 20{,}010 \\ 000{,}000 \\ +2{,}001{,}000 \\ \hline 2{,}021{,}010 \end{array}$$

Result: $2{,}001 \times 1{,}010 = 2{,}021{,}010$

The product is read: Two million, twenty-one thousand, ten.

1.4.2 Properties of Multiplication

- The Commutative Property

$$\boxed{7 \times 8 = 8 \times 7}$$

- The Associative Property

The way the factors are grouped does not change the product.

$$\boxed{7 \times (4 \times 5) = (4 \times 7) \times 5}$$

- The Distributive Property

$$\boxed{2 \times (3 + 4) = (2 \times 3) + (2 \times 4)}$$

- The Identity Property

The product of any factor and 1 equals the factor.

$$\boxed{45 \times 1 = 45}$$

- The Zero Property

The product of any factor and 0 equals 0.

$$\boxed{45 \times 0 = 0}$$

1.4.3 Common Factors

A common factor is a factor of two or more numbers.

Examples:

3 is a common factor of 6 and 9
$(3 \times 2 = 6; 3 \times 3 = 9)$

5 is a common factor of 10, 15, and 20

$(5 \times 2 = 10; 5 \times 3 = 15; 5 \times 4 = 20)$

1.4.4 Greatest Common Factor (GCF)

The greatest common factor of a set of numbers is the greatest number in the list of common factors.

Example:

Find the greatest common factor of 24 and 36.

Step 1: List all the factors of 24:

$1 \times 24 = 24$; $2 \times 12 = 24$; $3 \times 8 = 24$; $4 \times 6 = 24$

Factors of 24: 1, 2, 3, 4, 6, 8, 12

Step 2: List all the factors of 36:

$1 \times 36 = 36$; $2 \times 18 = 36$; $3 \times 12 = 36$; $4 \times 9 = 36$; $6 \times 6 = 36$

Factors of 36: 1, 2, 3, 4, 6, 9, 12, 18

Common factors: 1, 2, 3, 4, 6, 12

The greatest common factor of 24 and 36 is 12.

1.4.5 Common Multiples

A common multiple of two or more numbers is a number that is a multiple of each of them.

Example:

Find the common multiples of 6 and 12.
Step 1: List the multiples of 6:

0, 6, **12**, 18, **24**, 30, **36**, 42, **48**, 54, **60**, 66, **72**...

Step 2: List the multiples of 12:

0, **12**, **24**, **36**, **48**, **60**, **72**...

Step 3: Compare multiples and find the common numbers:

0, 12, 24, 36, 48, 60, 72...

Result: Some common multiples of 6 and 12

are 0, 12, 24, 36, 48...

1.4.6 Least Common Multiple (LCM)

The least common multiple (LCM) is the least nonzero number of the common multiples.

Example:

Find the least common multiple (LCM) of 4, 8, and 12.

Step 1: Multiples of 4:

0, 4, 8, 12, 16, 20, **24**, 28, 32, 36, 40, 44, **48**…

Step 2: Multiples of 8:

0, 8, 16, **24**, 32, 40, **48**, 56, 64…

Step 3: Multiples of 12:

0, 12, **24**, 36, **48**, 60, 72…

Step 4: Finding the LCM of 4, 8, 12:

0, **24**, 48…

The least common multiple is 24.

1.5 Division

Division is an operation which determines how many times a given number goes into another number, that is, how many times the given number can be subtracted from another number with a result greater than or equal to zero.

The signs of division are $\div$, /, —, and $\overline{)\quad}$.

For example, $8 \div 2 = 4$; $8/2 = 4$; $\begin{array}{r} 4 \\ 2\overline{)8} \end{array}$

The number 8 is called the **dividend**. The number 2 is called the **divisor**. The result, 4, is the **quotient**.

Examples:

1) Solve $225 \div 15$

Step 1: Compare the numbers 225 and 15. In the number 225 we take as many figures, left to right, as we need to form a number equal to or greater than 15. 22 is such a number. 15 goes into that number one time, so we write 1 above it:

$$\begin{array}{r} 1 \\ 15\overline{)225} \\ -15 \\ \hline 7 \end{array}$$

Step 2: Multiply: $1 \times 15 = 15$; and subtract: $22 - 15 = 7$

Step 3: Write the next digit of 225 beside the difference (7):

$$\begin{array}{r} 1 \\ 15\overline{)225} \\ -15\downarrow \\ \hline 75 \end{array}$$

Step 4: 15 goes into 75 five times, so we write 5 above it:

$$\begin{array}{r} 15 \\ 15\overline{)225} \\ -15\downarrow \\ \hline 75 \end{array}$$

(To determine how many times 15 goes into 75, subtract 15 from 75 as many times as you can and get a result greater than or equal to 0. The number of times you can subtract is what you write above).

Step 5: We write that product under 75 and subtract:

$$75 - 75 = 0.$$

$$
\begin{array}{r}
15 \\
15\overline{)225} \\
-15 \\
\hline
75 \\
-75 \\
\hline
0
\end{array}
$$

Since the result is 0, and we have used all the digits of 225, the operation is complete.

The result 15 is written on top.

Check your work: $15 \times 15 = 225$.

2) Solve $267 \div 12$

Step 1: Compare the numbers 267 and 12. In the number 267 we take as many digits, left to right, as we need to form a number equal to or greater than 12. 26 is such a number. 12 goes into 26 twice, so we write 2 above it.

$$
\begin{array}{r}
2 \\
12\overline{)267}
\end{array}
$$

Step 2: Multiply: $2 \times 12 = 24$; and subtract: 26-24=2

$$
\begin{array}{r}
2 \\
12\ \overline{267} \\
-24 \\
\hline
2
\end{array}
$$

Step 3: Write the next digit of 267, which is 7, next to the difference 2.

$$\begin{array}{r} 2 \\ 12\overline{)267} \\ -24\downarrow \\ \hline 27 \end{array}$$

Step 4: 12 goes into 27 two times. Write 2 above.

$$\begin{array}{r} 22 \\ 12\overline{)267} \\ -24\downarrow \\ \hline 27 \end{array}$$

Step 5: Multiply: $2 \times 12 = 24$.

We write that product under 27 and subtract: $27 - 24 = 3$. Since 3 is less than 12 the operation is complete.

$$\begin{array}{r} 22 \\ 12\overline{)267} \\ -24 \\ \hline 27 \\ -24 \\ \hline 3 \end{array}$$

Result: twenty-two and a remainder of 3.

$$\begin{array}{r} 22R3 \\ 12\overline{)267} \end{array}$$

Check: $22 \times 12 + 3 = 267$ 3 is the remainder

1.5.1 Divisibility Rules. Even and Odd Numbers

A number is divisible by another number when there is no remainder.

A number is **divisible by two** when the rightmost digit of that number is 0, or when it can be divided by 2 without a remainder. ***Such numbers are called even numbers. All other numbers are called odd numbers***

Examples:

181**4** is an even number because 4 ÷ 2 = 2

72**0** is an even number because the rightmost digit is 0

1**9** is an odd number because 9 ÷ 2 = 4 with a remainder of 1

A number is **divisible by 4** when the two rightmost digits of a number are 00 or can be divided by 4 without a remainder.

Examples:

6**00** is divisible by four because the two rightmost digits are 00.
600 ÷ 4 = 150.

5**84:** 84 ÷ 4 = 21, and 584 ÷ 4 = 146

A number is **divisible by three** if the sum of its digits can be divided by 3 with no remainder.

Example: 26,835: The sum of 2 + 6 + 8 + 3 + 5 = 24
24 ÷ 3 = 8
26,835 ÷ 3 = 8,945

A number is **divisible by 5** if the rightmost digit is 0 or 5.

Examples:

12**0** ÷ 5 = 24

14**5** ÷ 5 = 29

A number is **divisible by 25** if the two rightmost digits are 00, 25, 50, or 75.

Examples:

200 $200 \div 25 = 8$

425 $425 \div 25 = 17$

150 $150 \div 25 = 6$

375 $375 \div 25 = 15$

A number is **divisible by 6** if it is divisible by both 2 and 3.

Examples:

162 $2 \div 2 = 1$ (divisible by 2)

$1 + 6 + 2 = 9$; $9 \div 3 = 3$ (divisible by 3)

$162 \div 6 = 27$

1.6 Powers

A shorter way to write expressions of the following type:

$4 \times 4 \times 4 \times 4 = 256$ ***or*** $12 \times 12 \times 12 \times 12 \times 12 = 248{,}832$

is to use a power:

$$4 \times 4 \times 4 \times 4 = 4^4 = 256$$
$$12 \times 12 \times 12 \times 12 \times 12 = 12^5 = 248{,}832$$

Power expressions use the exponent to show how many times the base is used as a factor.

Examples:

$$6^2 = 6 \times 6 = 36$$
$$5^4 = 5 \times 5 \times 5 \times 5 = 625$$

If the exponent is 0, the power is always equal to 1.

For example, $2^0 = 1$; $5^0 = 1$; $125^0 = 1$.

1.7 Order of Operations

There are rules in calculation when a numerical expression contains two or more operations:

1. *Solve the power before other operations.*
2. *Then do the operation inside the parentheses.*
3. *Then do all multiplication and divisions, from left to right.*
4. *Finally, do all the additions and subtractions, from left to right.*

Examples:

1) $85 - (4 + 6^2 \times 2) + 2$

Step 1: $6^2 = 36$

Step 2: $36 \times 2 = 72$

Step 3: $72 + 4 = 76$

Step 4: $85 - 76 = 9$

Step 5: $9 + 2 = 11$

Result: $85 - (4 + 6^2 \times 2) + 2 = 11$

2) $17 + 8 \times 4 - 12 \div 2$

Step 1: $8 \times 4 = 32$

Step 2: $12 \div 2 = 6$

Step 3: $17 + 32 = 49$

Step 4: $49 - 6 = 43$

Result: $17 + 8 \times 4 - 12 \div 2 = 43$

1.8 Prime and Composite Numbers

A prime number is a whole number greater than 1 with only itself and 1 as factors. 2 is the only even number that is prime.

Examples of prime numbers:

2	193	449	733	1031	1321	1637	1997	2333
3	197	457	739	1033	1327	1657	1999	2339
5	199	461	743	1039	1361	1663	2003	2341
7	211	463	751	1049	1367	1667	2011	2347
11	223	467	757	1051	1373	1669	2017	2351
13	227	479	761	1061	1381	1693	2027	2357
17	229	487	769	1063	1399	1697	2029	2371
19	233	491	773	1069	1409	1699	2039	2377
23	239	499	787	1087	1423	1709	2053	2381
29	241	503	797	1091	1427	1721	2063	2383
31	251	509	803	1093	1429	1723	2069	2389
37	257	521	811	1097	1433	1733	2081	2393
41	263	523	821	1103	1439	1741	2083	2399
43	269	541	823	1109	1447	1747	2087	2411
47	271	547	827	1117	1451	1753	2089	2417
53	277	557	829	1123	1453	1759	2099	2423
59	281	663	839	1129	1459	1777	2111	2437
61	283	569	853	1151	1471	1783	2113	2441
67	293	571	857	1153	1481	1787	2129	2447
71	307	577	859	1163	1483	1789	2131	2459
73	311	587	863	1171	1487	1801	2137	2467
79	313	593	877	1181	1489	1811	2141	2473
83	317	599	781	1187	1493	1823	2143	2477
89	331	601	883	1193	1499	1831	2153	2503
97	337	607	887	1201	1511	1847	2161	2521
101	347	613	907	1213	1523	1861	2179	2531
103	349	617	911	1217	1531	1867	2203	2539
107	353	619	919	1223	1543	1871	2207	2543
109	359	631	929	1229	1519	1873	2213	2549
113	367	641	937	1231	1553	1877	2221	2551
127	373	643	941	1237	1559	1879	2237	2557
131	379	647	947	1249	1567	1889	2239	2579
137	383	653	953	1259	1571	1901	2243	2591
139	389	659	967	1277	1579	1987	2251	2593
149	397	661	971	1279	1583	1913	2267	2609
151	401	673	917	1283	1597	1931	2269	2617
157	409	677	983	1289	1601	1933	2273	2621
163	419	683	991	1291	1607	1949	2281	2633
167	421	691	997	1297	1609	1951	2287	2647
173	431	701	1009	1301	1613	1973	2293	2657
179	433	709	1013	1303	1619	1979	2297	2659
181	439	719	1019	1307	1621	1987	2309	2663
191	443	727	1021	1319	1627	1993	2311	2671

A **composite number** is a whole number greater than 1 that has factors other than itself and 1.

Example:

8 is a composite number. Its factors are 1, 2, 4, and 8.

All even numbers (except 2) are composite numbers

Every composite number can be written as the product of prime numbers. This is called **prime factorization**.

A factor tree can help you find the prime factorization of a number.

Example:

Two factor trees for 48

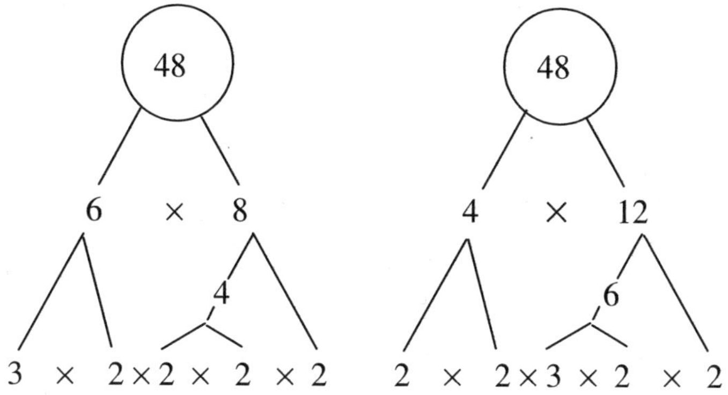

The prime factorization of 48 is $2 \times 2 \times 2 \times 2 \times 3$.

Any given composite number can be represented as a product of a set of prime factors that is unique.

For example, $36 = 2 \times 2 \times 3 \times 3 = 2^2 \times 3^2$; $45 = 3 \times 3 \times 5 = 3^2 \times 5$.

For large numbers, the following method of prime factoring can be used:

Example: 1421.

It is necessary to find the smallest prime number by which 1421 can be divided without a remainder. According to the rules of divisibility, the number 1421 cannot be divided by 2, 3, or 5. Let's try to divide by 7:

$$1421 \div 7 = 203$$

We write

$$\begin{array}{r|l} 1421 & 7 \\ 203 & \end{array}$$

We will test the divisibility of the number 203 in the same way:

$$203 \div 7 = 29$$

We write

$$\begin{array}{r|l} 1421 & 7 \\ 203 & 7 \\ 29 & 29 \end{array}$$

The number 29 is a prime number.
Therefore the result of prime factoring is

$$1421 = 7 \times 7 \times 29$$

1.9 Fractions

A fraction is a number that names part of a whole or part of a group.

Example:

$\frac{3}{4}$, where 3 is the numerator and 4 is the denominator

The **numerator** shows how many units one has (pieces of bread, slices of pie, etc.).
The **denominator** shows how many units make up the whole.

For example, there are 12 months in a year. Each month is $\frac{1}{12}$ year. Read $\frac{1}{12}$ as "one twelfth."

1.9.1 Proper Fractions

A proper fraction is a fraction with a numerator that is less than the denominator.

Examples:

$$\frac{1}{2}; \frac{2}{3}; \frac{7}{9}; \frac{12}{15}$$

1.9.2 Improper Fractions and Mixed Numbers

An improper fraction is a fraction with a numerator that is greater than or equal to the denominator.

Examples:

$$\frac{3}{2}; \frac{5}{3}; \frac{12}{5}; \frac{42}{31}$$

An improper fraction can be written as a whole or a mixed number. One needs only to divide the numerator by the denominator.

If the numerator is equal to the denominator, the fraction equals 1.

Examples:

$$\frac{5}{5} \qquad 5 \div 5 = 1 \qquad \frac{5}{5} = 1$$

$$\frac{12}{12} \qquad 12 \div 12 = 1 \qquad \frac{12}{12} = 1$$

If the numerator is greater than the denominator, there are two possibilities: division may produce a whole quotient, or a quotient with a remainder.

Examples of the first possibility: $\frac{4}{2}=2;\frac{6}{3}=2;\frac{21}{7}=3;\ \frac{25}{5}=5$

The fraction is changed into a whole number.

Examples of the second possibility:

$$\frac{3}{2} \qquad \begin{array}{r} 1R1 \\ 2\overline{)3} \\ -\ 2 \\ \hline 1 \end{array} \qquad 3\div 2=1\text{ R1} \qquad \frac{3}{2}=1\frac{1}{2}$$

$1\frac{1}{2}$ is a mixed number

A mixed number is a number that is made up of a whole number and a fraction.

The mixed number $1\frac{1}{2}$ is equivalent to $1+\frac{1}{2}$

Other mixed numbers: $2\frac{3}{4}\left(2+\frac{3}{4}\right);\ 4\frac{1}{3}\left(4+\frac{1}{3}\right);$ $7\frac{1}{7}\left(7+\frac{1}{7}\right)$, etc.

How can a mixed number be written as an improper fraction?

Step 1: Multiply the whole number and the denominator.

Step 2: Add this product to the numerator.

Step 3: Write the sum over the denominator.

Examples:

1) The mixed number $2\frac{3}{4}$:

Step 1: $2 \times 4 = 8$

Step 2: $8 + 3 = 11$

Step 3. $\frac{11}{4}$

So, $2\frac{3}{4} = \frac{11}{4}$

2) The mixed number $4\frac{1}{2}$:

Step 1: $4 \times 2 = 8$

Step 2: $8 + 1 = 9$

Step 3: $\frac{9}{2}$

So, $4\frac{1}{2} = \frac{9}{2}$

1.9.3 Equivalent Fractions

Fractions that name the same amount are called **equivalent fractions**.

We can find an equivalent fraction by multiplying the numerator and denominator by the same nonzero number.

Examples:

$$\frac{3}{4} = \frac{3 \times 2}{4 \times 2} = \frac{6}{8}$$

$$\frac{3}{4}=\frac{3\times4}{4\times4}=\frac{12}{16}$$

$$\frac{2}{3}=\frac{2\times4}{3\times4}=\frac{8}{12}$$

$$\frac{2}{3}=\frac{2\times5}{3\times5}=\frac{10}{15}$$

So, $\frac{3}{4}=\frac{6}{8}=\frac{12}{16}$; and $\frac{2}{3}=\frac{8}{12}=\frac{10}{15}$

We can also find an equivalent fraction by dividing the numerator and denominator by the same nonzero number.

Examples:

$$\frac{6}{8}=\frac{6\div2}{8\div2}=\frac{3}{4}$$

$$\frac{12}{16}=\frac{12\div4}{16\div4}=\frac{3}{4}$$

$$\frac{8}{12}=\frac{8\div4}{12\div4}=\frac{2}{3}$$

$$\frac{10}{15}=\frac{10\div5}{15\div5}=\frac{2}{3}$$

1. 9. 4 Least Common Denominator (LCD)

The least common denominator (LCD) is the least common multiple of the denominators of two or more fractions.

For example, the LCD of $\frac{1}{3}$ and $\frac{3}{5}$ is 15 because the LCM of 3 and 5 is 15.

1.9.5 Comparing Fractions: Reduce to a Common Denominator

To compare fractions the denominators of the fractions must be alike. Then the fraction is greater if it has a greater numerator.

Example:

Compare the fractions $\frac{3}{8}$ and $\frac{5}{8}$

$5 > 3$, so $\frac{5}{8} > \frac{3}{8}$

If the denominators are not equal, they must be reduced to a common denominator (common to all fractions)

Examples:

Compare the fractions $\frac{1}{2}$ and $\frac{3}{4}$

$\frac{1}{2} = \frac{1\times 2}{2\times 2} = \frac{2}{4}$, so $\frac{3}{4} > \frac{2}{4}$

Compare the fractions $\frac{1}{3}, \frac{3}{5}$, and $\frac{5}{6}$

Find the LCM of the numbers 3, 5, and 6. It is 30.

$$\frac{1}{3} = \frac{1\times 10}{3\times 10} = \frac{10}{30};\ \frac{3}{5} = \frac{3\times 6}{5\times 6} = \frac{18}{30};\ \frac{5}{6} = \frac{5\times 5}{6\times 5} = \frac{25}{30}$$

Compare the numbers 10, 18, and 25.

$25 > 10$; $25 > 18$

So the greatest of the three fractions is $\frac{5}{6}$.

When you find the answer to a problem with fractions, you might need to change the fraction to an equivalent form in simplest terms. To simplify a fraction, divide both the numerator and the denominator by the greatest number possible. This operation is called **simplifying a fraction.**

Examples: *1)* Simplify: $\frac{6}{10}$.

Step 1: Find the GCF [1.4.4.] of the numbers 6 and 10. It is the number 2.

Step 2: Divide the numerator and the denom i-nator by 2:

$$\frac{6}{10}=\frac{6\div 2}{10\div 2}=\frac{3}{5}$$

In simplest terms, the fraction is $\frac{3}{5}$.

2) Simplify: $\frac{124}{320}$

Step 1: Find the GCF of the numbers 124 and 320. It is the number 4.

$$\frac{124}{320}=\frac{124\div 4}{320\div 4}=\frac{31}{80}$$

In simplest terms, the fraction is $\frac{31}{80}$.

1.10 Addition and Subtraction of Fractions

- Addition and Subtraction of Fractions with Like Denominators

To add or subtract fractions with like denominators:

Step 1: Add or subtract the numerators.

Step 2: Simplify the answer.

Examples:

$$\frac{2}{7}+\frac{1}{7}=\frac{2+1}{7}=\frac{3}{7}$$

$$\frac{2}{5}+\frac{3}{5}=\frac{2+3}{5}=\frac{5}{5}=1$$

$$\frac{1}{12}+\frac{3}{12}=\frac{1+3}{12}=\frac{4}{12}=\frac{1}{3}$$

$$\frac{3}{5}-\frac{1}{5}=\frac{3-1}{5}=\frac{2}{5}$$

$$\frac{3}{12}-\frac{1}{12}=\frac{3-1}{12}=\frac{2}{12}=\frac{1}{6}$$

1.10.1 Addition and Subtraction of Fractions with Different Denominators

To add or subtract fractions with different denominators:

Step 1: Rewrite the fractions as fractions with like denominators (reduce to a common denominator [1.9.5.]).

Step 2: Add or subtract the nominators.

Step 3: Simplify the answer.

Examples:

$$\frac{3}{8}+\frac{1}{2}=\frac{3}{8}+\frac{4}{8}=\frac{7}{8}$$

$$\frac{1}{4}+\frac{3}{7}=\frac{7}{28}+\frac{12}{28}=\frac{19}{28}$$

$$\frac{1}{3}-\frac{1}{6}=\frac{2}{6}-\frac{1}{6}=\frac{1}{6}$$

$$\frac{4}{9}-\frac{2}{18}=\frac{8}{18}-\frac{2}{18}=\frac{6}{18}=\frac{1}{3}$$

1.10.2 Adding Mixed Numbers and Fractions

When adding mixed numbers and fractions:

Step 1: Write mixed numbers and fractions as fractions with like denominators (reduce to a common denominator).

Step 2: Add the fractions.

Step 3: Add the whole numbers.

Step 4: Simplify the answer.

Example:

Solve $3\frac{1}{3}+\frac{3}{4}$

Step 1: $3\frac{4}{12}+\frac{9}{12}$

Step 2: $\frac{4}{12}+\frac{9}{12}=\frac{4+9}{12}=\frac{13}{12}$

Step 3: $3+\frac{13}{12}=3\frac{13}{12}$

Step 4: $3\frac{13}{12} = 3 + 1\frac{1}{12} = 4\frac{1}{12}$

Result: $3\frac{1}{3} + \frac{3}{4} = 4\frac{1}{12}$

1.11 Subtraction of Fractions with Different Denominators

To subtract fractions with different denominators:

Step 1: Rewrite the fractions as fractions with like denominators (reduce to a common denominator).

Step 2: Subtract the fractions.

Step 3: Simplify the answer.

Examples:

1) Find $\frac{1}{3} - \frac{1}{4}$

Step 1: $\frac{4}{12} - \frac{3}{12}$

Step 2: $\frac{4}{12} - \frac{3}{12} = \frac{4-3}{12} = \frac{1}{12}$

Result: $\frac{1}{3} - \frac{1}{4} = \frac{1}{12}$

2) Find $\frac{1}{2} - \frac{3}{10}$

Step 1: $\frac{5}{10} - \frac{3}{10}$

Step 2: $\frac{5-3}{10}=\frac{2}{10}$

Step 3: $\frac{2}{10}=\frac{1}{5}$

Result: $\frac{1}{2}-\frac{3}{10}=\frac{1}{5}$

1.11.1 Subtraction of Fractions and Mixed Numbers from Whole Numbers

To subtract a fraction from a whole number:

Step 1: Write the whole number as a mixed number with a like denominator.

Step 2: Subtract the fractions.

Step 3: Subtract the whole numbers.

Step 4: Add the fraction and the whole number.

Example:

Solve $7-1\frac{2}{5}$

Step 1: $7=6+\frac{5}{5}=6\frac{5}{5}$

Step 2: $\frac{5}{5}-\frac{2}{5}=\frac{5-2}{5}=\frac{3}{5}$

Step 3: $6-1=5$

Step 4: $5+\frac{3}{5}=5\frac{3}{5}$

Result: $7-1\frac{2}{5}=5\frac{3}{5}$

- Subtraction of Mixed Numbers

To subtract mixed numbers:

Step 1: Write the mixed numbers as fractions with like denominators (reduce to a common denominator).

Step 2: Subtract the fractions.

Step 3: Subtract the whole numbers.

Step 4: Add the fractions and the whole number.

It may be necessary to simplify the answer.

Example:

Solve $4\frac{1}{5}-2\frac{1}{10}$

Step 1: $4\frac{2}{10}-2\frac{1}{10}$

Step 2: $\frac{2}{10}-\frac{1}{10}=\frac{2-1}{10}=\frac{1}{10}$

Step 3: $4-2=2$

$$\textit{Step 4:}\quad 2+\frac{1}{10}=2\frac{1}{10}$$

$$\text{Result:}\quad 4\frac{1}{5}-2\frac{1}{10}=2\frac{1}{10}$$

It may be necessary to regroup the mixed number.

Examples:

1) Solve $5\frac{1}{8}-3\frac{3}{4}$

$$\textit{Step 1:}\quad 5\frac{1}{8}-3\frac{6}{8}$$

$$\textit{Step 2:}\quad \frac{1}{8}-\frac{6}{8}=?$$

$\frac{6}{8}$ is greater than $\frac{1}{8}$. We can't subtract it from $\frac{1}{8}$.

To get over this problem, write 5 as a mixed number: $5=4\frac{8}{8}$

$$\textit{Step 2.1:}\quad 5\frac{1}{8}=4\frac{8}{8}+\frac{1}{8}=4\frac{9}{8}$$

$$\textit{Step 2.2:}\quad \frac{9}{8}-\frac{6}{8}=\frac{3}{8}$$

$$\textit{Step 3:}\quad 4-3=1$$

$$\textit{Step 4:}\quad 1+\frac{3}{8}=1\frac{3}{8}$$

Result: $5\frac{1}{8}-3\frac{3}{4}=1\frac{3}{8}$

2) Solve $6\frac{2}{5}-4\frac{1}{2}$

Step 1: $6\frac{4}{10}-4\frac{5}{10}$

Step 2: $4<5$, so regroup: $6=5\frac{10}{10}$

Step 2.1: $5\frac{10}{10}+\frac{4}{10}=5\frac{14}{10}$

Step 2.2: $\frac{14}{10}-\frac{5}{10}=\frac{14-5}{10}=\frac{9}{10}$

Step 3: $5-4=1$

Step 4: $1+\frac{9}{10}=1\frac{9}{10}$

Result: $6\frac{2}{5}-4\frac{1}{2}=1\frac{9}{10}$

1.12 Multiplication of Fractions

To multiply fractions:

Step 1: Multiply the numerators. The product is the new numerator.

Step 2: Multiply the denominators. The product is the new denominator.

It may be necessary to simplify the answer.

Examples:

1) Solve $\frac{1}{2}\times\frac{3}{4}$

Step 1: $\frac{1}{2}\times\frac{3}{4}=\frac{1\times 3}{}=\frac{3}{}$

Step 2: $\frac{1}{2}\times\frac{3}{4}=\frac{1\times 3}{2\times 4}=\frac{3}{8}$

Result: $\frac{1}{2}\times\frac{3}{4}=\frac{3}{8}$

2) Solve $\frac{2}{6}\times\frac{3}{4}$

Step 1: $\frac{2}{6}\times\frac{3}{4}=\frac{2\times 3}{}=\frac{6}{}$

Step 2: $\frac{2}{6}\times\frac{3}{4}=\frac{2\times 3}{6\times 4}=\frac{6}{24}$

$\frac{2}{6}\times\frac{3}{4}=\frac{6}{24}=\frac{1}{4}$

Result: $\frac{2}{6}\times\frac{3}{4}=\frac{1}{4}$

1.12.1 Multiplication of Fractions using Cancellation

Instead of simplifying fractions after they have been multiplied, it may be possible to use cancellation before multiplying. To cancel, find a common factor of a numerator and a denominator. Divide the numerator and the denominator

by the common factor. Then multiply the new numerator and denominator.

Examples:

1) Solve $\frac{5}{6}\times\frac{1}{10}$

The common factor of 5 and 10 is 5.

Cancel: $\frac{\cancel{5}^{1}}{6}\times\frac{1}{\cancel{10}_{2}}=\frac{1}{12}$

Result: $\frac{5}{6}\times\frac{1}{10}=\frac{1}{12}$

2) Solve $\frac{3}{4}\times\frac{2}{21}$

Cancel: $\frac{{}^{1}\cancel{3}}{{}_{2}\cancel{4}}\times\frac{\cancel{2}^{1}}{\cancel{21}_{7}}=\frac{1}{14}$

Result: $\frac{3}{4}\times\frac{2}{21}=\frac{1}{14}$

1.12.2 Multiplication of Mixed Numbers by Whole Numbers, Mixed Numbers, and Fractions

To multiply a mixed number write the mixed number and the whole number as improper fractions.

Examples:

1) Solve $1\frac{1}{2}\times 3$

$$1\frac{1}{2}\times 3=\frac{3}{2}\times\frac{3}{1}=\frac{3\times 3}{2\times 1}=\frac{9}{2}=4\frac{1}{2}$$

Result: $1\frac{1}{2}\times 3=4\frac{1}{2}$

2) Solve $2\frac{3}{81}\times 3$

$$2\frac{3}{81}\times 3=\frac{165}{81}\times\frac{3}{1}=\frac{165\times \cancel{3}^{1}}{{}_{27}\cancel{81}\times 1}=\frac{165\times 1}{27\times 1}=\frac{165}{27}=6\frac{3}{27}$$

Result: $2\frac{3}{81}\times 3=6\frac{3}{27}$

1.13 Division of Fractions by Fractions

To divide a fraction by a fraction:

Step 1: Multiply the numerator of the first fraction by the denominator of the second fraction. The product is the numerator of the new fraction.

Step 2: Multiply the denominator of the first fraction by the numerator of the second fraction. The product is the denominator of the new fraction.

Step 3: Simplify the answer.

Examples:

1) Solve $\frac{1}{3}\div\frac{4}{6}$

Step 1: $\frac{1}{3} \div \frac{4}{6} = \frac{1 \times 6}{\quad} = \frac{6}{\quad}$

Step 2: $\frac{1}{3} \div \frac{4}{6} = \frac{1 \times 6}{3 \times 4} = \frac{6}{12}$

Step 3: $\frac{6}{12} = \frac{1}{2}$

Result: $\frac{1}{3} \div \frac{4}{6} = \frac{1}{2}$

2) Solve $\frac{4}{9} \div \frac{8}{9}$

Step 1: $\frac{4}{9} \div \frac{8}{9} = \frac{4 \times 9}{\quad} = \frac{36}{\quad}$

Step 2: $\frac{4}{9} \div \frac{8}{9} = \frac{4 \times 9}{9 \times 8} = \frac{36}{72}$

Step 3: $\frac{36}{72} = \frac{1}{2}$

Result: $\frac{4}{9} \div \frac{8}{9} = \frac{1}{2}$

1.13.1 Division of Mixed Numbers by Whole Numbers

To divide a mixed number by a whole number, write the mixed number as an improper fraction.

Examples:

$$1\frac{1}{3} \div 2 = \frac{4}{3} \div \frac{2}{1} = \frac{4 \times 1}{3 \times 2} = \frac{4}{6} = \frac{2}{3}$$

Result: $1\frac{1}{3} \div 2 = \frac{2}{3}$

1.13.2 Division of Fractions by Fractions as Multiplication by the Reciprocal

A reciprocal is an inverted fraction, that is a fraction with the numerator and the denominator switched. The reciprocal is 1 divided by the fraction.

Example:

Fraction	Reciprocal
$\frac{1}{3}$	$1 \div \frac{1}{3} = \frac{1}{1} \div \frac{1}{3} = \frac{3}{1}$
$\frac{2}{3}$	$\frac{3}{2}$
$\frac{5}{12}$	$\frac{12}{5}$

Multiplying a fraction by its reciprocal always equals 1. Division of a fraction by a fraction can be changed to multiplication by the reciprocal.

Examples:

Solve $\frac{1}{2} \div \frac{2}{3}$

Find the reciprocal of the fraction $\frac{2}{3}$. It is $\frac{3}{2}$.

Multiply: $\frac{1}{2}\times\frac{3}{2}=\frac{1\times3}{2\times2}=\frac{3}{4}$

Result: $\frac{1}{2}\div\frac{2}{3}=\frac{3}{4}$

1.14 Decimal Fractions (Decimals)

The decimal system expresses fractions based on denominators that are powers of 10 (10; 100; 1000; 10,000…). A **decimal** is a number expressed using a decimal point.

0.25 — a decimal
5.5 — a mixed decimal

Each digit in a decimal has a value based on its place in the decimal.

Rule for reading a decimal:

- Read the whole number part;
- Read the decimal point as 'and';
- Read the decimal part as a whole number and then name the place value of the last digit.

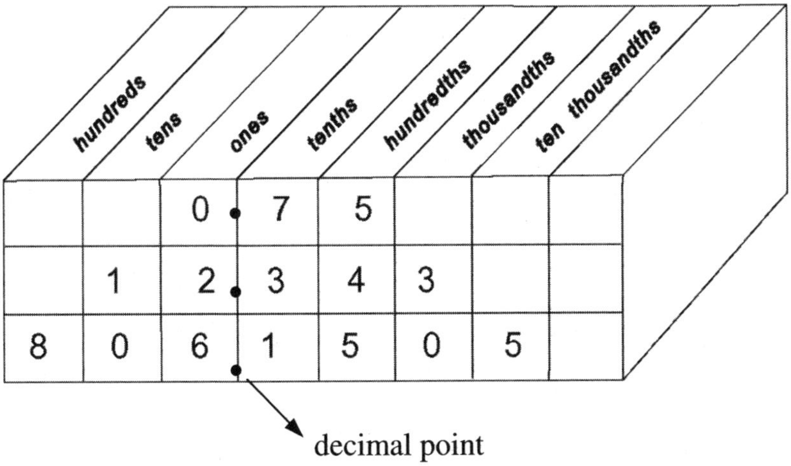

The decimals given on the place-value chart are read as follows:

0.75 — seventy-five hundredths

12.343 — twelve and three hundred forty-three thousandths

806.1505 — eight hundred six and one thousand five hundred five ten thousandths

1.14.1 Converting a Decimal to a Fraction

To convert a decimal to a fraction, read the decimal name and make it a fraction whose denominator is a power of 10. If possible, simplify the answer.

Examples:

$$0.75 = \frac{75}{100} = \frac{3}{4}$$

$$12.374 = 12\frac{374}{1000} = 12\frac{187}{500}$$

$$806.1505 = 806\frac{1505}{10{,}000} = 806\frac{301}{2000}$$

1.14.2 Properties of Decimals

1. Adding any quantity of zeros to a decimal does not change the decimal.

Examples:

$$0.25 + 0 = 0.25$$

$$0.125 + 0 = 0.125$$

2. Moving the decimal point one digit to the right *increases* the decimal by a factor of ten.

Examples:

$$0.25 = \frac{25}{100} = \frac{1}{4}$$

$$2.5 = 2\frac{5}{10} = \frac{25}{10} = \frac{10}{4}\text{; that is, } \frac{1}{4}\times 10$$

$$25.0 = \frac{100}{4}\text{; that is, } \frac{1}{4}\times 100$$

3. Transferring the decimal point one digit to the left *decreases* the decimal by a factor of ten.

Examples:

$$2.5 = 2\frac{5}{10} = \frac{25}{10} = \frac{5}{2} = \frac{10}{4}$$

$$0.25 = \frac{25}{100} = \frac{1}{4}\text{; that is, } \frac{10}{4} \div 10$$

$$0.025 = \frac{25}{1000} = \frac{1}{40} = \frac{10}{400}\text{; that is, } \frac{10}{4} \div 100$$

1.14.3 Addition and Subtraction of Decimals

To add decimals, line up the decimal points. Then add or subtract as usual, carrying to the next column. Be sure to write a decimal point in the sum/difference. Write zeroes as needed.

Examples:

1) Solve 8.42 + 4.5

$$\begin{array}{r} 8.42 \\ +4.50 \\ \hline 12.92 \end{array}$$

Result: 8.42 + 4.5 = 12.92

2) Solve 0.95 + 6.16

$$\begin{array}{r} 0.95 \\ +6.16 \\ \hline 7.11 \end{array}$$

Result: 0.95 + 6.16 = 7.11

3) Solve 8 + 3.4 + 0.7

$$\begin{array}{r} 8.0 \\ 3.4 \\ +0.7 \\ \hline 12.1 \end{array}$$

Result: 8 + 3.4 + 0.7 = 12.1

4) Solve 42.3 – 15.94

$$\begin{array}{r} 42.30 \\ -15.94 \\ \hline 26.36 \end{array}$$

Result: 42.3 – 15.94 = 26.36

Check: 26.36 + 15.94 = 42.3

1.15 Multiplying Decimals by Whole Numbers

To multiply a decimal by a whole number:

Step 1: Multiply as if you were multiplying whole numbers.

Step 2: Place the decimal point in the product. Count the number of decimal digits to the right of the decimal point in the numbers you have multiplied. The product should have the same number of decimal digits.

Examples:

1) Solve 15×0.3

$$\begin{array}{r} 15 \\ \times 0.3 \\ \hline 4.5 \end{array}$$

Result: $15 \times 0.3 = 4.5$

2) Solve 4.51×34

$$\begin{array}{r} 4.51 \\ \times 34 \\ \hline 1{,}804 \\ +13{,}530 \\ \hline 153.34 \end{array}$$

Result: $4.51 \times 34 = 153.34$

3) Solve 0.03×11

$$\begin{array}{r} 0.03 \\ \times 11 \\ \hline 003 \\ +0030 \\ \hline 0.33 \end{array}$$

Result: $0.03 \times 11 = 0.33$

1.15.1 Multiplying Decimals by Decimals

To multiply a decimal by another decimal:

Step 1: Multiply as if you were multiplying whole numbers.

Step 2: Place the decimal point in the product by counting the number of decimal places to the right of the decimal point in both numbers.

Examples:

*1)*Solve 1.7×0.2

$$\begin{array}{r} 1.7 \\ \times 0.2 \\ \hline 0.34 \end{array}$$

Result: $1.7 \times 0.2 = 0.34$

2) Solve 0.03×0.001

$$\begin{array}{r} 0.03 \\ \times 0.001 \\ \hline 0.00003 \end{array}$$

Result: $0.03 \times 0.001 = 0.00003$

3) Solve 114.701×12.18

$$\begin{array}{r} 114.701 \\ \times 12.18 \\ \hline 917{,}608 \\ 1{,}147{,}010 \\ 22{,}940{,}200 \\ +114{,}701{,}000 \\ \hline 1{,}397.05818 \end{array}$$

Result: $114.701 \times 12.18 = 1{,}397.05818$

1.16 Dividing Decimals by Whole Numbers

To divide a decimal by a whole number:

Step 1: Place the decimal point above the decimal point in the quotient.

Step 2: Divide as with whole numbers.

Examples:

1) Solve $1.71 \div 3$

Step 1: $3\overline{)1.71}$ (with the decimal point placed above)

Step 2:

$$\begin{array}{r} 0.57 \\ 3\overline{)1.71} \\ \underline{-15} \\ 21 \\ \underline{-\;\;21} \\ 0 \end{array}$$

Result: $1.71 \div 3 = 0.57$

Check: $3 \times 0.57 = 1.71$

2) Solve $66.4 \div 8$ $\quad 8\overline{)66.4}$ (with the decimal point placed above)

$$\begin{array}{r} 8.3 \\ 8\overline{)66.4} \\ \underline{-64\downarrow} \\ 2\,4 \\ \underline{-\;\;2\,4} \\ 0 \end{array}$$

Result: $66.4 \div 8 = 8.3$

Check: $8 \times 8.3 = 66.4$

3) Solve $24.816 \div 8$

$$
\begin{array}{r}
3.102 \\
8\overline{)24.816} \\
-24\downarrow \\
\hline
8 \\
-8 \\
\hline
016 \\
-16 \\
\hline
0
\end{array}
$$

Result: $24.816 \div 8 = 3.102$

Check: $8 \times 3.102 = 24.816$

1.16.1 Dividing Decimals by Decimals

To divide by a decimal:

Step 1: Change the divisor to a whole number by moving the decimal point.

Step 2: Move the decimal point in the dividend the same number of places.

Step 3: Divide as in dividing decimals by whole numbers.

Examples:

1) *Solve* $4.35 \div 0.5$

Step 1: $0.5 \rightarrow 5$

Step 2: $4.35 \rightarrow 43.5$

Step 3:

$$\begin{array}{r} 8.7 \\ 5\overline{)43.5} \\ -40 \\ \hline 35 \\ -35 \\ \hline 0 \end{array}$$

Result: $43.5 \div 0.5 = 8.7$
Check: $0.5 \times 8.7 = 43.5$

2) Solve $7.332 \div 0.26$

$$\begin{array}{r} 28.2 \\ 26\overline{)733.2} \\ -52 \\ \hline 213 \\ -208 \\ \hline 52 \\ -52 \\ \hline 0 \end{array}$$

Result: $7.332 \div 0.26 = 28.2$
Check: $0.26 \times 28.2 = 7.332$

3) Solve: $15.18 \div 0.33$

$$\begin{array}{r} 46 \\ 33\overline{)1{,}518} \\ -132 \\ \hline 198 \\ -\ \ 198 \\ \hline 0 \end{array}$$

Result: $15.8 \div 0.33 = 46$
Check: $0.33 \times 46 = 15.18$

1.16.2 Dividing Whole Numbers by Decimals

To divide a whole number by a decimal number:

Step 1: Change the decimal number to a whole number by moving the decimal point.

Step 2. Count the number of decimal places and add the same number of zeros to the right of the whole number.

Step 3: Divide as in dividing by whole numbers.

Examples:

1) Solve: $154 \div 1.4$

Step 1: $1.4 \longrightarrow 14$

Step 2: $154.0 \longrightarrow 1540$

Step 3:

$$\begin{array}{r} 110 \\ 14\overline{)1540} \\ -14 \\ \hline 14 \\ -14 \\ \hline 00 \end{array}$$

Result: $154 \div 1.4 = 110$

Check: $1.4 \times 110 = 154$

2) Solve $51 \div 0.34$

$$51 \longrightarrow 5100;\ 0.34 \longrightarrow 34$$

$$\begin{array}{r} 150 \\ 34\overline{)5100} \\ -\ 34 \\ \hline 170 \\ -\ 170 \\ \hline 00 \end{array}$$

Result: $51 \div 0.34 = 150$

Check: $0.34 \times 150 = 51$

3) Solve: $27 \div 0.003$

$$27 \longrightarrow 27000;\ 0.003 \longrightarrow 3$$

$$\begin{array}{r} 9000 \\ 3\overline{)27000} \\ -27 \\ \hline 0000 \end{array}$$

Result: $27 \div 0.003 = 9000$

Check: $0.003 \times 9000 = 27$

1.16.3 Infinite Decimals

Sometimes when you divide, the quotient may be an infinite decimal. In some of these cases you may have to quit dividing when you have achieved sufficient exactness.

Examples:

1) Solve $19 \div 3$

$$\begin{array}{r} 6.333\ldots \\ 3\overline{)19.000} \\ -18 \\ \hline 10 \\ -9 \\ \hline 10 \\ -9 \\ \hline 10 \end{array}$$

Result: $19 \div 3 = 6.333\ldots$, or $6.\overline{3}$

2) Solve $22 \div 7$

$$\begin{array}{r} 3.14285 \\ 7\overline{)22.00000} \\ -21 \\ \hline 10 \\ -7 \\ \hline 30 \\ -28 \\ \hline 20 \\ -14 \\ \hline 60 \\ -56 \\ \hline 40 \\ -35 \\ \hline 5 \end{array}$$

Result: $22 \div 7 = 3.14285\ldots \approx 3.14$

1.16.4 Multiplying and Dividing by Powers of 10

To multiply decimals by powers of ten (10, 100, 1000…), move the decimal point in the factor to the right as many places as there are zeros in the multiplier.

Examples:

$10 \times 0.62 = 6.2$

$10 \times 7.4 = 74$

$100 \times 0.62 = 62$

$100 \times 7.4 = 740$

$1000 \times 0.62 = 620$

$1000 \times 7.4 = 7400$

To divide a decimal by a power of ten, move the decimal point in the dividend to the left as many places as there are zeros in the divider.

Examples:

$0.62 \div 10 = 0.062$

$7.4 \div 10 = 0.74$

$0.62 \div 100 = 0.0062$

$7.4 \div 100 = 0.074$

1.17 Percentages

A percentage is a way of expressing the quotient of any number divided by 100. The symbol % is read 'percent.' A percentage is always expressed as an equivalent decimal or a common fraction.

For example, 15% = 15 hundredths, written as 0.15 or $\frac{15}{100}$.

35% = 0.35

4% = 0.04

380% = 3.8

$100\% = \frac{100}{100} = 1$

To change a decimal to a percentage, move the decimal point 2 places to the right and write a percent symbol.

Examples:

0.526 = 52.6%

0.6 = 60%

0.01 = 1%

20.1 = 2010%

To change a fraction to a percentage, first change the fraction to a decimal by dividing the numerator by the denominator. Then rewrite the decimal quotient as a percentage.

Examples:

1) Write ½ as a percentage.

$$\begin{array}{r} 0.5 \\ 2\overline{)1.00} \\ -10 \\ \hline 0 \end{array} \qquad 0.5 = 50\%$$

2) Write $\frac{3}{20}$ as a percentage

$$\begin{array}{r} 0.15 \\ 20\overline{)3.00} \\ -20 \\ \hline 100 \\ -100 \\ \hline 0 \end{array} \quad 0.15 = 15\%$$

To convert a whole number into a percentage, multiply it by 100.

Examples:

$0.5 = 0.5 \times 100 = 50\%$

$1 = 1 \times 100 = 100\%$

$2 = 2 \times 100 = 200\%$

$10 = 10 \times 100 = 1000\%$

To find a percentage of a number, change the percentage into a decimal and then multiply the decimal by the number.

Examples:

1) Find 15% of 600.

$15\% = 0.15$

$0.15 \times 600 = 90$

2) Find 50% of 200.

$50\% = 0.5$

$0.5 \times 200 = 100$

3) Find 25% of 20.

$25\% = 0.25$

$0.25 \times 20 = 5$

Example: There are 600 students in high school. 30% of all students are girls. How many boys are there in high school?

Step 1: How many girls in high school?

$30\% = 0.3$

$0.3 \times 600 = 180$

Step 2: How many boys in high school?

$600 - 180 = 420$

To find what percentage one number is of another number, multiply the first number by 100 and then divide by the second number.

Examples:

1) 20 is what percent of 200?

$20 \times 100 = 2000$

$2000 \div 200 = 10\%$

2) 125 is what percent of 250?

$125 \times 100 = 12{,}500$

$12{,}500 \div 250 = 50\%$

1.18 Estimation. Rounding Numbers

To estimate sums, differences, products, or quotients, you must learn to round numbers.

- The Rule of Rounding: To round a number off to a given decimal place, add one to the digit in that decimal place if the first digit of the part of the number taken away is greater than or equal to 5. Otherwise, simply remove the unnecessary digits.

Examples:

1) Round the number 25.874 to one decimal place.
Since 7>5, write 25.9.

$$25.874 \approx 25.9$$

2) Round the number 2.2361 to three decimal places.
Since 1<5, $2.2361 \approx 2.236$

Estimation of decimal sums and differences

To estimate decimal sums, first round the decimals to the same place. Then add the rounded numbers.

Example:

Estimate \$5.69 + \$3.18 to the dollar.

$$\$5.69 \approx \$6; \; \$3.18 \approx \$3$$

$$\$6 + \$3 = \$9$$

To estimate decimal differences, first round the decimals to the same place. Then subtract the rounded numbers.

Example:

Estimate 12.33 – 5.78 to the nearest tenth.

$$12.33 \approx 12.3; \; 5.78 \approx 5.8$$

$$12.3 - 5.8 = 6.5$$

1.19 Finding a Pattern

The answer to a problem may be found by recognizing a pattern. Read the problem carefully. Write the pattern and determine how the numbers are related. Find the rule that makes the pattern. Then solve the problem.

Example 1:

What is the next number in this number pattern?

$$7, 21, 63, 189, \ldots$$

Determine the relationship:

Rule: multiply by 3

The next number will be 189×3, or 567.

Example 2:

What is the next number in this number pattern?

$$2\frac{1}{4}, \ 2\frac{7}{8}, \ 3\frac{1}{2}, \ldots$$

Rule: Add $\frac{5}{8}$.

The next number will be $3\frac{1}{2} + \frac{5}{8} = 4\frac{1}{8}$

1.20 Numerical Sequences

Mathematics uses several different numerical sequences.

- An **arithmetical progression** is one in which the *difference* between each number is constant.

Examples:

1, 2, 3, 4, 5…

2, 5, 8, 11, 14…

- A **geometrical progression** is one in which the *ratio* between each number is constant.

Examples:

2, 4, 8, 16, 32…

1, 3, 9, 27, 81…

- A **palindrome** is a symmetrical numerical sequence around a central digit.

Examples:

These are palindromes: 4**3**4, 13**2**31, 22**2**22

These are not palindromes: 305, 41304, 2022

There are different methods to transform a nonpalindrome to a palindrome. One method is the addition method. In that method we add the inverse form of the number.

Example:

Basic form of the number	23453
Inverse form of the number	+ 35432
	58**8**85

The addition method has the following steps:

Step 1: Write the basic number.

Step 2: Write the inverse of that number.

Step 3: Add the basic and inverse numbers.

Step 4: If the sum is a palindrome, the process is finished.

This is a "Class 1" palindrome.

Step 5: If the sum is not a palindrome, repeat the process as needed.

The palindrome received after two such operations is a "Class 2" palindrome, etc.

Examples:

1) Derive a palindrome from 712.

Step 1: Write the basic number 712

Step 2: Write the inverse form 217

Step 3:

$$\begin{array}{r} 712 \\ +217 \\ \hline 919 \end{array}$$

This is a Class 1 palindrome.

2) Derive a palindrome from 162.

Step 1: Write the basic number 162

Step 2: Write the inverse form 261

Step 3:

$$\begin{array}{r} 162 \\ +261 \\ \hline 423 \end{array}$$

423 is not a palindrome, so

Step 4: Write the inverse form 324

Step 5:

$$\begin{array}{r} 423 \\ +324 \\ \hline 747 \end{array}$$

This is Class 2 palindrome.

3) Derive a palindrome from 627.

Step 1: Write the basic number 627

Step 2: Write the inverse form 726

Step 3:

$$\begin{array}{r} 627 \\ +726 \\ \hline 1353 \end{array}$$

1353 is not palindrome, so

Step 4: Write the inverse form 3531

Step 5:

$$\begin{array}{r} 1353 \\ +3531 \\ \hline \mathbf{4884} \end{array}$$

↑↑

88 are the central digits,

and $\frac{8+8}{2} = 8$

The palindrome is 484

The **Fibonacci series** is one in which each digit equals the sum of the two preceding digits.

Example:

1, 2, 3, 5, 8, 13…

(2+1) (3+2) (5+3) (8+5)

Numerical sequences can be based on different rules:

SEQUENCE	RULE
4, 7, 10, 13, 16…	+ 3
17, 15, 13, 11, 9…	- 2
10, 20, 40, 80, 160…	× 2
64, 32, 16, 8, 4…	÷ 2
1, 2, 3, 6, 12, 24, 25, 26, 27…	+ 1 (3 places), × 2 (3 places)

1.21 Commonly Asked Questions: Arithmetic

1) **Q:** What is the difference between a digit and a number?

A: For the whole numbers 0, 1, 2, 3, 4, 5, 6, 7, 8, 9, there is no difference between digits and numbers. But for numbers 10 and larger, the numbers are represented by certain combinations of digits. ***For example,*** the number 2,115 is represented by a combination of 4 digits: 2, 1, 1, and 5. It is a four-digit number.

2) **Q:** In a large number, 2,376,843, what is the largest digit?

A: The digit 8 is the largest digit in the example. 9 is the largest digit of all. The digit 2 has the greatest value in the number, as it represents the number 2 million.

3) **Q:** What is the difference between natural or counting numbers and whole numbers?

A: Whole numbers include the number zero (0, 1, 2, 3...), while the natural numbers don't (1, 2, 3...). Ancient peoples long used the natural numbers, while the number zero is a relatively recent "discovery."

4) **Q:** What's the largest number that can be carried in adding two whole numbers?

A: The number 1. ***For example:***

$$\begin{array}{lr} \text{Carried numbers} & 11 \\ & 199 \\ & +99 \\ \hline & 298 \end{array}$$

5) **Q:** How can I memorize the multiplication table most readily?

A: You should imagine the table as a series of 10 columns:

0×0=0	1×0=0	2×0=0	3×0=0	4×0=0
0×1=0	1×1=1	2×1=0	3×1=3	4×1=4
0×2=0	1×2=2	2×2=4	3×2=6	4×2=8
0×3=0	1×3=3	2×3=6	3×3=9	4×3=12
0×4=0	1×4=4	2×4=8	3×4=12	4×4=16
0×5=0	1×5=5	2×5=10	3×5=15	4×5=20
0×6=0	1×6=6	2×6=12	3×6=18	4×6=24
0×7=0	1×7=7	2×7=14	3×7=21	4×7=28
0×8=0	1×8=8	2×8=16	3×8=24	4×8=32
0×9=0	1×9=9	2×9=18	3×9=27	4×9=36

5×0=0	6×0=0	7×0=0	8×0=0	9×0=0
5×1=5	6×1=6	7×1=7	8×1=8	9×1=9
5×2=10	6×2=12	7×2=14	8×2=16	9×2=18
5×3=15	6×3=18	7×3=21	8×3=24	9×3=27
5×4=20	6×4=24	7×4=28	8×4=32	9×4=36
5×5=25	6×5=30	7×5=35	8×5=40	9×5=45
5×6=30	6×6=36	7×6=42	8×6=48	9×6=54
5×7=35	6×7=42	7×7=49	8×7=56	9×7=63
5×8=40	6×8=48	7×8=56	8×8=64	9×8=72
5×9=45	6×9=54	7×9=63	8×9=72	9×9=81

You can learn the multiplication table more readily by learning each column.

6) **Q:** When multiplying by a number that contains zeros, do you have to carry out the operation for all the zeros?

A: No. Instead of multiplying by zero, you can simply move the result of the next multiplication to the left as many columns as there are zeros.

For example:

$$\begin{array}{r} 1031 \\ \times\ 2001 \\ \hline 1031 \\ +\ 2062 \\ \hline 2{,}063{,}031 \end{array}$$

7) **Q:** Why is it necessary to have the same denominator in fractions when adding and subtracting them?

A: The denominator of a fraction tells us what part of the whole we are dealing with in the problem. For example, if we are dealing with quarters of an apple, we can only add or subtract quarter apples. If we add two quarters to one quarter, we will get three quarters. If we operate at the same time with quarters and thirds of apples, for example, then we have to add values of different magnitudes (as if you were trying to add pints and quarts). That is why it is always necessary, when adding or subtracting fractions, to reduce them to a common denominator, like with our quarter and third of an apple:

$$\frac{1}{4}+\frac{1}{3}=\frac{1\times3}{4\times3}+\frac{1\times4}{3\times4}=\frac{3}{12}+\frac{4}{12}=\frac{7}{12}$$

So, if we have a quarter and a third of an apple, all together we have seven twelfths of an apple.

8) **Q:** When you write a mixed number it looks like multiplying a whole number by a fraction.

For example, $1\frac{1}{3}$ is similar to $1\times\frac{1}{3}$. How can I tell the difference?

A: The difference here is only in the presence or absence of a multiplication sign. If there is no sign, then $1\frac{1}{3}=1+\frac{1}{3}$, but if there is a multiplication sign, $1\times\frac{1}{3}=\frac{1}{3}$. In arithmetic, multiplication is most often represented by the sign ×, while in other areas of mathematics it is represented by ‘ ’ or even by no sign at all.

9) **Q:** Which way of dividing simple fractions is better: cross multiplication of the numerator by the denominator or multiplying by the reciprocal?

A: Both methods give the correct result, but the method of using the reciprocal causes most people fewer problems, since schoolchildren often forget in which order they should complete the cross multiplication.

10) **Q:** What advantages do decimal fractions have over regular fractions?

A: The major advantage of decimal fractions is that the value of the denominator is easily convertible. For fractions with large denominators, this eliminates the difficulty of finding a common denominator.

For example:

$$4.462 + 5.5 \longrightarrow 4.462 + 5.500 = 9.962$$

Decimal fractions are more compact since you do not write the denominator, which is instead determined by the position of the decimal point in the number. Another advantage is that a decimal fraction can easily be converted into a regular fraction.

For example:

$$4.205 = 4\frac{205}{1000}$$

Regular fractions also have advantages over decimal fractions. For example, one-third can be expressed exactly as a fraction: $\frac{1}{3}$, but as a decimal it is infinite: 0.33333333.... If you calculate with the decimal (for example, in your calculator), your results will always be inexact, while calculating with the fraction easily gives exact results.

***11)* Q:** When I am doing operations on decimals that represent dollars and cents, to how many decimal points do I need to calculate the result?

A: Up to the second digit after the decimal point, because a cent is one hundredth of a dollar, and there is no coin smaller.

For example, $\$20 \div 3 = \$6.66666\ldots \approx \$6.66$

However, often when calculating tax or interest, businesses and banks will calculate to the third digit after the decimal and round the number to the nearest hundredth (or cent). Using such a method, the above example would become $6.67.

2 CHAPTER

ALGEBRA

Algebra is a big part of mathematics. Elementary algebra includes operations on variables, solving algebraic equations, logarithms, and several other operations. Algebra, as opposed to arithmetic, deals mostly with variable expressions.

2.1 Negative Numbers. Absolute Value

A temperature of 20 degrees above zero is a positive number (+20°), and 20 degrees below zero is a negative number (-20°). 200 meters above sea level is a positive number (+200m); 200 meters below sea level is a negative number (-200m). A number line gives a visual representation of positive and negative numbers.

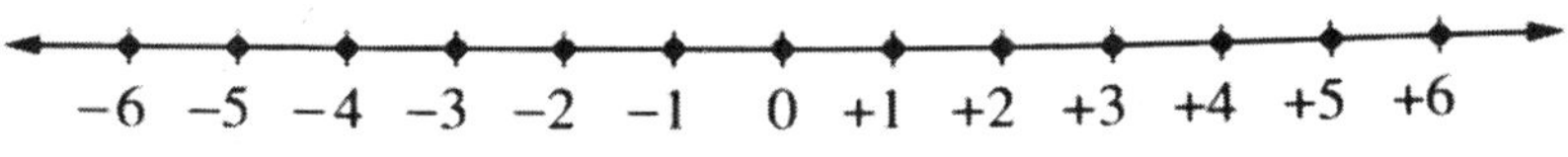

A positive number may be written without its sign. Thus, positive 20 is either +20 or just 20, but negative 20 must be written −20.

The** <u>**absolute**</u> **value** ***of a number is that number regardless of its sign. The absolute value of a number is represented by two straight lines: $|...|$. For example, $|-30| = 30$. The absolute value of −30 is 30.

The set of positive numbers, zero, and the negative numbers together are called <u>integers.</u> Numbers that can be written as a ratio of two integers are called <u>rational numbers.</u>

Addition, Subtraction, Multiplication and Division of Rational Numbers (the Rules of Signs)

- **Addition**. When adding two numbers with the same sign, use that sign for the sum as well.

Examples: (+8) + (+10) = 18
(-8) + (-10) = -18

To add two numbers with different signs it is necessary to subtract the lesser absolute value from the greater absolute value. The sum has the sign of the greater absolute value.

Examples: (-4) + (+12) = 8
(-4) + (+2) = -2

- **Subtraction**. Subtraction may be replaced by addition; in that case, the minuend keeps its sign and the subtrahend takes the opposite sign.

Examples: (+6) – (+4) = (+6) + (-4) = 6 – 4 = 2
(+6) – (-4) = (+6) + (+4) = 6 + 4 = 10
(-6) – (-4) = (-6) + (+4) = -2
(-6) – (-6) = (-6) + (+6) = -6 + 6 = 0

- **Multiplication**. When multiplying two numbers with the same signs, the product is always a positive number. If the signs are different, the product is a negative number.

Examples:

$$(+2.4) \cdot (-5) = -12$$

$$(-2.4) \cdot (-5) = 12$$

$$(-8) \cdot (+3) = -24$$

- **Division**. When dividing two numbers with the same signs, the quotient is always a positive number. If the signs of the two numbers are different, the quotient is a negative number.

Examples:

(-8) ÷ (+2) = -4
(+8) ÷ (-2) = -4
(+8) ÷ (+2) = 4
(-8) ÷ (-2) = 4

or: $\frac{-8}{2} = -4$

$\frac{8}{-2} = -4$

$\frac{8}{2} = 4$

$\frac{-8}{-2} = 4$

Table of Signs for Multiplication and Division

Sign of Multiplicand (or Dividend)	Sign of Factor (or Divisor)	Sign of Product (or Quotient)
+	+	+
+	-	-
-	+	-
-	-	+

2.2 Properties of Addition

- The Commutative Property

The order of the addends does not change the sum:

$$\boxed{a+b=b+a}$$

- The Associative Property

The way the addends are grouped does not change the sum:

$$\boxed{(a+b)+c=a+(b+c)}$$

- The Identity Property

$$\boxed{n+0=n}$$

2.3 Properties of Multiplication

- The Commutative Property

The order of the factors does not change the product:

$$\boxed{a\cdot b=b\cdot a}$$

- The Associative Property
  The way the factors are grouped does not change the product:

$$\boxed{a\cdot(b\cdot c)=(b\cdot a)\cdot c}$$

- The Distributive Property

$$\boxed{a\cdot(b+c)=a\cdot b+a\cdot c}$$

- The Identity Property

$$\boxed{a\cdot 1=a}$$

- The Zero Property

The product of any factor and zero equals zero:

$$\boxed{a\cdot 0=0}$$

2.4 Sets, Intersections, and Unions

A **set** is a well-defined collection of objects called **members** or **elements**.

Set-Builder Notation

Sets can be written in **roster notation** and **set-builder notation**.

Roster notation for the set of whole numbers greater than 30 is written

$$\{31, 32, 33, 34\ldots\}$$

Set-builder notation gives a description of how the set is built.

Set-builder notation for the set of whole numbers greater than 30 is written

$$\{x \mid x \text{ is a whole number and } x > 30\}$$

We read this as "the set of all x such that x is a whole number and x is greater than 30."

2.4.1 Intersection of Sets

The intersection of two sets A and B, written $A \cap B$, is the set of all members that are common to both sets. $A \cap B$ is read "A intersection B." In the diagram below, which is called a **Venn diagram**, the circles represent sets A and B. The shaded region represents $A \cap B$.

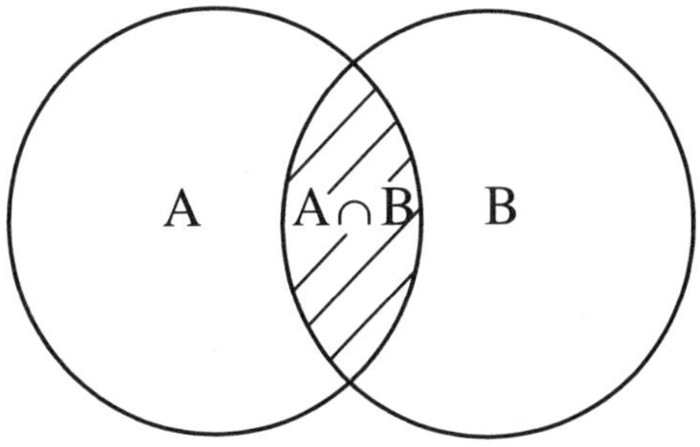

Example:

Let A = {5, 6, 7, 8, 9}
Let B = {5, 6, 12, 14, 15}

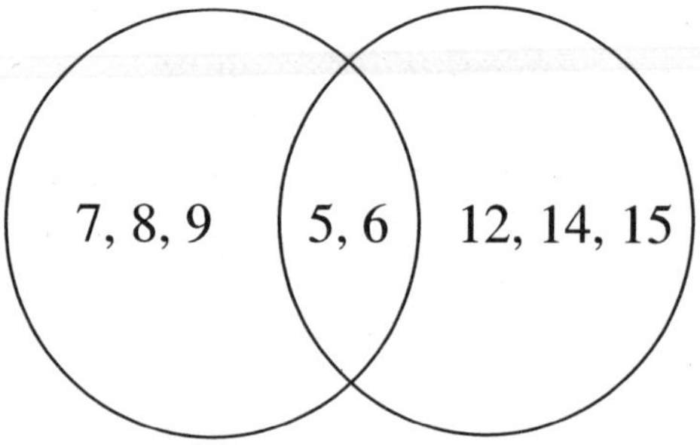

Find $A \cap B$
$A \cap B = \{5, 6\}$

2.4.2 Union of Sets

The union of two sets A and B, written $A \cup B$, is the set of all members that are in A or in B (or in both). In the diagram below, the circles represent the sets. The shaded region represents the union of the sets.

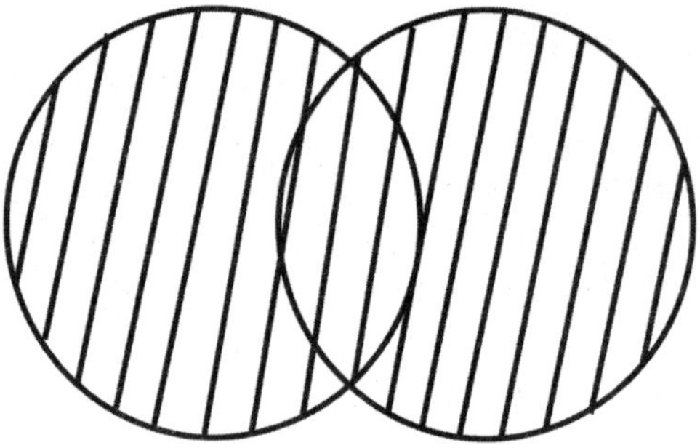

Example: Let A = {7, 9, 11, and 12}
Let B = {9, 10, 12, 15}

Find $A \cup B$
$A \cup B = \{7, 9, 10, 11, 12, 15\}$

2.4.3 Properties of the Intersection and Union Operations

- The Commutative Property

$$A \cup B = B \cup A$$
$$A \cap B = B \cap A$$

- The Associative Property

$$(A \cup B) \cup C = A \cup (B \cup C)$$
$$(A \cap B) \cap C = A \cap (B \cap C)$$

- The Distributive Property

$$(A \cup B) \cap C = (A \cap C) \cup (B \cap C)$$
$$(A \cap B) \cup C = (A \cup C) \cap (B \cup C)$$

2.5 Algebraic Terms

The product of two or more factors, each of which is either a number, a letter, or an exponent, is called an algebraic term.

Example: $4xy^2$

This term contains: the number 4 (the coefficient)

x (a variable)

y (a variable base)

2 (an exponent)

A separate letter or number can also be called a term.

A single term is also called a **monomial** (except for terms in which the variable is situated in the denominator).

Example: $3x^2y^2$ is a monomial

$\dfrac{3x^2}{y^2}$ is not a monomial.

Like terms have the same variable base and the same exponent.

Example: $4xy^2$, $2xy^2$, xy^2

Addition and Subtraction.

Only like terms can be added or subtracted. To find the sum or difference of like terms, add or subtract the coefficients.

Examples:

$$2x^2y^2 - 5x^2y^2 + 6x^2y^2 = 3x^2y^2$$

$$4x^3y^2 - 2x^2y^2 - x^3y^2 + 5x^2y^2 + 5xy = 3x^3y^2 + 3x^2y^2 + 5xy$$

The sum or difference of monomials that cannot be combined is called a **polynomial**. If there are two items, it is a **binomial**. If there are three items, it is a **trinomial**.

Examples:

$3x^2 + 4$ is a binomial
$2x^2y^2 - x^3y^2$ is a binomial
$3x^3y^2 + 3x^2y^2 + 5xy$ is a trinomial
$2x^4y^3 + 3x^3y^2 - 4x^2y + 3xy^2 + 5xy$ is a polynomial in five terms

2.6 Algebraic Powers

When multiplying or dividing a polynomial by a monomial or polynomial, often it is necessary to complete operations with powers.

In the expression 4^3, 4 is the **base** and 3 is the **exponent**.

$$4^3 = 4 \cdot 4 \cdot 4$$
$$a^n = a \cdot a \cdot a \cdot a \cdot a\ldots \text{ (n times)}$$

Multiplication and division of powers can only take place if the terms have the same base.

Examples:

1) $5^2 \cdot 5^3 = 5 \cdot 5 \times 5 \cdot 5 \cdot 5 = 5^{(2+3)} = 5^5$

Check: $5^2 = 25$; $5^3 = 125$; $5^5 = 25 \cdot 125 = 3125$

So, $\boxed{a^n \cdot a^m = a^{n+m}}$

2) $2^4 \div 2^2 = \dfrac{2^4}{2^2} = \dfrac{2 \cdot 2 \cdot 2 \cdot 2}{2 \cdot 2} = \dfrac{16}{4} = 4 = 2^{(4-2)} = 2^2$

$3^5 \div 3^2 = \dfrac{3 \cdot 3 \cdot 3 \cdot 3 \cdot 3}{3 \cdot 3} = 3^{(5-2)} = 3^3 = 9$

So, $\boxed{\dfrac{a^n}{a^m} = a^{n-m}}$

And some new formulas:

$$\boxed{\left(\frac{a}{b}\right)^n = \frac{a^n}{b^n}}$$

Check: $a = 4, b = 2, n = 3$ $\left(\dfrac{4}{2}\right)^3 = 8$;

$\dfrac{4^3}{2^3} = \dfrac{4 \cdot 4 \cdot 4}{2 \cdot 2 \cdot 2} = \dfrac{64}{8} = 8$

$$\boxed{(a \cdot b)^n = a^n \cdot b^n}$$

Check: $a = 2, b = 3, n = 2$ $(2 \cdot 3)^2 = 2^2 \cdot 3^2$, or $36 = 36$

$$\boxed{(a^n)^m = a^{n \cdot m}}$$

Check: $a = 3, n = 2, m = 3$ $\quad (3^2)^3 = 3^{2 \cdot 3} = 3^6$

$$9^3 = 3^6$$

$$729 = 729$$

2.7 Multiplication of a Polynomial by a Monomial or Polynomial

To multiply a polynomial by a monomial, each term of the polynomial is multiplied by the monomial.

Examples:

1) Multiply $(4x^4 + 2x^3 - x^2)$ ***by*** $2x^2$

$$2x^2\ (4x^4 + 2x^3 - x^2) =$$
$$= 2x^2\ (4x^4) + 2x^2(2x^3) + 2x^2(-x^2) = 8x^6 + 4x^5 - 2x^4$$

2) Multiply $2x(4x^3y + 7x^2y^2 - 2x - 4)$

$$2x(4x^3y + 7x^2y^2 - 2x - 4) =$$
$$= 2x(4x^3y + 7x^2y^2) + 2x(-2x - 4) = 8x^4y + 14x^3y^2 - 4x^2 - 8x$$

To multiply a polynomial by a polynomial, each term of one polynomial is multiplied by each term of a second polynomial. After multiplication, simplify the answer.

Examples:

1) Multiply $(3x^2 + 3)$ ***by*** $(2x^3 + 3)$

$(3x^2 + 3)\ (2x^3 + 3) = 6x^5 + 9x^2 + 6x^3 + 9$ (cannot be simplified)

2) Multiply $(2x^3+x^2-1)(4x^4-2x^3-x^2)$

$$(2x^3+x^2-1)(4x^4-2x^3-x^2)=$$
$$8x^7-4x^6-2x^5+4x^6-2x^5-x^4-4x^4+2x^3+x^2$$

Simplify the answer:

$$8x^7-4x^6-2x^5+4x^6-2x^5-x^4-4x^4+2x^3+x^2=$$
$$=8x^7+(-4x^6+4x^6)+(-2x^5-2x^5)+(-x^4-4x^4)+2x^3+x^2=$$
$$=8x^7-4x^5-5x^4+2x^3+x^2$$

This expression can also be written

$$8x^7-4x^5-5x^4+2x^3+x^2=2x^3(4x^4-2x^2+1)-5x^4+x^2$$

2.7.1 Formulas for Simplifying Multiplication

There are some formulas, which often help to simplify multiplication by polynomials, and to simplify the results.

1. $(a+b)^2=a^2+2ab+b^2$

2. $(a-b)^2=a^2-2ab+b^2$

3. $(a+b)(a-b)=a^2-b^2$

4. $(a+b)^3=a^3+3a^2b+3ab^2+b^3$

5. $(a-b)^3=a^3-3a^2b+3ab^2-b^3$

6. $$\boxed{(a+b)(a^2-ab+b^2)=a^3+b^3}$$

7. $$\boxed{(a-b)(a^2+ab+b^2)=a^3-b^3}$$

Examples:

1) Multiply $9x^2y^4-5y^4x^2+0.4xy$ by $4y^4x^2-0.4xy$

Step 1: Simplify the first trinomial:

$9x^2y^4-5y^4x^2+0.4xy = 4y^4x^2+0.4xy$

Step 2: Let $4y^4x^2=a$ and $0.4xy=b$.

Then $(4y^4x^2+0.4xy)\,(4y^4x^2-0.4xy)= (a+b)(a-b)$

Step 3: Apply formula number 3 and obtain the result:

$(9x^2y^4-5y^4x^2+0.4xy)\,(4y^4x^2-0.4xy)=$

$= (4y^4x^2)^2-(0.4xy)^2 =$

$= 16y^8x^4-0.16x^2y^2$

2) Multiply $2x^3+5$ by $4x^6-10x^3+25$

If $2x^3=a$ and $5=b$, then $a^2=(2x^3)^2=4x^6$; $b^2=5^2=25$

Apply formula 6 and obtain the result:

$(2x^3+5)(4x^6-10x^3+25) = (a+b)(a^2-ab+b^2)=a^3+b^3$

Then $(2x^3+5)(4x^6-10x^3+25) = (2x^3)^3+(5)^3=$

$= 8x^9+5^3=8x^9+125$

2.8 Dividing by a Monomial or a Polynomial

To divide a sum of numbers or monomials by a monomial, divide each term by the divisor.

Examples:

1) $\dfrac{24x+48x+16x}{8}=\dfrac{24x}{8}+\dfrac{48x}{8}+\dfrac{16x}{8}=3x+6x+2x=11x$

2) $\dfrac{48x^2+16x}{8x}=\dfrac{48x^2}{8x}+\dfrac{16x}{8x}=6x+2$

To divide a polynomial by a polynomial, follow these steps:

Step 1: Write each polynomial in *descending* order so that the exponents of a particular variable decrease as we move from left to right.

For example,

the polynomial $2x^2+4x^5-4x+x^3-7$

must be written $4x^5+x^3+2x^2-4x-7$

Dividing any polynomial A by another polynomial B is possible only if the largest exponent of A is larger than the largest exponent of B.

Step 2: Divide the first term of the dividend by the first term of the divisor. The result is the first term of the quotient.

Step 3: Multiply the term of the quotient by the divisor.

Step 4: Continue as in arithmetic division until reaching a remainder of 0 or a remainder whose degree is less than the degree of the divisor.

Examples:

1) Divide $10x + x^2 + 16$ by $x + 8$

Step 1: Write the first polynomial in descending order.

$$x^2 + 10x + 16$$

Step2:

$$\begin{array}{r|l} & x \\ \hline x+8 & x^2 + 10x + 16 \end{array} \qquad x^2 \div x = x$$

Step 3:

$$\begin{array}{r|l} & x \\ \hline x+8 & x^2 + 10x + 16 \\ & -(x^2 + 8x) \\ \hline & 2x \end{array} \qquad x(x+8) = x^2 + 8x$$

Step 4:

$$\begin{array}{r|l} & x + 2 \\ \hline x+8 & x^2 + 10x + 16 \\ & -(x^2 + 8x) \\ \hline & 2x + 16 \end{array}$$

$$\begin{array}{r} x+2 \\ x+8\overline{)x^2+10x+16} \\ -(x^2+8x) \\ \hline 2x+16 \\ -(2x+16) \\ \hline 0 \end{array}$$

2(x + 8)=2x + 16

Result: $\dfrac{x^2+10x+16}{x+8}=x+2$

Check: $(x+2)(x+8)=x^2+8x+2x+16=x^2+10x+16$

2) Divide $8x^3+16x^2-2x+4$ by $4x^2-2x+1$

$$\begin{array}{r} 2x+5R6x-1 \\ 4x^2-2x+1\overline{)8x^3+16x^2-2x+4} \\ -(8x^3-4x^2+2x) \\ \hline 20x^2-4x+4 \\ -(20x^2-10x+5) \\ \hline 6x-1 \end{array}$$

R=6x-1

The remainder has a degree less than the degree of the divisor, so the process is complete.

Result: $\dfrac{8x^3+16x^2-2x+4}{4x^2-2x+1}=2x+5$, with a remainder of 6$x$ – 1

Check:

$$(2x+5)(4x^2-2x+1)=8x^3-4x^2+2x+20x^2-10x+5=$$

$$=8x^3+16x^2-8x+5$$

$8x^3 + 16x^2 - 8x + 5 + R = 8x^3 + 16x^2 - 8x + 5 + 6x - 1 =$

$= 8x^3 + 16x^2 - 2x + 4$, the dividend

3) Divide $x^4 + x^3 + 3x^2 + 3x + 2$ by $x^2 + x + 1$

$$\begin{array}{r} x^2 + 2\ Rx \\ x^2 + x + 1 \overline{) x^4 + x^3 + 3x^2 + 3x + 2} \\ -(x^4 + x^3 + x^2) \\ \hline 2x^2 + 3x + 2 \\ -\ (2x^2 + 2x + 2) \\ \hline x \end{array}$$

Result: $\dfrac{x^4 + x^3 + 3x^2 + 3x + 2}{x^2 + x + 1} = x^2 + 2$, with a remainder of x.

Check:
$(x^2+2)(x^2+x+1) = x^4 + x^3 + x^2 + 2x^2 + 2x + 2 = x^4 + x^3 + 3x^2 + 2x + 2$

$x^4 + x^3 + 3x^2 + 2x + 2 + R = x^4 + x^3 + 3x^2 + 2x + 2 + x = x^4 + x^3 + 3x^2 + 3x + 2$, the dividend.

2.9 Algebraic Fractions

An algebraic fraction is a quotient of two algebraic expressions.

For example: $\dfrac{x}{3}, \dfrac{3}{x}, \dfrac{x+3}{x-2}, \dfrac{x^2+10x+16}{x+8}$

When an algebraic fraction is a quotient of two polynomials, it is called a **rational expression**. An algebraic fraction cannot have a denominator equal to 0.

Examples:

If $x = 0$, then the fraction $\frac{5}{x}$ is not defined.

This rule also applies to the expression $\frac{25}{x^2 - 9}$ where $x = 3$.

To reduce fractions to their simplest form, or **lowest terms**, factor them and then cancel common factors. This procedure can be applied to rational expressions as well as rational numbers.

Examples:

1) Express $\frac{14x^5}{7x^2}$ in its lowest terms.

$$\frac{14x^5}{7x^2} = \frac{7 \cdot 2 \cdot x^2 \cdot x^3}{7 \cdot x^2} = \frac{2x^3}{1} = 2x^3$$

Solution: $\frac{14x^5}{7x^2} = 2x^3$

2) Express $\frac{2x^2 + 3x - 5}{x^2 - 1}$ in its lowest terms.

Write the numerator and denominator as a product of two binomials:

$$2x^2 + 3x - 5 = (2x + 5)(x - 1)\ ;\ x^2 - 1 = x^2 - 1^2 = (x + 1)(x - 1)$$

$$\frac{2x^2 + 3x - 5}{x^2 - 1} = \frac{(2x + 5)(x - 1)}{(x + 1)(x - 1)} = \frac{2x - 5}{x + 1}$$

Solution: $\frac{2x^2 + 3x - 5}{x^2 - 1} = \frac{2x + 5}{x + 1}$

This answer is incorrect if $x = -1$. Then $\frac{2x+5}{-1+1} = \frac{2x+5}{0}$

The fully correct answer is written

$$\frac{2x^2+3x-5}{x^2-1} = \frac{2x+5}{x+1} \quad (x \neq -1)$$

2.10 Multiplying Algebraic Fractions

To multiply two fractions $\frac{a}{b}$ and $\frac{x}{y}$ ($b \neq 0$ and $y \neq 0$):

Step 1: Multiply the numerators $\quad a \cdot x$

Step 2: Multiply the denominators $\quad b \cdot y$

Step 3: Write the answer $\quad \frac{a}{b} \cdot \frac{x}{y} = \frac{ax}{by}$

Step 4: Simplify the answer (Simplification can be done before multiplying).

Example:

Solve $\frac{4a^2b}{3c^2d} \cdot \frac{2c^3d^2}{ab^3}$

Step 1: $4a^2b \cdot 2c^3d^2 = 8a^2bc^3d^2$

Step 2: $3c^2d \cdot ab^3 = 3ab^3c^2d$

Step 3: $\frac{4a^2b}{3c^2d} \cdot \frac{2c^3d^2}{ab^3} = \frac{8a^2bc^3d^2}{3ab^3c^2d}$

Step 4: $\frac{8a^2bc^3d^2}{3ab^3c^2d} = \frac{8acd}{3b^2}$

Or: $\frac{4a^2b}{3c^2d}\cdot\frac{2c^3d^2}{ab^3}=\frac{4a\cdot 2cd}{3\cdot b^2}=\frac{8acd}{3b^2}$

Solution: $\frac{4a^2b}{3c^2d}\cdot\frac{2c^3d^2}{ab^3}=\frac{8acd}{3b^2}$

2.11 Dividing Algebraic Fractions

To divide two fractions $\frac{a}{b}$ and $\frac{x}{y}$ ($b \neq 0, x \neq 0, y \neq 0$):

Step 1: Multiply the numerator of the first fraction by the denominator of the second fraction. The product is a numerator of the new fraction.

Step 2: Multiply the numerator of the first fraction by the numerator of the second fraction. The product is the denominator of the new fraction.

Step 3: Simplify the answer.

We can multiply the first fraction by the reciprocal of the second fraction.

Multiply the first fraction by the reciprocal of the second fraction.

$\frac{x}{y}$ is the fraction, and $\frac{y}{x}$ is the reciprocal of the fraction.

$$\frac{a}{b}\div\frac{x}{y}=\frac{a}{b}\cdot\frac{y}{x}$$

Example:

Divide $\frac{x^2-1}{x}\div\frac{x+1}{3x^2}$

Solution:

Step 1 and 2: $\frac{x^2-1}{x} \div \frac{x+1}{3x^2} = \frac{(x^2-1)3x^2}{x(x+1)}$

Step 3:

$$\frac{x^2-1}{x} \div \frac{x+1}{3x^2} = \frac{(x^2-1)3x^2}{x(x+1)} = \frac{(x^2-1^2)3x^2}{x(x+1)} = \frac{(x+1)(x-1)3x^2}{x(x+1)} = 3x(x-1)$$

Solution:

$$\frac{x^2-1}{x} \div \frac{x+1}{3x^2} = 3x(x-1) \qquad (x \neq 0,\ x \neq -1)$$

2.12 Addition and Subtraction of Algebraic Fractions

Addition and subtraction of algebraic fractions occurs in the same way as the addition and subtraction of arithmetic fractions.

Examples:

1) $\frac{m}{a^2b} + \frac{n}{ab^2} = \frac{m}{a^2b} \cdot \frac{b}{b} + \frac{n}{ab^2} \cdot \frac{a}{a} = \frac{mb+na}{a^2b^2}$

2) $\frac{a-b}{2a^2-ab-3b^2} - \frac{a+b}{2a^2-5ab+3b^2}$

Factor the denominators:

$2a^2 - ab - 3b^2 = (2a-3b)(a+b)$

$2a^2 - 5ab + 3b^2 = (2a-3b)(a-b)$

$$\frac{a-b}{(2a-3b)(a+b)} - \frac{a+b}{(2a-3b)(a-b)} = \frac{(a-b)^2-(a+b)^2}{(2a-3b)(a+b)(a-b)} = \frac{-4ab}{(2a-3b)(a^2-b^2)}$$

2.13 Ratios and Proportions

A **ratio** is a comparison of two numbers using division.

The ratio of 2 to 3 can be expressed in the following ways:

$$\frac{2}{3},\ 2:3,\ 2\div 3,\ 0.\overline{6}$$

In general, the ratio of a to b is written $\frac{a}{b}$ or $a:b$. The numbers a and b are called the **terms of the ratio**.

If the ratios name the same number, then they are **equivalent ratios**.

Example: The ratio of 56 to 200 $\left(\frac{56}{200}\right)$ can be simplified to the ratio of 7 to 25 $\left(\frac{7}{25}\right)$. $\frac{56}{200}$ and $\frac{7}{25}$ name the same number. They are equivalent ratios.

A ratio is in its simplest form if no whole numbers (other than 1) can divide both its terms evenly.

A **proportion** is an equation of the form $\frac{a}{b}=\frac{c}{d}$, which states that the two ratios are equivalent.

a, b, c, and *d* are the four terms of the proportion. *a* and *d* are called the **extremes** and *b* and *c* are the **means**.
In a proportion, the product of the means is equal to the product of the extremes.

$$\text{If } \frac{a}{b}=\frac{c}{d}, \text{ then } ad=bc.$$

The process that uses this property is called **cross multiplication**.

Examples:

1) Solve the proportion $\frac{5}{6}=\frac{x}{72}$

$$\frac{5}{6}=\frac{x}{72}$$

$$6x=5\cdot 72 \quad \text{(Cross multiplication)}$$

$$6x=360$$

Solution: $x=60$

2) Solve the proportion $\frac{3}{7}=\frac{x-2}{x+2}$

$$\frac{3}{7}=\frac{x-2}{x+2}$$

$$3(x+2)=7(x-2) \text{ (Cross Multiplication)}$$

$$3x+6=7x-14$$

$$4x=20$$

$$x=5$$

3) Two angles are complementary. Their measures are in the ratio of 2:3. Find the measures.

Step 1: Define a variable: Let x represent the lesser angle. Then $90-x$ represents the greater angle.

Step 2: Write a proportion: $\frac{x}{90-x}=\frac{2}{3}$

Step 3: Solve the proportion.

$$3x = 2(90 - x)$$

$$3x = 180 - 2x$$

$$5x = 180$$

$$x = 36$$

Since $x = 36$, $90 - x = 54$.

Therefore, the measures are 36° and 54°.

A **percentage** is a ratio of a number to 100.

Examples:

1) What is 5% of 80?

$$5\% = \frac{5}{100}$$

Let x represent the number.

$$\frac{x}{80} = \frac{5}{100} \text{ (Some number is compared to 80)}$$

$$100x = 80 \cdot 5 \qquad \text{(Cross Multiplication)}$$

$$x = 4$$

Therefore, 4 is 5% of 80.

2) Tom paid $0.30 sales tax on a $7.50 purchase.

What percentage does the government take in sales tax?

$$\frac{0.30}{7.50} = \frac{x}{100}$$

$$\frac{30}{750} = \frac{x}{100}$$

$$75x = 300$$

$$x = 4$$

Therefore, the sales tax is 4%.

2.14 Equations (First Degree and One Variable)

An equation is a statement that two algebraic expressions are equal.

To solve an equation is to find the value of the variable.

To find a missing addend, subtract the known addend from both sides of the equations.

Example: $x + 7 = 12$

$$x + 7 - 7 = 12 - 7$$

$\text{x} = 5$ This is the root of the equation.

To find a missing factor, divide both sides of the equation by the known factor.

Example: $4x = 36$

$$\frac{4x}{4} = \frac{36}{4}$$

$x = 9$ This is the root of the equation.

To find a variable in general, add, subtract, multiply, or divide the same number on both sides of the equal sign. Apply the distribution property to separate the variable from its coefficient.

Examples:

1) Find x in $3x - 6 = 30$

$$3x - 6 + 6 = 30 + 6$$

$$3x = 36$$

$$x = \frac{36}{3} = 12$$

Check: $3 \cdot 12 - 6 = 30$

$$30 = 30$$

2) Find x in $\frac{1}{2}x + 6x = 13$

$$x\left(\frac{1}{2} + 6\right) = 13$$

$$6\frac{1}{2}x = 13$$

$$x = \frac{13}{6\frac{1}{2}} = 2$$

Check: $\frac{1}{2} \cdot 2 + 6 \cdot 2 = 13$

3) Find x in $5x - 9 = 1 + 3x$

$$5x - 9 + 9 = 1 + 3x + 9$$

$$5x = 3x + 10$$

$$5x - 3x = 3x - 3x + 10$$

$$2x = 10$$

$$x = \frac{10}{2} = 5$$

Check: $5 \cdot 5 - 9 = 1 + 3 \cdot 5$

4) Find x in $2x + 3(2x - 6) = 2x + 6$

$$2x + 6x - 18 = 2x + 6$$

$$8x - 18 = 2x + 6$$

$$8x - 18 + 18 = 2x + 6 + 18$$

$$8x = 2x + 24$$

$$8x - 2x = 2x + 24 - 2x$$

$$6x = 24$$

$$x = \frac{24}{6} = 4$$

Check: $2 \cdot 4 + 3(2 \cdot 4 - 6) = 2 \cdot 4 + 6$

$$14 = 14$$

5) Find x in $\frac{x+2}{4} + \frac{x+4}{5} = \frac{4(x-1)}{5}$

Multiply each term of equation by the LCM of the denominators. The LCM of 4, 5, and 5 is 20.

$$20\frac{x+2}{4} + 20\frac{x+4}{5} = 20\frac{4(x-1)}{5}$$

$$5(x+2)+4(x+4)=16(x-1)$$

$$9x+26=16x-16$$

$$9x-9x+26=16x-9x-16$$

$$26=7x-16$$

$$26+16=7x-16+16$$

$$42=7x$$

$$x=\frac{42}{7}=6$$

Check: $\frac{6+2}{4}+\frac{6+4}{5}=\frac{4(6-1)}{5}$

$$4=4$$

2.14.1 Using Equations to Solve Problems

1. A pair of shoes, a purse, and a dress cost \$140 all together. The shoes cost twice as much as the purse, and the dress costs twice as much as the shoes. What does each of these three things cost?

Let x = the price of the purse. Then $2x$ = the price of the shoes. $2 \cdot 2x = 4x$ = the price of the dress. This relationship can be expressed in an equation as:

$$x+2x+4x=\$140$$

$$7x=\$140$$

$$x=\frac{140}{7}=\$20$$

So the purse costs x, or \$20. The shoes cost $2x$, or \$40. The dress costs $4x$, or \$80.

Check: \$20 + \$40 + \$80 = \$140

2. At the end of 1995, David was half as old as his grandmother. The sum of the years in which they were born is 3839. How old will David be at the end of 2000?

Let x = Grandmother's age at the end of 1995. The year of her birth is therefore $1995 - x$. David's age at the end of 1995 is $\frac{x}{2}$.

His year of birth is $1995 - \frac{x}{2}$. Since the sum of the years in which they were born is 3839, we have an equation:

$$1995 - x + (1995 - \frac{x}{2}) = 3839$$

$$1995 - x + 1995 - \frac{x}{2} = 3839$$

$$1995 + 1995 - 3839 = 1.5x$$

$$x = \frac{150}{1.5} = 100$$

David's age at the end of 1995 was $\frac{x}{2} = \frac{100}{2} = 50$ years. In the year 2000, David is 5 years older, or $50 + 5 = 55$.

2.15 Systems of Linear Equations

If in a single equation there are two or more unknown quantities, then there is no simple solution to the equation. The number of equations in the system of equations must not be less than the number of unknowns.

Algebraic Methods

- First Method: Elimination of one variable by substitution.

Example: Solve the system of equations

$$x + 4y = 12$$

$$3x + 3y = 18$$

Step 1: Find x from the first equation:

$$x + 4y - 4y = 12 - 4y$$

$$x = 12 - 4y$$

Step 2: Replace x by 12 - 4y in the second equation and solve for y:

$$3(12 - 4y) + 3y = 18$$

$$36 - 12y + 3y = 18$$

$$36 - 9y = 18$$

$$36 - 9y - 36 = 18 - 36$$

$$-9y = -18$$

$$y = \frac{-18}{-9} = 2$$

Step 3: Substitute $y = 2$ into the first equation and solve for x:

$$x + 4 \cdot 2 = 12$$

$$x + 8 - 8 = 12 - 8$$

$$x = 4$$

Answer: $x = 4,\ y = 2$

Check:

$$x + 4y = 4 + 4 \cdot 2 = 12$$

$$3x + 3y = 3 \cdot 4 + 3 \cdot 2 = 18$$

- Second Method: Elimination of one variable by addition or subtraction.

This method requires that the coefficients of one variable be equal in absolute value.

Examples:

1) Solve the system of equations: $5x + 3y = 27$

$$x + y = 7$$

Step 1: Make the coefficients of variable y equal by multiplying both sides of the second equation by 3.

$$5x + 3y = 27$$

$$3(x + y) = 7 \cdot 3$$

$$3(x + y) = 7 \cdot 3$$

$$3x + 3y = 21$$

Step 2: Subtract the second equation from the first and find x.

$$5x + 3y = 27$$

$$-(3x + 3y) = 21$$

$$2x \quad = 6$$

$$x = \frac{6}{2} = 3$$

Step 3: Substitute $x = 3$ into the second original equation and find y.

$$3 + y = 7$$

$$3 + y - 3 = 7 - 3$$

y=4

Answer: x=3, y=4

Check: $5x + 3y = 5 \cdot 3 + 3 \cdot 4 = 27$

$$x + y = 3 + 4 = 7$$

2) Solve the system of equations:

$$0.3x - 0.5y = -0.9$$

$$2.1x + y = 7.2$$

Step 1: Make the coefficients of variable y equal by multiplying both sides of the second equation by 0.5.

$$0.3x - 0.5y = -0.9$$

$$0.5(2.1x + y) = 0.5 \cdot 7.2$$

$$0.3x - 0.5y = -0.9$$

$$1.05x + 0.5y = 3.6$$

Step 2: Add the first and second equations and find x.

$$\begin{array}{r} 0.3x - 0.5y = -0.9 \\ +(1.05x + 0.5y) = 3.6 \\ \hline 1.35x \qquad = 2.7 \end{array}$$

$$x = \frac{2.7}{1.35} = 2$$

Step 3: Substitute $x = 2$ into the second original equation and find y.

$$2.1 \cdot 2 + y = 7.2$$

$$4.2 + y = 7.2$$

$$4.2 + y - 4.2 = 7.2 - 4.2$$

$$y = 3$$

Check: $0.3 \cdot 2 - 0.5 \cdot 3 = -0.9$

$2.1 \cdot 2 + 3 = 7.2$

Answer: $x = 2, y = 3$

2.15.1 Special Formulas

The solution of the equation system: $ax + by = c$

$a_1x + b_1y = c_1$

may be found quickly by using the following formula:

$$x = \frac{b_1c - bc_1}{ab_1 - a_1b}$$

$$y = \frac{ac_1 - a_1c}{ab_1 - a_1b}$$

Example:

Solve the system
$$2x+3y=18$$
$$x+2y=11$$

$$x=\frac{2\cdot 18-3\cdot 11}{2\cdot 2-1\cdot 3}=\frac{36-33}{4-3}=\frac{3}{1}=3$$

$$y=\frac{2\cdot 11-1\cdot 18}{2\cdot 2-1\cdot 3}=\frac{22-18}{4-3}=\frac{4}{1}=4$$

Check:
$$2\cdot 3+3\cdot 4=18$$
$$3+2\cdot 4=11$$

2.16 Graphical Method

Solve the system of equations:
$$x+4y=12$$
$$3x+3y=18$$

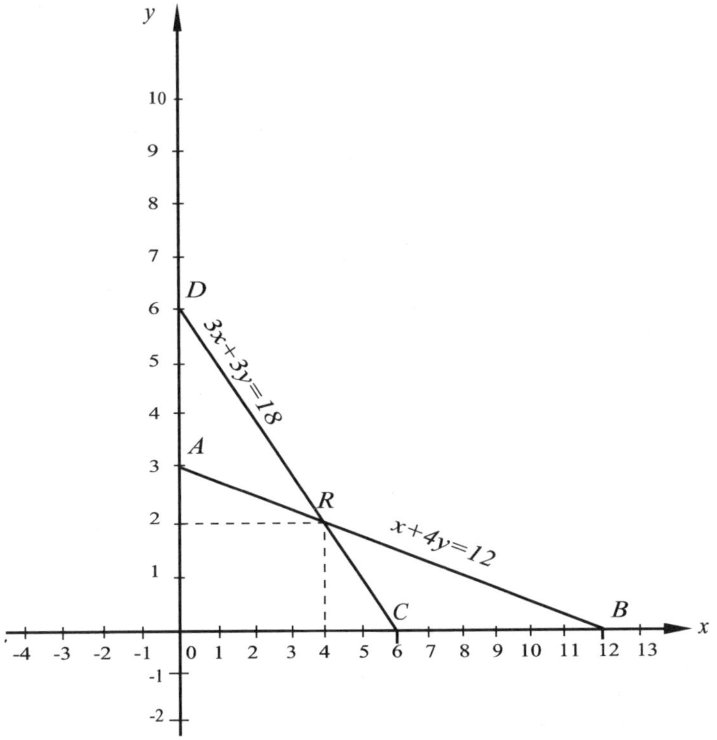

Step 1: Let x = 0 in the first equation.

Then $4y = 12$; $y = 3$.

The coordinates of the first point (A) on the graph are {0;3}.

Step 2: Let $y = 0$ in the first equation.

Then $x = 12$.

The coordinates of the second point (B) on the graph are {12;0}.

Draw a straight line through points A and B on the graph. That line corresponds to the first equation.

Step 3: Let $x = 0$ in the second equation.

Then $3y = 18$; $y=6$.

The coordinates of the first point (C) on the graph are {0;6}.

Step 4: Let $y = 0$ in the second equation.

Then $3x = 18$; $x = 6$.

The coordinates of the second point D on the graph are {6;0}.

Draw a straight line through points C and D on the graph. This line corresponds to the second equation. The point (R) of intersection of the lines AB and CD is the solution of the system of equations. The coordinates of that point are the roots of the system, x=4, y=2.

2.17 Negative, Zero, and Fractional Exponents

$$a^n = b$$

A power is the product of equal factors.

Examples:

$$a^3 = a \cdot a \cdot a$$

$$a^5 = a \cdot a \cdot a \cdot a \cdot a$$

If *a, b,* and *c* are positive integers:

$$\boxed{x^a \cdot x^b = x^{a+b}}$$

$$\boxed{\frac{x^a}{x^b} = x^{a-b}}$$

$$\boxed{(x^a)^c = x^{a \cdot c}}$$

$$\boxed{(x \cdot y)^a = x^a \cdot y^a}$$

$$\boxed{\left(\frac{x}{y}\right)^a = \frac{x^a}{y^a} (y \neq 0)}$$

The zero exponent:

$$x^0 = 1 \text{ if } x \neq 0$$

For example:

$$5^0 = 1$$

$$(-5)^0 = 1$$

$$(5x)^0 = 1$$

$$(-5x)^0 = 1$$

The negative exponent:

$$x^{-n} = \frac{1}{x^n} \text{ if } x \neq 0$$

For example:

$$x^{-1} = \frac{1}{x}$$

$$2^{-1} = \frac{1}{2} = 0.5$$

$$x^{-n} \cdot x^n = x^{(-n+n)} = x^0 = 1$$

$$x^{-2} \cdot x^2 = \left(\frac{1}{x}\right)^2 \cdot x^2 = \frac{1^2}{x^2} \cdot x^2 = 1$$

$$3^{-2} \cdot 3^2 = \frac{1^2}{3^2} \cdot 3^2 = 1$$

$$\frac{x^n}{x^{-n}} = \frac{x}{\frac{1}{x^n}} = x^n \cdot x^n = x^{2n}$$

$$\frac{2^3}{2^{-3}} = 2^3 \cdot 2^3 = 64$$

The fractional exponent:

$$x^{\frac{m}{n}} = \sqrt[n]{x^m} \quad (n \neq 0)$$

For example:

$$2^{\frac{1}{2}} = \sqrt{2} \approx 1.4$$

$$\sqrt[3]{2^3} = 2^{\frac{3}{3}} = 2$$

$$2^{\frac{5}{2}} = \sqrt{2^5} \approx 5.7$$

2.18 Roots

Extracting a root is the reverse operation of raising to a power.

If $5^3 = 5 \cdot 5 \cdot 5 = 125$, then $\sqrt[3]{125} = 5$

RADICAL SIGN

INDEX → $\sqrt[n]{N}$ ← RADICAND

If n = 2, then the number two is not written ($\sqrt[2]{x} = \sqrt{x}$).

This is read "the square root of x."

$\sqrt[3]{x}$ is read "the cube root of x."

If the index n is an odd number, then the solution has the same sign as the radicand N.

For example:

$$\sqrt[3]{125} = 5$$

$$\sqrt{144} = 12$$

Check: $(5)(5)(5) = 125$

$$(12)(12) = 144$$

If the index n is an even number, then there are two solutions: positive and negative.

For example:

$$\sqrt{16} = 4 \text{ and } \sqrt{16} = -4$$

We can abbreviate this as $\sqrt{16} = \pm 4$

The square root of a negative number does not exist in the set of real numbers.

Usually a square root is found using a calculator (the square root key typically looks like this: $\boxed{\sqrt{x}}$).

Sometimes it is necessary to find the approximate value of a square root.

Examples:

1) Solve $x = \sqrt{120}$

Step 1: Determine the nearest whole number to $\sqrt{120}$. It is 11 ($11^2 = 121$).

Step 2: $a = \dfrac{120}{11} = 10.91$

Step 3: $b = \dfrac{11 + 10.91}{2} = 10.95$

Solution: $x = \sqrt{120} \approx 10.95$

2) Solve $x = \sqrt{10{,}500}$

Step 1: The nearest whole number is

100 ($100^2 = 10{,}000$).

Step 2: $a = \dfrac{10{,}500}{100} = 105$

Step 3: $b = \dfrac{100 + 105}{2} = 102.5$

Solution: $x \approx 102.5$

2.18.1 Adding and Subtracting Radicals

Like radicals are radicals that have the same index and the same radicand.

For example: $3\sqrt{5}$ and $5\sqrt{5}$ are like radicals

$4\sqrt[3]{6}$ and $7\sqrt[3]{6}$ are like radicals

$9\sqrt{7}$ and $9\sqrt[3]{7}$ are unlike radicals

$5\sqrt{7}$ and $5\sqrt{5}$ are unlike radicals

To add and subtract like radicals, use the following formulas:

$$a\sqrt[n]{x}+b\sqrt[n]{x}+c\sqrt[n]{x}+\ldots=(a+b+c+\ldots)\sqrt[n]{x}$$

$$a\sqrt[n]{x}-b\sqrt[n]{x}-c\sqrt[n]{x}-\ldots=(a-b-c-\ldots)\sqrt[n]{x}$$

Examples:

$$2\sqrt{3}+4\sqrt{3}+7\sqrt{3}=(2+4+7)\sqrt{3}=13\sqrt{3}$$

$$3\sqrt[3]{5}+\frac{1}{2}\sqrt[3]{5}+\frac{1}{4}\sqrt[3]{5}=(3+\frac{1}{2}+\frac{1}{4})\sqrt[3]{5}=3\frac{3}{4}\sqrt[3]{5}$$

$$7\sqrt{2}-4\sqrt{2}-\sqrt{2}=(7-4-1)\sqrt{2}=2\sqrt{2}$$

Adding and subtracting unlike radicals cannot always be expressed in single terms. For example the sum of $\sqrt{2}$ and $\sqrt{3}$ is nothing other than $\sqrt{2}+\sqrt{3}$.

Sometimes, however, it is possible to transform unlike radicals into like radicals.

For example:

$\sqrt{20}+\sqrt{45}+4\sqrt{5}=\sqrt{4\cdot 5}+\sqrt{9\cdot 5}+4\sqrt{5}=2\sqrt{5}+3\sqrt{5}+4\sqrt{5}=(2+3+4)\sqrt{5}=9\sqrt{5}$

Solution: $\sqrt{20}+\sqrt{45}+4\sqrt{5}=9\sqrt{5}$

2.18.2 Multiplication of Roots with the Same Index

$$\boxed{\sqrt[n]{a}\cdot\sqrt[n]{b}\cdot\sqrt[n]{c}=\sqrt[n]{abc}}$$

Examples:

1) $\sqrt{4}\cdot\sqrt{9}\cdot\sqrt{16}=\sqrt{4\cdot 9\cdot 16}=\sqrt{576}=24$

Check: $\sqrt{4}=2,\ \sqrt{9}=3,\ \sqrt{16}=4$

$2\cdot 3\cdot 4=24$

2) $\sqrt[3]{8}\cdot\sqrt[3]{27}\cdot\sqrt[3]{64}=\sqrt[3]{8\cdot 27\cdot 64}=\sqrt[3]{13{,}824}=24$

Check: $\sqrt[3]{8}=2,\ \sqrt[3]{27}=3,\ \sqrt[3]{64}=4$

$2\cdot 3\cdot 4=24$

3) $(2\sqrt{16})(3\sqrt{144})=(2\cdot 3)\sqrt{16\cdot 144}=6\sqrt{2304}=6\cdot 48=288$

2.18.3 Division of Roots with the Same Index

Formula: $\boxed{\dfrac{\sqrt[n]{a}}{\sqrt[n]{b}}=\sqrt[n]{\dfrac{a}{b}}}$

Example: $\dfrac{\sqrt{16}}{\sqrt{4}}=\sqrt{\dfrac{16}{4}}=\sqrt{4}=2$

2.19 Irrational Numbers

In the classification of numbers, real numbers can be subdivided into rational and irrational numbers.

> Irrational numbers cannot be expressed as the ratio of two integers. In general, irrational numbers are:
>
> 1) the roots of nonperfect powers,
> 2) decimals that do not end or repeat, and
> 3) the number π (the ratio of a circle's circumference to its diameter.)

When writing an irrational number, we use three dots (…) after a series of digits to indicate that the number does not terminate.

Examples:

$$\sqrt{2} = 1.4142135\ldots$$

$$\sqrt{3} = 1.7320508\ldots$$

$$\sqrt{5} = 2.2360679\ldots$$

$$\pi = 3.141592\ldots$$

The quantity of figures in an irrational number depends on how many you need for your approximation.

2.20 Complex Numbers

Solving some mathematical problems requires the square root of a negative number. Unfortunately, this is impossible to find, since the square of both a positive and a negative number yields a positive number.

For example,

$\sqrt{-9}$ has no solution, since $(-3)^2 = +9$ and $(3)^2 = +9$.

In order to solve such problems, an imaginary number is used.

i is defined this way: $i = \sqrt{-1}$. Therefore, $i^2 = -1$.

This imaginary unit is the basis of a new set of numbers, called **imaginary numbers**. All numbers that are not imaginary are called **real numbers**.

We can use the imaginary number *i* just as we would any other number:

$$\sqrt{-9} = \sqrt{(+9)(-1)} = \sqrt{9} \cdot \sqrt{-1} = 3i$$

$$\sqrt{-72} = \sqrt{36} \cdot \sqrt{2} \cdot \sqrt{-1} = 6i\sqrt{2}$$

$$\sqrt{-64} + 2\sqrt{-9} = \sqrt{64} \cdot \sqrt{-1} + 2\sqrt{9} \cdot \sqrt{-1} = 8i + 6i = 14i$$

All powers of *i* can be expressed with just four values:

$$i^2 = (\sqrt{-1})^2 = -1$$

$$i^3 = i^2 \cdot i = -1 \cdot i = -i$$

$$i^4 = i^2 \cdot i^2 = 1$$

$$i^5 = i^4 \cdot i = 1 \cdot i = i$$

$$i^6 = i^5 \cdot i = i \cdot i = -1$$

$$i^7 = -i$$

$$i^7 = -i$$

$$i^8 = 1$$

$$i^9 = i$$

et cetera

Addition and Subtraction of Imaginary Numbers

$$\sqrt{-81}+\sqrt{-36}+\sqrt{-225}=\sqrt{81}\cdot\sqrt{-1}+\sqrt{36}\sqrt{-1}+\sqrt{225}\cdot\sqrt{-1}=$$

$$=9i+6i+15i=30i$$

$$\sqrt{-49}-\sqrt{-16}=\sqrt{49}\cdot\sqrt{-1}-\sqrt{16}\cdot\sqrt{-1}=7i-4i=3i$$

Multiplication of Imaginary Numbers

$$\sqrt{-49}\cdot\sqrt{-9}=\sqrt{49}\cdot\sqrt{-1}\cdot\sqrt{9}\cdot\sqrt{-1}=7i\cdot 3i=21i^2=21(-1)=-21$$

$$\sqrt{-49}\cdot\sqrt{-9}\cdot\sqrt{-16}=\sqrt{49}\cdot\sqrt{-1}\cdot\sqrt{9}\cdot\sqrt{-1}\cdot\sqrt{16}\cdot\sqrt{-1}=$$

$$=7i\cdot 3i\cdot 4i=84i^3=84(-i)=-84i$$

Division of Imaginary Numbers

$$\frac{\sqrt{-16}}{\sqrt{-9}}=\frac{\sqrt{16}\sqrt{-1}}{\sqrt{9}\sqrt{-1}}=\frac{4i}{3i}=\frac{4}{3}$$

A **complex number** is any number that can be expressed in the form $a+bi$, where a and b and real numbers.

$$\begin{array}{cc} a & +bi \\ \downarrow & \downarrow \\ \text{real \#} & \text{imaginary \#} \end{array}$$

If $a=0$, $\quad a+bi=0+bi=bi$, a pure imaginary number

If $b=0$, $\quad a+bi=a+0=a$, a pure real number.

Addition and Subtraction of Complex Numbers

$$(-3+5i)+(4-8i)=-3+5i+4-8i=1-3i$$

$(3+0i)+(6+0i)=3+6=9$

$(-2+3i)+(-2-3i)=-2+3i-2-3i=-4$

$(-5+2i)-(3-5i)=-5+2i-3+5i=-8+7i$

$(3+2i)-(-3+2i)=3+2i+3-2i=6$

Multiplication of Complex Numbers

$(1-2i)(3+2i)=3+2i-6i-4i^2=3-4i-4(-1)=7-4i$

$(3+2i)(3-2i)=9-6i+6i-4i^2=9-4(-1)=3^2+2^2=13$

Pairs of expressions such as $(a + bi)$ and $(a - bi)$ are called **conjugate** complex numbers. The product of two conjugate complex numbers is always a real number.

$(a+bi)(a-bi)=a^2+b^2$

Division of Complex Numbers

1) Solve $\frac{7-4i}{3+2i} \quad (3+2i \neq 0)$

Multiply the numerator and denominator by $(3-2i)$ so as to eliminate the conjugate complex numbers.

$$\frac{(7-4i)(3-2i)}{(3+2i)(3-2i)}=\frac{21-14i-12i+8i^2}{9+4}=\frac{13-26i}{13}=1-2i$$

Solution: $\frac{(7-4i)}{3+2i}=1-2i$

2.21 Inequalities

An inequality is a statement that uses one of these symbols: $>, <, \geq, \leq$.

The Symbol	is called...
$>$	is greater than
$<$	is less than
$\geq$	is greater than or equal to
$\leq$	is less than or equal to

For example: $3 > 2$
$2 < 3$
$1 > -1$

2.21.1 Fundamental Properties of Inequalities

1. If $a > b$, then $b < a$.

Example: If $5x-1 > 2x+1$, then $2x+1 < 5x-1$

2. If $a > b$ and $b > c$, then $a > c$.

If $a < b$ and $b < c$, then $a < c$

For example, if $x > 2y$ and $y > 10$, then $x > 20$.

3. If $a > b$, then $a+c > b+c$ (and $a-c > b-c$).

If $a < b$, then $a+c < b+c$ (and $a-c < b-c$).

Therefore we can add (or subtract) equal numbers to the left and right part of the expression.

Example: Given the inequality $x+8 > 3$
$x+8-8 > 3-8$ (subtract 8)
$x > -5$

4. If $a > b$ and $c > d$, then $a + c > b + d$
If $a < b$ and $c < d$, then $a + c < b + d$

Examples: $-8 > -10$ and $5 > 2$
$-8 + 5 > -10 + 2$
$-3 > -8$

Given the system $\frac{1}{2}x + \frac{1}{2}y < 18$; $\frac{1}{2}x - \frac{1}{2}y < 4$ find x

Solution: $\frac{1}{2}x + \frac{1}{2}x + \frac{1}{2}y - \frac{1}{2}y < 18 + 4$

Add the terms: $x < 22$

5. If $a > b$ and $c < d$, then $a - c > b - d$
If $a < b$ and $c > d$, then $a - c < b - d$

Examples:

Given that $12 < 20$ and $17 > 15$,

$12 – 17 < 20 – 15$
$-5 < 5$

Given the system $\frac{1}{2}x + \frac{1}{2}y < 18$; $\frac{1}{2}x - \frac{1}{2}y > 8$
Find y

Subtract the second equation from the first:

$\frac{1}{2}x - \frac{1}{2}x + \frac{1}{2}y + \frac{1}{2}y < 10$
$y < 10$

6. If $a > b$ and $m > 0$, then $ma > mb$ and $\frac{a}{m} > \frac{b}{m}$.

We can therefore multiply or divide both sides of the expression by equal numbers.

Example:

Given $2x < 12$, find x

Divide both parts by 2:

$$\frac{2x}{2} < \frac{12}{2}$$

$$x < 6$$

If you are multiplying or dividing by a negative number, you must reverse the inequality sign.

Example:

$$25 > 20$$

Divide both parts by –5:

$$-\frac{25}{5} < -\frac{20}{5}$$

$$-5 < -4$$

2.21.2 Solution of Linear Inequalities

Linear inequalities are solved the same way as linear equations.

One model of a linear inequality:

$$ax > b$$

Solution: $x > \frac{b}{a}$ if $a > 0$

$$x < \frac{b}{a} \text{ if } a < 0$$

Examples:

1) $5x-3>8x+1$

$5x-3+3>8x+1+3$ (Add 3)

$5x>8x+4$

$-3x>4$

Solution: $x<-\dfrac{4}{3}$

2) $5x+2<7x+6$

$5x+2-2<7x+6-2$ (Subtract 2)

$5x<7x+4$

$5x-7x<+4$

$-2x<4$

Solution: $x>-2$

3) $(x-1)^2<x^2+8$

$x^2-2x+1<x^2+8$

$x^2-x^2-2x+1<x^2-x^2+8$ (Subtract x^2)

$-2x+1-1<8-1$ (Subtract 1)

$-2x<7$

Solution: $x>-\dfrac{7}{2}$

2.21.3 Solving Systems of Linear Inequalities

Examples:

1) $4x-3>5x-5$ and $2x+4<8x$

Solution of the first inequality:

$$4x-4x-3>5x-4x-5$$

$$-3>x-5$$

$$-3+5>x-5+5$$

$$2>x$$

$$x<2$$

Solution of the second inequality:

$$2x-2x+4<8x-2x$$

$$4<6x$$

$$\frac{2}{3}<x$$

Answer: $\frac{2}{3}<x<2$

2) $2x-3>3x-5$ and $2x+4>8x$

$$2x-2x-3>3x-2x-5$$

$$-3>x-5$$

$$-3+5>x-5+5$$

$$2 > x$$

$$x < 2$$

$$2x - 2x + 4 > 8x - 2x$$

$$4 > 6x$$

$$\frac{2}{3} > x$$

Answer: $x < \frac{2}{3}$

3) $2x < 16$ and $3x + 1 > 4x - 4$ and

$3x + 6 > 2x + 7$ and $x + 5 < 2x + 6$

Solution of the first inequality:

$$x < 8$$

Solution of the second inequality:

$$x < 5$$

Solution of the third inequality:

$$x > 1$$

Solution of the fourth inequality:

$$x > -1$$

Solution of the system:

$$1 < x < 5$$

2.22 Quadratic Equations

An equation of the form $ax^2 + bx + c = 0$ is called a quadratic equation (standard form).

A quadratic equation has two answers, or roots (x_1 and x_2). Therefore we say it is a degree 2 equation.

An equation of the form $ax^2 + c = 0$ $a \neq 0$, (a and c are real numbers) is called an **incomplete quadratic equation**.

There are some methods by which such an equation can be solved.

Example: $x^2 - 36 = 0$

First Method

$$x^2 - 36 + 36 = 0 + 36$$

$$x^2 = 36$$

$$x = \sqrt{36} = \pm 6$$

Second Method

$$x^2 - 36 = x^2 - 6^2 = (x-6)(x+6)$$

This product can equal 0 if $(x-6) = 0$ or $(x+6) = 0$

Therefore $x_1 = 6;\ x_2 = -6$

We can extend the square root method to quadratic operations of the form

$$(x+a)^2 = n$$

Examples:

1) $(x+3)^2 = 25$

$$\sqrt{(x+3)^2} = \sqrt{25}$$

$$x+3=\pm 5$$

$$x_1 = 2;\ x_2 = -8$$

2) $$x^2 + 4x + 4 = 16$$

$$(x+2)^2 = 16$$

$$x+2=\pm 4$$

$$x_1 = 2;\ x_2 = -6$$

The left side of the equation $ax^2 + bx + c = 0$ is a quadratic trinomial that can be factored into the product of two binomials.

Example: Solve $2x^2 - 11x + 5 = 0$

$$2x^2 - 11x + 5 = (2x-1)(x-5) = 0$$

$$2x - 1 = 0; \text{ or}$$

$$x - 5 = 0$$

Roots: $x_1 = \frac{1}{2};\ x_2 = 5$

How did we expand $2x^2 - 11x + 5$ into $(2x-1)(x-5)$?

The factors of the first term, $2x^2$, are $2x$ and x. They become the first terms of the binomials: $(2x \quad)(x \quad)$

The factors of the last term, +5, become the second terms of the binomials, but they must be chosen in such a way that the inner and outer cross products of the binomials add up to the middle term, $-11x$, of the original trinomial. Try –1 and –5 as the factors of +5.

$$(2x-1)(x-5)=0$$

Since $(-x)+(-10x)=-11x$, these are the correct factors.
If the product of two factors is 0, either factor may equal 0.

$$2x-1=0\text{, or}$$
$$x-5=0$$

Find the roots: $x_1=\dfrac{1}{2}; x_2=5$

More examples:

1) Solve $5x^2+9x-18=0$

$$5x^2+9x-18=(5x-6)(x+3)$$

$$5x-6=0\text{, or}$$

$$x+3=0$$

Roots: $x_1=\dfrac{6}{5}; x_2=-3$

2) Solve $3x^2-14x-24=0$

$$3x^2-14x-24=(3x+4)(x-6)$$

$$3x+4=0\text{, or } x-6=0$$

Roots: $x_1=\dfrac{-4}{3}; x_2=6$

To find the roots x_1 and x_2, we can use the quadratic formula.

$$x_{1,2} \frac{-b \pm \sqrt{b^2 - 4ac}}{2a}$$

Example:

Solve the equation $3x^2 - 10x + 3 = 0$

$a = 3, b = -10, c = 3$

First root:

$$x_1 = \frac{-(-10) + \sqrt{(-10)^2 - 4 \cdot 3 \cdot 3}}{2 \cdot 3} = \frac{10 + \sqrt{100 - 36}}{6} = \frac{10 + \sqrt{64}}{6} = \frac{10 + 8}{6} = 3$$

$x_1 = 3$

Second root:

$$x_2 = \frac{10 - \sqrt{64}}{6} = \frac{10 - 8}{6} = \frac{2}{6} = \frac{1}{3}$$

$$x_2 = \frac{1}{3}$$

Check: $3{x_1}^2 - 10x_1 + 3 = 3 \cdot 3^2 - 10 \cdot 3 + 3 = 27 - 30 + 3 = 0$

$$3{x_2}^2 - 10x_2 + 3 = 3\left(\frac{1}{3}\right)^2 - 10\left(\frac{1}{3}\right) + 3 = 3 \cdot \frac{1}{9} - \frac{10}{3} + 3 = \frac{1}{3} - 3\frac{1}{3} + 3 = 0$$

Not every root of a quadratic equation can be a real number.

In the quadratic formula $x_{1,2} = \dfrac{-b \pm \sqrt{b^2 - 4ac}}{2a}$, the expression $b^2 - 4ac$ is called a **discriminator**. If $|b^2| > |4ac|$, the discriminator is a positive number and the roots are real numbers. If $|b^2| < |4ac|$, the discriminator is a negative number and the roots are imaginary numbers.

Example:

Solve $x^2 - 8x + 17 = 0$

$$x_{1,2} = \frac{-(-8) \pm \sqrt{(-8)^2 - 4 \cdot 1 \cdot 17}}{2 \cdot 1} = \frac{8 \pm \sqrt{64-68}}{2} = \frac{8 \pm \sqrt{-4}}{2} = \frac{8 \pm \sqrt{4}\sqrt{-1}}{2} = \frac{8}{2} \pm \frac{2i}{2} = 4 \pm i$$

Solution: $x_1 = 4 + i; x_2 = 4 - i$

Check: $x_1^{\ 2} = (4+i)^2 = 4^2 + 2(4i) + i^2 = 16 + 8i - 1 = 15 + 8i$

$8x_1 = 8(4+i) = 32 + 8i$

$x_1^2 - 8x_1 + 17 = 15 + 8i - (32 + 8i) + 17 = 15 + 8i - 32 - 8i + 17 = 0$

$x_2^2 = (4-i)^2 = 4^2 - 2(4i) + i^2 = 16 - 8i - 1 = 15 - 8i$

$8x_2 = 8(4-i) = 32 - 8i$

$x_2^{\ 2} - 8x_2 + 17 = 15 - 8i - (32 - 8i) + 17 = 15 - 8i - 32 + 8i + 17 = 0$

2.22.1 Properties of Roots of Quadratic Equations

The sum of the roots of the quadratic equation $x^2 + bx + c = 0$ equals $x_1 + x_2 = -b$.

The product of the roots of the same quadratic equation equals $x_1 \cdot x_2 = c$

If x_1 and x_2 are roots of the quadratic equation $ax^2 + bx + c = 0$

$$ax^2 + bx + c = a \cdot (x - x_1)(x - x_2)$$

These properties can be used to simplify the same quadratic trinomials.

Example:

Simplify the trinomial $2x^2 + 13x - 24$

Find the roots: $x_1 = \frac{3}{2}$; $x_2 = -8$ (using the quadratic formula)

Therefore $2x^2 + 13x - 24 = 2\left(x - \frac{3}{2}\right)(x+8) = (2x-3)(x+8)$

Solution: $2x^2 + 13x - 24 = (2x-3)(x+8)$

2.23 Quadratic Inequalities

There are some methods we can use to solve a quadratic inequality:

2.23.1 Expanding a Quadratic Trinomial into the Product of Two Binomials

If the inequality includes a ">0," the two factors must have the same sign. If the inequality includes a "<0," the two factors must have opposite signs.
Examples:

1) Solve $7x^2 - 19x + 10 > 0$

Solution: $7x^2 - 19x + 10 = (7x-5)(x-2)$

Case 1. Both factors > 0.

$$7x - 5 > 0 \text{ and } x - 2 > 0$$

$$x > \frac{5}{7}; x > 2$$

Answer: $x > \frac{5}{7}$ and $x > 2x \longrightarrow x > 2$

Case 2. Both factors < 0.

$$7x-5<0 \text{ and } x-2<0$$

$$x<\frac{5}{7}; x<2$$

Solution: $x<\frac{5}{7}$ and $x<2 \rightarrow x<\frac{5}{7}$

Final solution: $x<\frac{5}{7}$ or $x>2$ (both cases)

2) Solve $7x^2-19x+10<0$

Solution: $7x^2-19x+10=(7x-5)(x-2)$

Case 1. Factor the first term as > 0 and factor the second as < 0

$$7x-5>0 \text{ and } x-2<0$$

$$x>\frac{5}{7}; x<2$$

Solution: $\frac{5}{7}<x<2$

Case 2. Factor the first term as < 0 and the second as > 0

$$7x-5<0 \text{ and } x-2>0$$

$$x<\frac{5}{7}; x>2$$

Solution: $2<x<\frac{5}{7} \rightarrow$ which is impossible.

So, case 1 is the only possible case.

Final solution: $\frac{5}{7}<x<2$

2.23.2 Solution by Working with the Roots of the Related Quadratic Equation

Example:

$$\text{Solve } 7x^2 - 19x + 10 > 0$$

First, find the roots of the equation $7x^2 - 19x + 10 = 0$

$$x_{1,2} = \frac{-b \pm \sqrt{b^2 - 4ac}}{2a} = \frac{19 \pm \sqrt{19^2 - 4 \cdot 7 \cdot 10}}{2 \cdot 7} = \frac{19 \pm \sqrt{81}}{14} = \frac{19 \pm 9}{14}$$

$$x_1 = 2;\ x_2 = \frac{10}{14} = \frac{5}{7}$$

Choose a checkpoint, say the number one, which is between the roots. Substitute into the given inequality.

$$7 \cdot 1 - 19 \cdot 1 + 10 > 0$$

$-2 > 0$ This is false, therefore the solution is not between the roots.

$$\text{Solution: } x_1 > 2 \text{ or } x_2 < \frac{5}{7}$$

2.24 Equations with Fractional or Negative Exponents

We already know the following:

$$(x^a)^b = x^{ab}$$

$$x^{-n} = \frac{1}{x^n}$$

If a and b are reciprocals, their product is 1.

For example:

$$(x^3)^{\frac{1}{3}} = x^{3\cdot\frac{1}{3}} = x$$

$$(x^{\frac{5}{4}})^{\frac{4}{5}} = x^{\frac{5}{4}\cdot\frac{4}{5}} = x$$

$$(x^{-\frac{1}{2}})^{-2} = x^{-\frac{1}{2}(-2)} = x$$

This observation will simplify the solution of equations containing powers with fractional or negative exponents.

Examples:

1) $x^{-\frac{1}{4}} = 2$

$$x^{(-\frac{1}{4})(-4)} = 2^{(-4)}$$

$$x = 2^{-4} = \frac{1}{2^4} = \frac{1}{16}$$

Check: $x^{-\frac{1}{4}} = 2$

$$\left(\frac{1}{16}\right)^{-\frac{1}{4}} = 16^{\frac{1}{4}} = \sqrt[4]{16} = 2$$

2) $x^{-\frac{1}{2}} = \frac{1}{3}$

$$x^{(-\frac{1}{2})(-2)} = \left(\frac{1}{3}\right)^{-2}$$

$$x = \left(\frac{1}{3}\right)^{-2} = 3^2 = 9$$

Check: $x^{-\frac{1}{2}} = \frac{1}{3}$

$$9^{-\frac{1}{2}} = \frac{1}{9^{\frac{1}{2}}} = \frac{1}{\sqrt{9}} = \frac{1}{3}$$

3) $2x^{-\frac{1}{4}} + 5 = 6$

$$2x^{-\frac{1}{4}} = 6 - 5 = 1$$

$$x^{-\frac{1}{4}} = \frac{1}{2}$$

$$x^{\left(-\frac{1}{4}\right)(-4)} = \left(\frac{1}{2}\right)^{-4}$$

$$x = \left(\frac{1}{2}\right)^{-4} = 2^4 = 16$$

Check: $2x^{-\frac{1}{4}} + 5 = 6$

$$2 \cdot 16^{-\frac{1}{4}} = 2 \cdot \frac{1}{16^{\frac{1}{4}}} = \frac{2}{\sqrt[4]{16}} = \frac{2}{2} = 1$$

$$1 + 5 = 6$$

2.24.1 Exponential Equations

An equation where the unknown value is an exponent is called an exponential equation.

To solve an exponential equation:

Step 1. Express both sides of the equation as powers of the same base.

Step 2. Solve the equation.

Examples:

1) $2^{x+2} = 32$

Step 1. $2^{x+2} = 2^5$

Step 2. If $2^{x+2} = 2^5$, then

$x + 2 = 5$

$x = 3$

Check: $2^{3+2} = 32$

2) $4^{3x+4} = 16^{x+5}$

Step 1. $4^{3x+4} = (4^2)^{x+5} = 4^{2x+10}$

Step 2. $3x + 4 = 2x + 10$

$3x + 4 - 2x = 10$

$x + 4 = 10$

$x = 6$

Check: $3 \cdot 6 + 4 = 2 \cdot 6 + 10$

$22 = 22$

3) $2^{x+1} = 16^{\frac{1}{4}}$

Step 1. $2^{x+1} = (2^4)^{\frac{1}{4}} = 2^{\frac{4}{4}} = 2^1$

Step 2. $x + 1 = 1$

$x = 0$

Check: $0 + 1 = 1$

4) $9^{x^2+3x} = 3^{15x-10}$

Step 1. $(3^2)^{x^2+3x} = 3^{2x^2+6x} = 3^{15x-10}$

Step 2. $2x^2 + 6x = 15x - 10$

$2x^2 - 9x + 10 = 0$

$$x_{1,2} = \frac{-b \pm \sqrt{b^2 - 4ac}}{2a} = \frac{9 \pm \sqrt{9 \cdot 9 - 4 \cdot 2 \cdot 10}}{2 \cdot 2} = \frac{9 \pm \sqrt{81 - 80}}{4} = \frac{9 \pm \sqrt{1}}{4}$$

$$x_1 = \frac{9+1}{4} = 2.5; \; x_2 = \frac{9-1}{4} = 2$$

Check: $2(2.5)^2 - 9(2.5) + 10 = 12.5 - 22.5 + 10 = 0$

$2(2)^2 - 9(2) + 10 = 8 - 18 + 10 = 0$

2.25 Logarithms

Logarithms simplify multiplication, division, and powers. Addition can be substituted for multiplication, subtraction for division, and multiplication for power.

$$y = \log_a A$$

logarithm (exponent) — base — number

This expression is equivalent to the expression $a^y = A$

Examples:

$$\log_2 8 = 3 \ \ (2^3 = 8)$$

$$\log_{10} 1000 = 3 \ \ (10^3 = 1000)$$

When no base is written in the logarithmic form of a number, the base is understood to be 10.

Example:

$\log N$ is equivalent to $\log_{10} N$.

Properties of Logarithms

1. The Product Rule

If $a > 0$ and $a \neq 1$

$$\boxed{\log_a (A \cdot B) = \log_a A + \log_a B}$$

Example:

$$A = 100;\ B = 1000;\ a = 10$$

$$\log AB = \log(100 \cdot 1000) = \log 100{,}000 = 5 \ \ (10^5 = 100{,}000)$$

$$\log A = 2 \ \ (10^2 = 100)$$

$$\log B = 3 \ \ (10^3 = 1000)$$

$$\log A + \log B = 2 + 3 = 5$$

Therefore $\log(100 \cdot 1000) = \log 100 + \log 1000$

$$5 = 5$$

2. The Quotient Rule

If $a > 0$ and $a \neq 1$

$$\log_a \frac{A}{B} = \log_a A - \log_a B$$

Example:

$$A = 1000;\ B = 10;\ a = 10$$

$$\log \frac{A}{B} = \log \frac{1000}{10} = \log 100 = 2\ (10^2 = 100)$$

$$\log A = \log 1000 = 3\ (10^3 = 1000)$$

$$\log B = \log 10 = 1\ (10^1 = 10)$$

$$\log \frac{A}{B} = \log A - \log B = 3 - 1 = 2$$

3. The Power Rule

If $a > 0$ and $a \neq 1$

$$\log_a A^b = b \cdot \log_a A$$

Example:

$$A = 100;\ b = 2;\ a = 10$$

$$\log 100^2 = 2 \cdot \log 100 = 2 \cdot 2 = 4$$

Check: $\log 100^2 = \log 10{,}000 = 4$

4. The Root Rule

$$\log_a (\sqrt[n]{A}) = \frac{1}{n} \cdot \log_a A$$

Examples:

1) $A = 1000; n = 3; a = 10$

$$\frac{1}{3} \cdot \log 1000 = \frac{1}{3} \cdot 3 = 1$$

Check: $\log(\sqrt[3]{1000}) = 1 \ (\log 10 = 1)$ $\quad$ 1=1

2)

$$\log \frac{2a^2b}{\sqrt[3]{m^2}} = \log \frac{2a^2b}{m^{\frac{2}{3}}} = \log(2a^2 \cdot b \cdot m^{-\frac{2}{3}}) = \log 2 + 2\log a + \log b - \frac{2}{3}\log m$$

On a scientific calculator, the [LOG] key is used to display the **common** logarithm of a number (a common logarithm is an exponent to base 10).

Check (with the calculator):

$$\log 0.05 = -2.3010$$

$$\log 43{,}112 = 4.6246$$

If $\log A = x$, then A is the number whose logarithm is x. When x is known, you can find A, which is the **antilogarithm** of x.

To find the antilogarithm on a calculator, press the 10^x key, which is usually accessed by the [2nd] ("shift") key.

Example:

Find x if $\log x = 1.3106$

Answer: $x = 20.450$

Sometimes it is convenient to use logarithms with the base e, which equals 2.71828183. The logarithm $\log_e N$ is called a natural logarithm.

The conversion of $\log N$ to $\log_e N$ is accomplished with the following formulas:

$$\log_e N \approx 2.30259 \log N$$

$$\log N \approx 0.43429 \log_e N$$

2.26 Logarithmic Equations

When an equation contains a variable that is a logarithm of a number, it is a logarithmic equation.

If the logarithms have the same base, follow the rule

$$\text{If } \log A = \log B \text{ then } A = B$$

and solve using the properties of logarithms.

Examples:

Solve for x:

1) $\log_a 4 + \log_a x = \log_a 16$

Step 1. $\log_a (4 \cdot x) = \log_a 16$

Step 2. $4x = 16$

$$x = \frac{16}{4} = 4$$

Check: $\log_a 4 + \log_a 4 = \log_a (4 \cdot 4) = \log_a 16$

2) $\log_9 x = \frac{1}{2}$

$$x = 9^{\left(\frac{1}{2}\right)} = \sqrt{9} = 3 \quad x = 3$$

Check: $\log_9 3 = \dfrac{1}{2}$

3) $\log_4 \log_5 \log_2 x = 0$

$$\log_4 1 = 0$$

$$\log_4 \log_3 \log_2 x = \log_4 1$$

Therefore $\quad \log_3 \log_2 x = 1,$ *or*

$$3^1 = \log_2 x$$
$$x = 8$$

4) Find the roots:

$$\frac{\log(35 - x^3)}{\log(5 - x)} = 3$$

$$\log(35 - x^3) = 3\log(5 - x)$$

$$\log(35 - x^3) = \log(5 - x)^3$$

$$35 - x^3 = (5 - x)^3 = 5^3 - 3 \cdot 5^2 x + 3 \cdot 5 \cdot x^2 - x^3 = 125 - 75x + 15x^2 - x^3$$

or

$$125 + x^3 - x^3 - 35 - 75x + 15x^2 = 0$$

$$15x^2 - 75x + 90 = 0$$

$$x^2 - 5x + 6 = 0$$

$$x_{1,2} = \frac{5 \pm \sqrt{5^2 - 4 \cdot 1 \cdot 6}}{2} = \frac{5 \pm 1}{2}$$

$$x_1 = \frac{5+1}{2} = 3; \;\; x_2 = \frac{5-1}{2} = 2$$

Check:

$$35 - x^3 = (5-x)^3$$

$$x_1 = 3$$

$$35 - 3^3 = 8; \quad (5-3)^3 = 8$$

$$x_2 = 2$$
$$35 - 2^3 = 27; \quad (5-2)^3 = 27$$

5) $\log_2(x+14) + \log_2(x+2) = 6$

$$\log_2(x+14)(x+2) = 6$$

or

$$(x+14)(x+2) = 2^6 = 64$$

$$x^2 + 2x + 14x + 28 = 64$$

$$x^2 + 16x - 36 = 0$$

$$\textit{Roots}: \quad x_1 = 2, \quad x_2 = -18$$

2.27 Progressions

Progressions can be subdivided into arithmetic and geometric progressions.

An **arithmetic progression** is a numerical sequence in which the *difference* between any two adjacent numbers is constant.

Example: 1, 2, 3, 4, 5…

Any arithmetic progression will fit the following formula:

$$a_n = a_1 + d(n-1)$$

where: a_1 is the first number of the progression
d is the difference between numbers
n is the number in the sequence that the formula describes

Example:

Given the arithmetic progression 2, 5, 8, 11, 14…, find a_7 (the seventh number in the sequence)

Solution: $a_7 = a_1 + d(n-1) = 2 + 3(7-1) = 20$

Check: 2, 5, 8, 11, 14, 17, <u>20</u>

1 2 3 4 5 6 7

The sum of the first n numbers of an arithmetic progression S_n can be found with the following formula:

$$S_n = \frac{(a_1 + a_n)n}{2}$$

Example:

Given the arithmetic progression 1, 2, 3, 4,5…, find S_3.

$$S_3 = \frac{(1+3)3}{2} = 6$$

Check: 1+2+3=6

A **geometric progression** is a numerical sequence in which the *ratio* between any two adjacent numbers is consistent.

Examples: 5, 10, 20, 40, 80…

$$8, 4, 2, 1, \frac{1}{2}, \frac{1}{4}....$$

Any number of a geometric progression can be determined with the following formula:

$$a_n = a_1 \cdot q^{n-1}$$

where q is the ratio between adjacent numbers.

Example:

Given the progression 5, 10, 20, 40…, find a_6

$$a_6 = a_1 + q^{n-1} = 5 \cdot 2^5 = 160$$

Check: 5, 10, 20, 40, 80, <u>160</u>
1 2 3 4 5 6

The sum of the first n numbers of an arithmetic progression S_n can be found with the following formula:

$$S_n = \frac{a_n q - a_1}{q-1}$$

Example:

Given the geometric progression 5, 10, 20, 40…, find S_4.

$$S_4 = \frac{40 \cdot 2 - 5}{2-1} = \frac{80-5}{1} = 75$$

Check: 5 + 10 + 20 + 40 = 75
1 2 3 4

2.28 Commonly Asked Questions: Algebra

1) **Q:** Why does any number to the zero power equal one?

A: We know that dividing a number by itself equals one:

$$\frac{3^5}{3^5}=1$$

We also know that

$$\frac{3^5}{3^5}=3^{5-5}=3^0$$

Therefore, $3^0=1$.

2) **Q:** Why isn't -10 more than -5? After all, 10 is more than 5.

A: Students often confuse the sign of a number with mathematical operations. Remember that –5 does not indicate subtraction. The "-" sign means that the number after it is the opposite of the positive number (remember the thermometer). Therefore, the bigger a number with a minus sign gets, the farther away it is from the positive side (this is just another way of saying that it gets smaller).

3) **Q:** What are conjugate numbers for? When is it convenient to use them in algebra?

A: Conjugate numbers look like this: $(a+b)(a-b)$. They multiply out like this: $(a+b)(a-b)=a^2-b^2$. This formula often helps to simplify an algebraic expression.

Example:

$$\frac{a+b}{a^2-b^2}=\frac{a+b}{(a+b)(a-b)}=\frac{1}{a-b}$$

Bringing in conjugate numbers can help avoid irrational expressions in a denominator.

Example:

$$\frac{4ab}{\sqrt{a}-\sqrt{2b}}$$

When we multiply the numerator and denominator by the conjugate number $(\sqrt{a}+\sqrt{2b})$, we receive:

$$\frac{4ab}{(\sqrt{a}-\sqrt{2b})(\sqrt{a}+\sqrt{2b})}=\frac{4ab(\sqrt{a}+\sqrt{2b})}{a-2b}$$

4) **Q:** Why is it possible to restate a fraction like this:

$$\frac{a+b}{n}=\frac{a}{n}+\frac{b}{n},$$

but not like this:

$$\frac{n}{a+b}=\frac{n}{a}+\frac{n}{b}?$$

A: The expression $\frac{a+b}{n}=\frac{a}{n}+\frac{b}{n}$ is a division of items by the same number (treated like the addition of fractions).

$$\frac{20+10}{5}=\frac{20}{5}+\frac{10}{5}=6$$

$\frac{n}{a+b}=\frac{n}{a}+\frac{n}{b}$ is a division of a number (n) by different numbers.

$$\frac{30}{2+5}=\frac{30}{2}+\frac{30}{5}=21$$ ← This equation is wrong.

5) **Q:** What is the relation of fractional exponents to roots? Why does $a^{\frac{1}{2}} = \sqrt{a}$?

A: The answer is based on the equality of two expressions:

$$(a^{\frac{1}{2}})^2 = a \quad \text{and} \quad (\sqrt{a})^2 = a$$

Therefore $a^{\frac{1}{2}} = \sqrt{a}$, and in general $a^{\frac{m}{n}} = \sqrt[n]{u^m}$

6) **Q:** What happens when we divide a number by 0?

A: If reduce the denominator of a fraction (also known as the divisor), the fraction will increase:

$$\frac{1}{100} = 0.01\,;\ \frac{1}{10} = 0.1\,;\ \frac{1}{0.1} = 10 \ldots \frac{1}{0.00001} = 100{,}000\,;$$

$$\frac{1}{0.0000000001} = 10000000000$$

As the denominator approaches zero, the resulting number becomes bigger and bigger, so we assume that a number divided by zero equals infinity:

$$\frac{1}{0} = \mathit{undefined}$$

7) **Q:** What does $\frac{0}{0}$ mean?

A: This is the result of an endless number of expressions:

$$\frac{1-1}{2-2} = \frac{0}{0};\ \frac{150-150}{12-12} = \frac{0}{0};\ \frac{0 \cdot 15}{0 \cdot 6} = \frac{0}{0}, \text{ et cetera.}$$

The expression $\frac{0}{0}$ is considered uncertain, so mathematical operations are not made with it.

8) **Q:** How can we accelerate the division of an algebraic fraction by a given value?

A: Incorporate the value into the denominator (divisor) and multiply.

Example: $$\frac{ab+c}{d+e} \div n$$

can be stated more conveniently as $$\frac{ab+c}{(d+e)\cdot n}$$

A practical example:

$$\frac{2\cdot 3+4}{2+3} \div 2 = \frac{2\cdot 3+4}{2+3} \div \frac{2}{1} = \frac{10}{5} \div \frac{2}{1} = \frac{10\cdot 1}{2\cdot 5} = 1$$

Accelerated method

$$\frac{2\cdot 3+4}{(2+3)\cdot 2} = 1$$

9) **Q:** What is a Pascal triangle for?

A: A Pascal triangle simplifies solutions to the binomial expression $(a+b)^n$

Formula for calculations:

$$(a+b)^n = a^n + na^{n-1}b + \frac{n(n-1)}{1\cdot 2}a^{n-2}b^2 + \frac{n(n-1)(n-2)}{1\cdot 2\cdot 3}a^{n-3}b^3 + ..b^n$$

Example:

$$(a+b)^5 = a^5 + 5a^4b + 10a^3b^2 + 10a^2b^3 + 5ab^4 + b^5$$

Coefficients for the formula $(a+b)^n$ can be found with a Pascal triangle. Every element of the triangle is formed by adding the two elements over it (on the left and on the right). In our example, coefficients under a are in the appropriate line of the triangle. Our coefficients are 1, 5, 10, 10, 5, 1.

$(a+b)^0 = 1$	1
$(a+b)^1 = 1a + 1b$	1 1
$(a+b)^2 = 1a^2 + 2ab + 1b^2$	1 2 1
$(a+b)^3 = 1a^3 + 3a^2b + 3ab^2 + 1b^3$	1 3 3 1
$(a+b)^4 = 1a^4 + 4a^3b + 6a^2b^2 + 4ab^3 + 1b^4$	1 4 6 4 1
$(a+b)^5 = 1a^5 + 5a^4b + 10a^3b^2 + 10a^2b^3 + 5ab^4 + 1b^5$	1 5 10 10 5 1

3 CHAPTER

GEOMETRY

By combining points, lines, and planes, geometry models the world in which we live.

3.1 Elementary Concepts

Name	Representation	Symbol	Explanation
Straight line *XY*	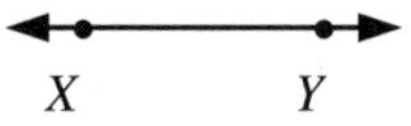	$\overleftrightarrow{XY}$	A line that is suggested by a stretched string, but one that is stretched without end in both directions
Ray *LM* Ray *ML*	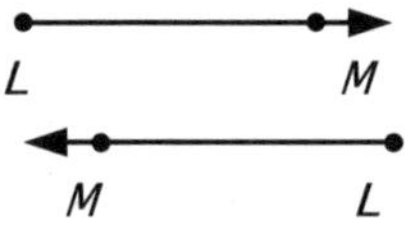	$\overrightarrow{LM}$ $\overleftarrow{ML}$	Part of a line that extends an infinite distance from an endpoint
Segment *AB*		$\overline{AB}$	Part of a line
Plane	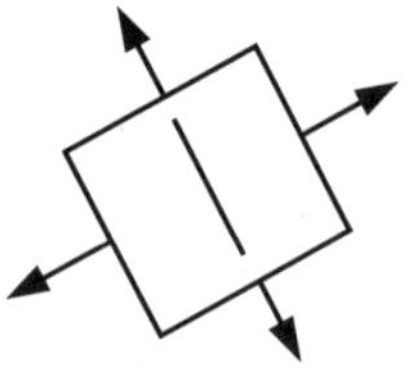		A set of points which extends a line into two dimensions

Congruent figures: figures that have the same shape and size. The symbol for congruence is ≅.
Congruent angles: angles that have the same degree measure.

3.2 Angles

An angle is the figure formed when two rays meet at a common endpoint, which is called the vertex.
The symbol of an angle is $\angle$.

The unit used in measuring angles is the degree.
The symbol for degrees is $\circ$.

1° is $\dfrac{1}{360}$ of complete circle.

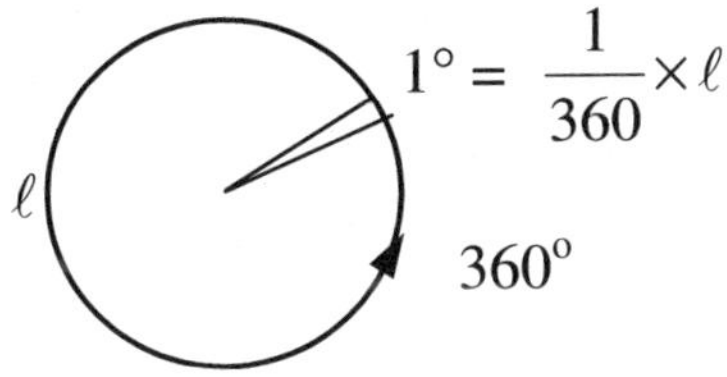

Angles can also be measured with another unit, the radian (see section 4.3)

Right Angle
A right angle is an angle that measures 90°.

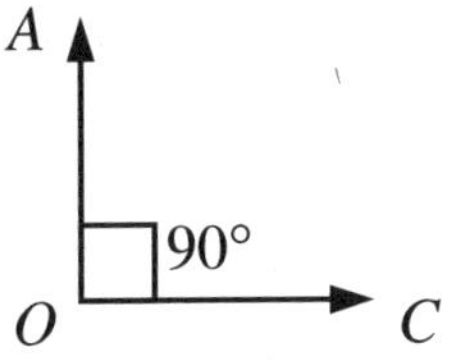

$\angle AOC$ is the right angle.

Acute Angle
An acute angle measures more than 0° and less than 90°.

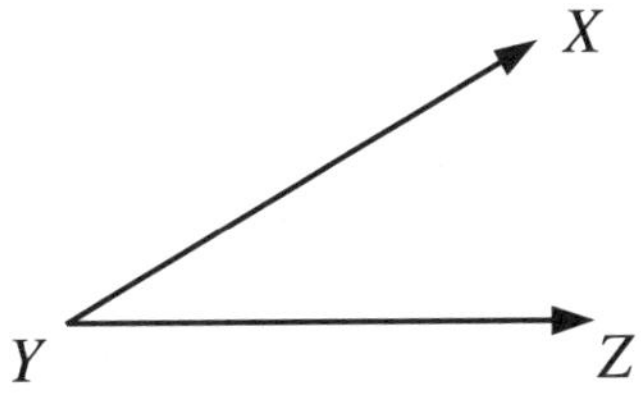

$\angle XYZ$ is an acute angle

Obtuse Angle

An obtuse angle measures more than $90°$ and less than $180°$.

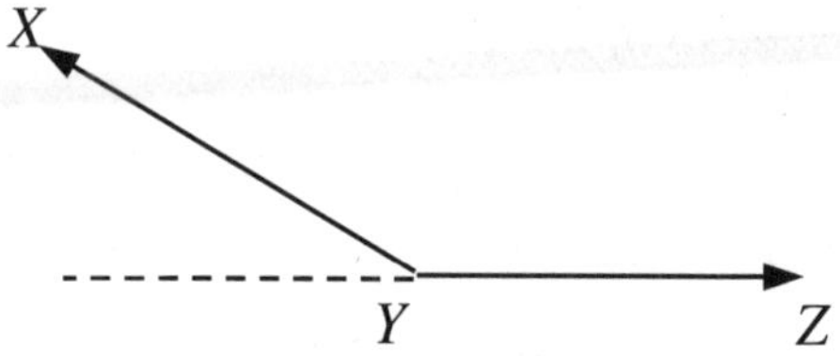

$\angle XYZ$ is an obtuse angle.

Bisector Angle

Every angle has a **bisector** that divides it into two congruent angles. $\angle ABQ \cong \angle QBC$

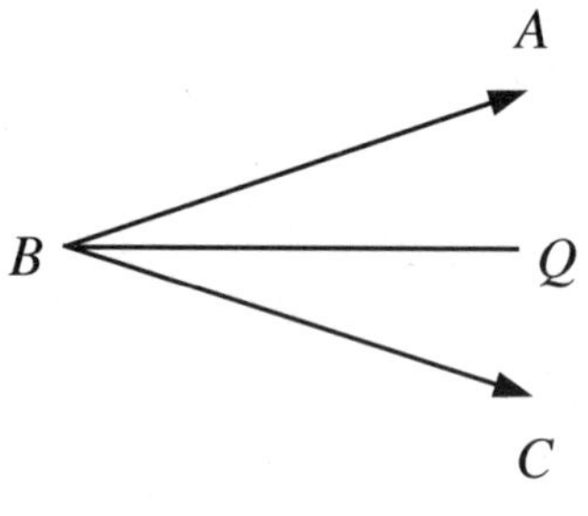

Straight Angle

A straight angle is an angle that measures $180°$.

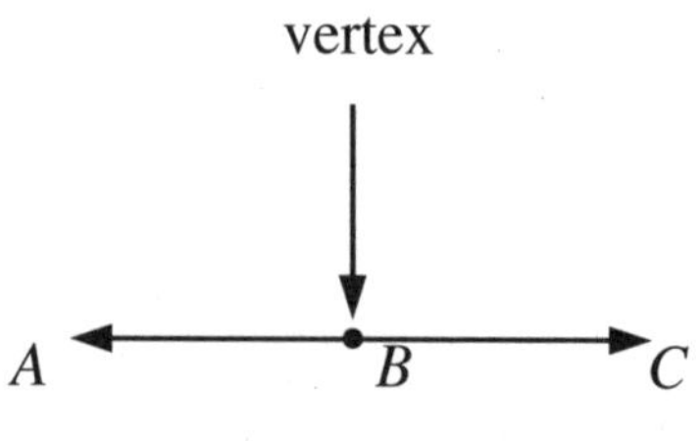

Additional Angle

An additional angle is one that adds to an existing angle to equal $180°$.

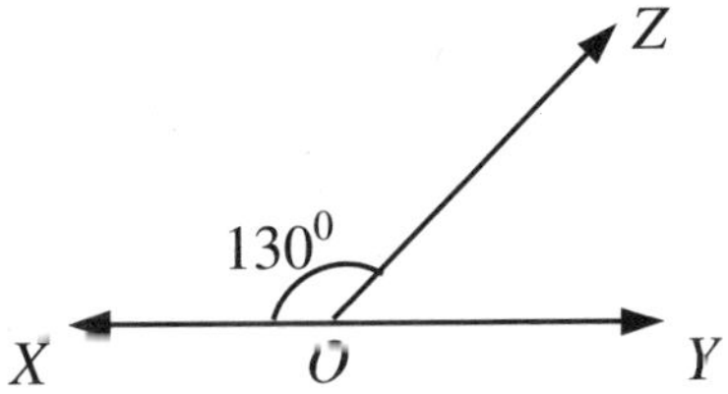

$\angle ZOY$ is the additional angle. $\angle ZOY = 180° - 130° = 50°$

Complementary Angles

Two angles whose sum equals $90°$ are complementary angles.

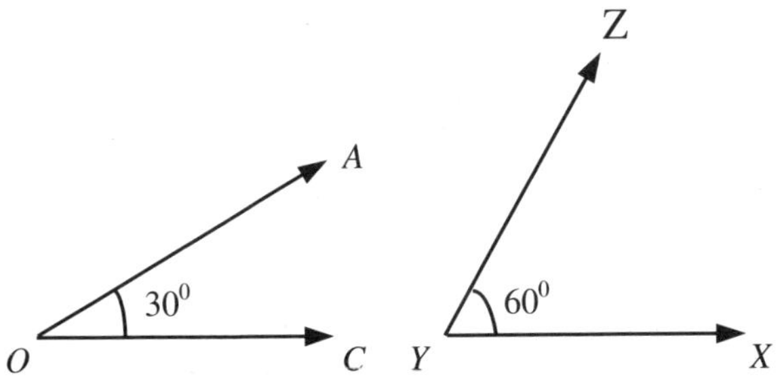

$\angle AOC$ and $\angle ZYX$ are complementary angles ($30^0 + 60^0 = 90^0$).

Supplementary Angles

Two angles whose sum equals $180°$ are supplementary angles.

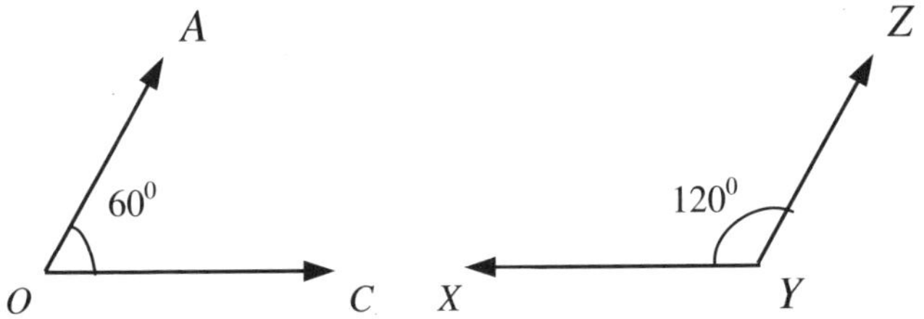

$\angle AOC$ and $\angle ZYX$ are supplementary angles ($60° + 120° = 180°$).

Corresponding Angles

Angles at similar places on a transversal that intersects two parallel lines are called corresponding angles.

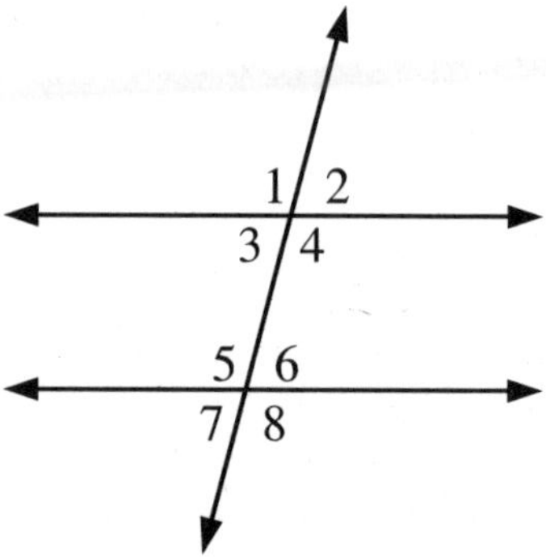

Corresponding angles:
1 and 5
3 and 7
2 and 6
4 and 8

Exterior Angles

The outside angles formed by a transversal that intersects two parallel lines are called exterior angles.

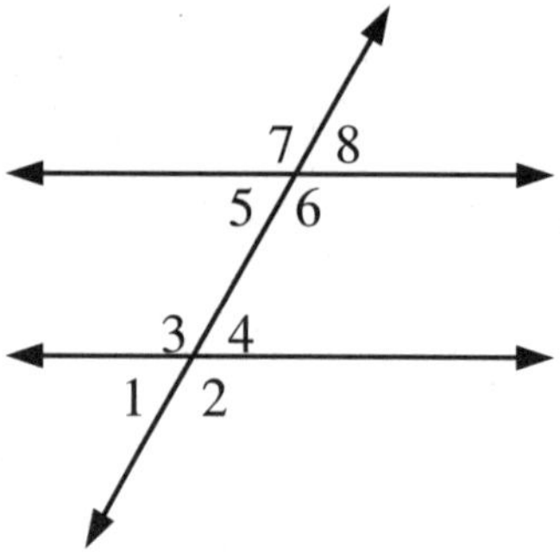

Exterior Angles: 1, 2, 7, and 8.

3.3 Perpendicular Lines and Parallel Lines

Two lines are perpendicular if they intersect to form a right angle.

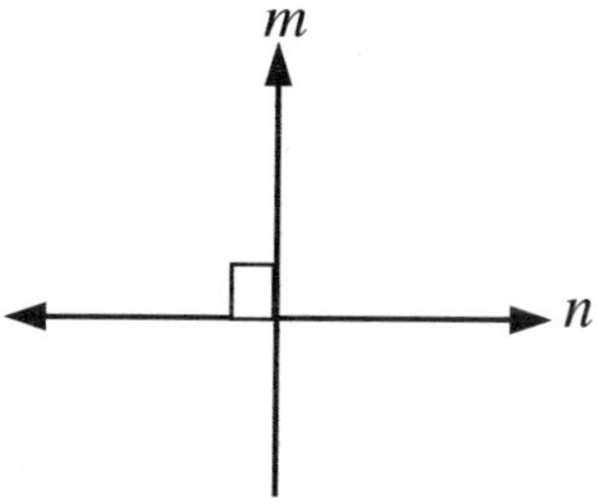

The symbol of perpendicular is "⊥." This is read as "perpendicular to."
In the diagram, line *m* is perpendicular to line *n*.

Two lines that lie in the same plane and never meet are called parallel lines.

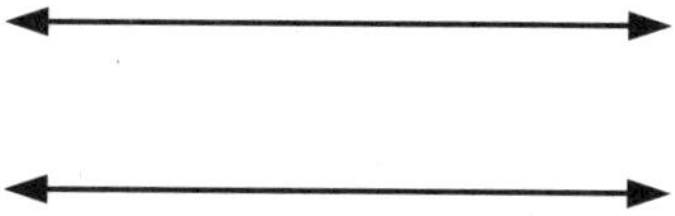

If two parallel lines are cut by a **transversal** (a transversal is a line that intersects two or more other lines) then:

- Alternate interior angles are congruent

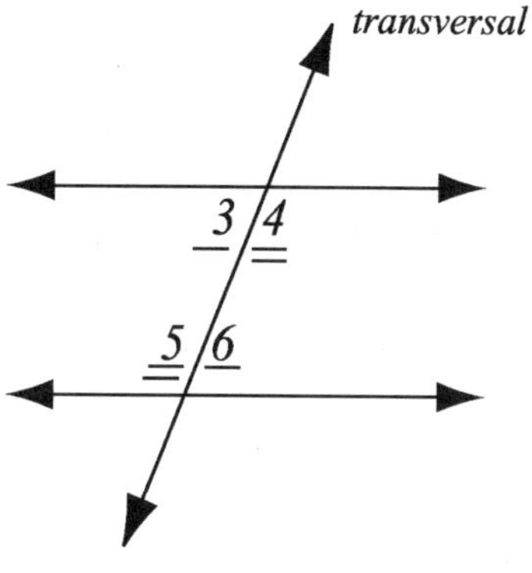

$$m\angle 3 = m\angle 6 \text{ and } m\angle 4 = m\angle 5$$

- Corresponding angles are congruent

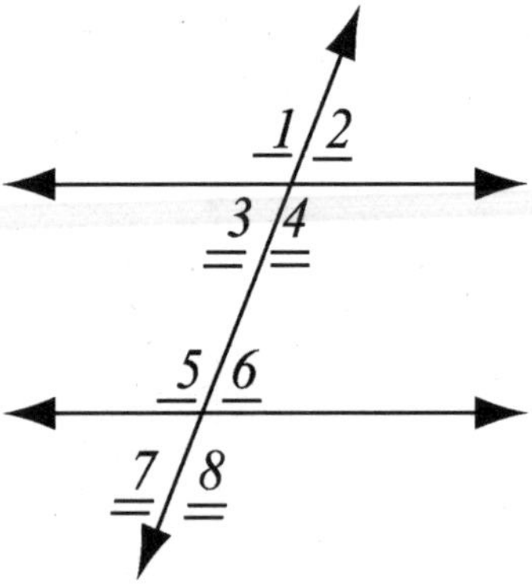

$$m\angle 1 = m\angle 5 \text{ and } m\angle 3 = m\angle 7$$
$$m\angle 2 = m\angle 6 \text{ and } m\angle 4 = m\angle 8$$

- Interior angles on the same side of the transversal are supplementary

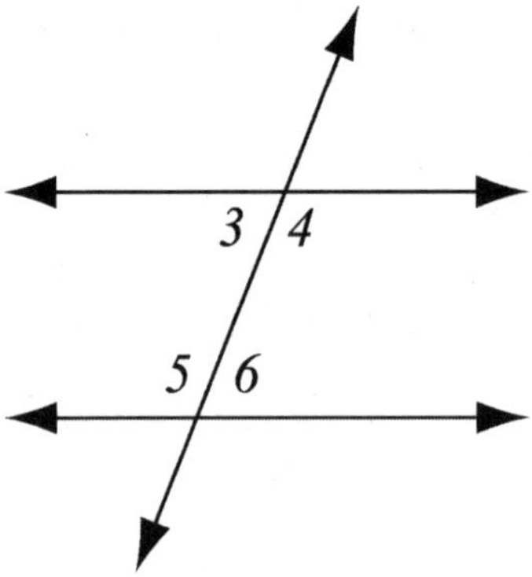

$$m\angle 3 + m\angle 5 = 180°$$
$$m\angle 4 + m\angle 6 = 180°$$

Examples:

1) $\overline{MN} \parallel \overline{KL}$

Given $m\angle 4 = 4x\text{-}10$
$m\angle 5 = 2x\text{-}20$

Find the measure of the $m\angle 4$ and $m\angle 5$.

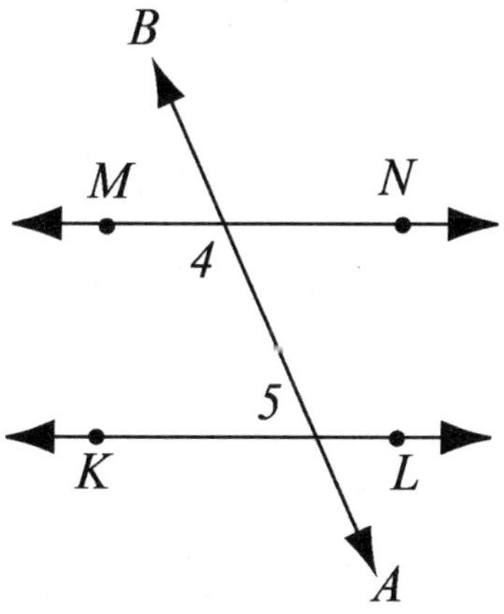

Statements	Reasons
$m\angle 4 + m\angle 5 = 180°$	If two parallel lines are cut by a transversal, then two interior angles on the same side of the transversal are supplementary.
$4x\text{-}10 + 2x\text{-}20 = 180$	Substitution of givens
$6x=210$	Calculations
$x=35°$	
$m\angle 4 = 4\cdot 35\text{-}10 = 130°$	Substitution for x
$m\angle 5 = 2\cdot 35\text{-}20 = 50°$	

Check $130° + 50° = 180°$

2) $\overline{DCE} \parallel \overline{AB}$

$\angle 1 \cong \angle 2$

Prove $\angle A \cong \angle B$

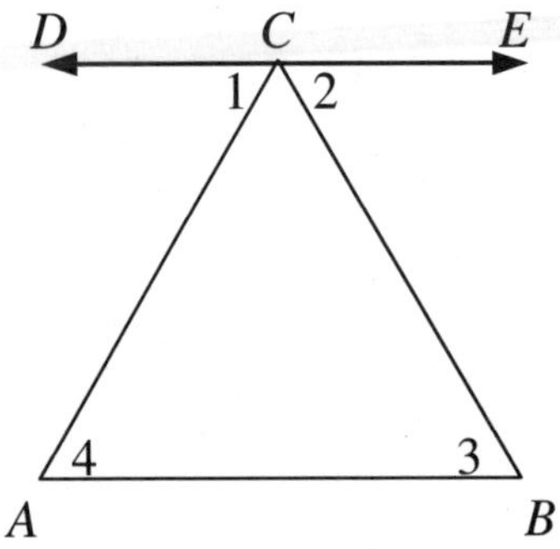

Statements	Reasons
$\angle 1 \cong \angle 2$	Given
$\angle 2 \cong \angle 3$	If two parallel lines are cut by a transversal, then the alternate interior angles formed are congruent (transversal $\overline{CB}$)
$\angle 1 \cong \angle 4$	If two parallel lines are cut by a transversal, then the alternate interior angles formed are congruent (transversal $\overline{CA}$)
$\angle A \cong \angle B$	Since $\angle 1 \cong \angle 2$ and $\angle 4\ (A) \cong \angle 1$ $\angle 3\ (B) \cong \angle 2$, therefore $\angle A \cong \angle B$

3.4 Polygons

Polygons are plane figures that are closed and have straight sides that meet only at their endpoints.

Examples:

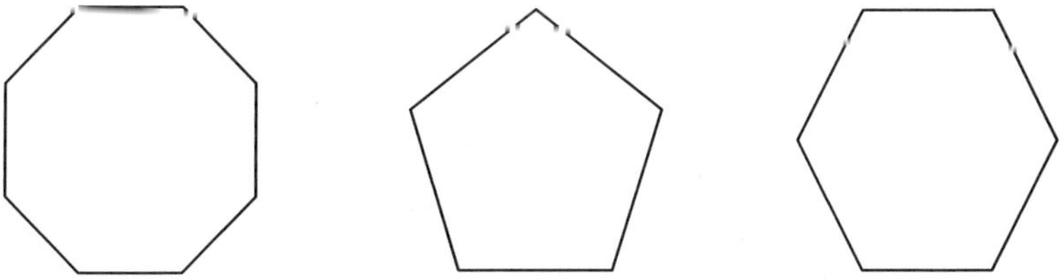

Name of Polygon	Number of Sides
Triangle	3
Quadrilateral	4
Pentagon	5
Hexagon	6
Septagon	7
Octagon	8
Nonagon	9
Decagon	10

The sum of the inside angles in any polygon always equals $180°(n-2)$, where n equals the number of sides in the polygon.

The **perimeter** is the number of unit lengths around a figure. For example, the perimeter of a hexagon can be expressed $P = S_1 + S_2 + S_3 + S_4 + S_5 + S_6$.

The area is the number of square units that covers a region or a figure.

3.5 Triangles

3.5.1 Classifying Triangles

Classifying by the type of angles

Acute Triangle

Contains three acute angles.

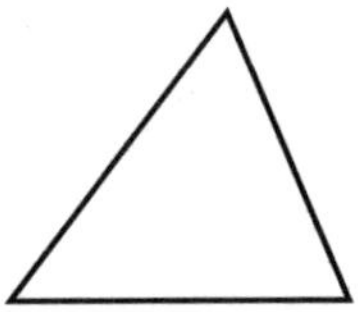

Right Triangle

Contains one right angle and two acute angles.

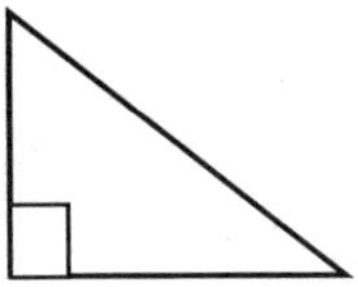

Obtuse Triangle

Contains one obtuse angle and two acute angles.

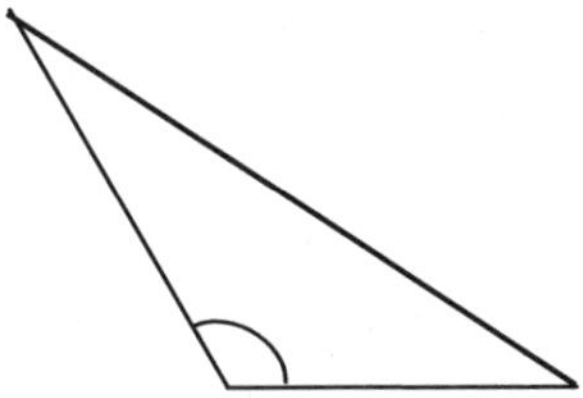

Classifying by Congruent Sides

Scalene Triangle

No congruent sides.

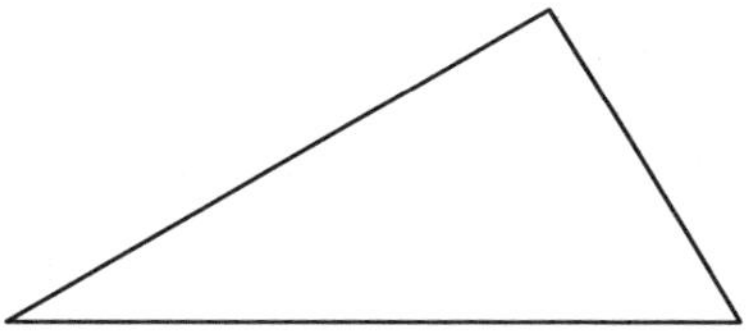

Isosceles Triangle

Two congruent sides.

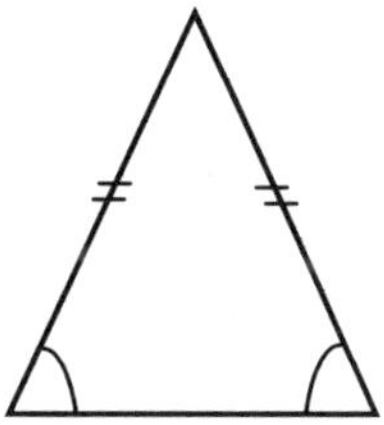

Equilateral Triangle

All sides congruent.

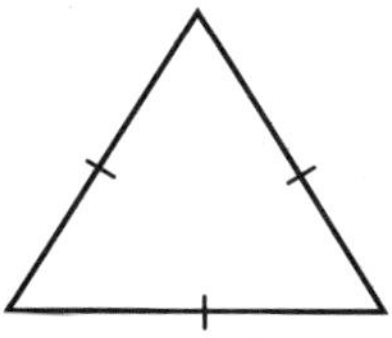

The sum of the three angles of any triangle is always $180°$.

Exterior Angles of a Triangle

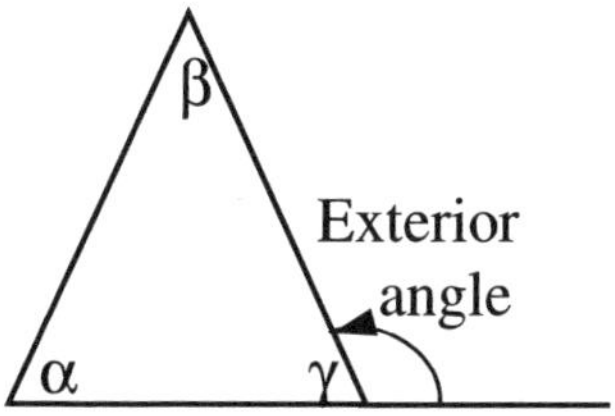

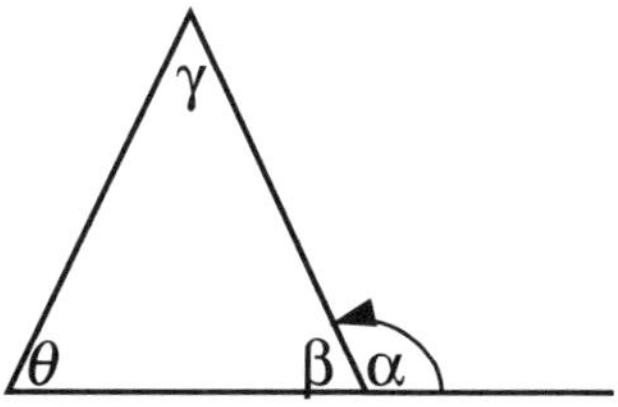

$m\angle\alpha + m\angle\beta + m\angle\gamma = 180°$ $\qquad$ $m\angle\alpha = m\angle\theta + m\angle\gamma$

3.5.2 Altitudes, Medians, Bisectors, Middle Lines, and Area of Triangles.

Altitudes are the line segments running from a vertex perpendicularly to the opposite side.

Altitudes in an acute triangle

Altitudes: $\overline{AD}, \overline{BF}, \overline{CE}$

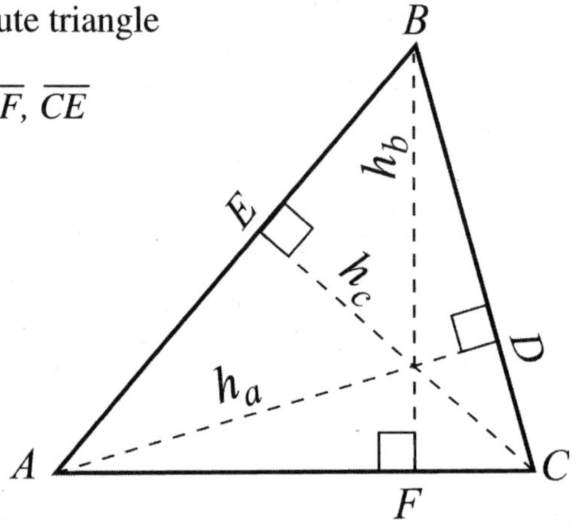

Altitudes in an obtuse triangle

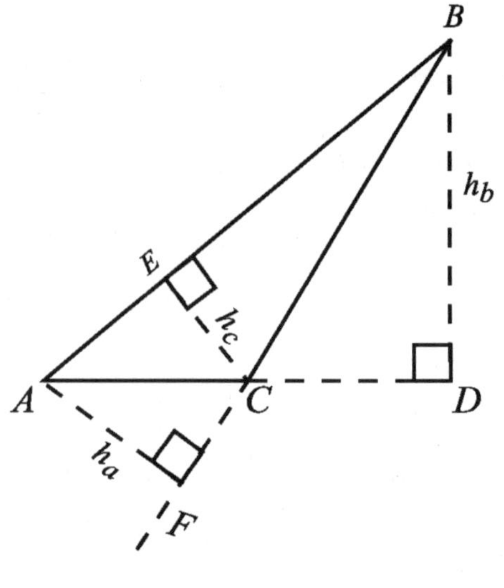

$AF=h_a$; $BD=h_b$; $CE=h_c$. Length of altitude h_a:

$$h_a = \frac{2\sqrt{p(p-a)(p-b)(p-c)}}{a}; \text{ where } p = \frac{a+b+c}{2}$$

Medians are the line segments running from a vertex to the midpoint of the opposite side.

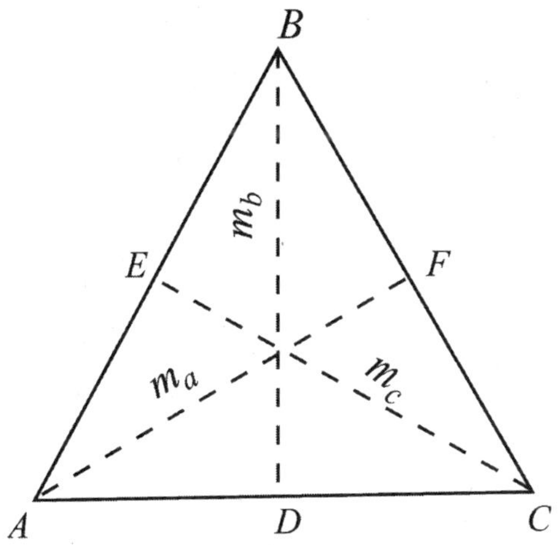

Medians: $AF=m_a$; $BD=m_b$; $CE=m_c$

$AE=EB$, $BF=FC$, $AD=DC$

Properties of Medians

1. The point where all three medians intersect divides each median in the ratio 2:1.

2. A median divides the triangle into two triangles of equal area.

Length of median m_a: $m_a = \frac{1}{2}\sqrt{2b^2 + 2c^2 - a^2}$

Bisectors are lines drawn from a vertex to the opposite side that bisect the angle at that vertex.

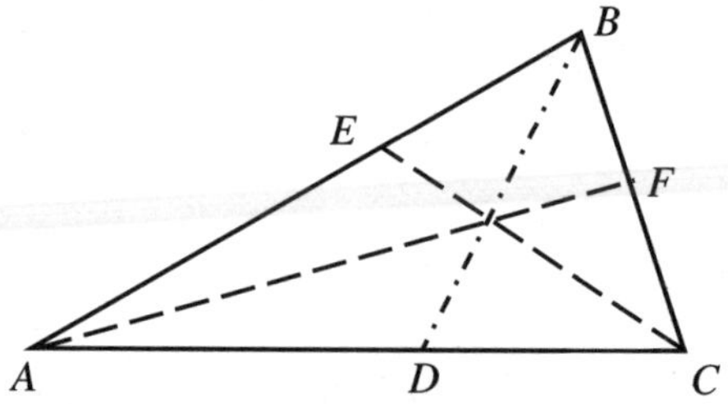

$AF; BD; CE$ are **bisectors** of the triangle.

Properties of Bisectors

1. The bisector divides the opposite side into parts that are proportional to the adjacent sides.

Example: $\frac{|BF|}{|FC|} = \frac{|AB|}{|AC|}$

2. The bisector divides the area of a triangle proportionally to its adjacent sides.

Example: $\frac{A(\Delta ABF)}{A(\Delta AFC)} = \frac{|AB|}{|AC|}$

DE, DF, EF are **middle lines** of the triangle.

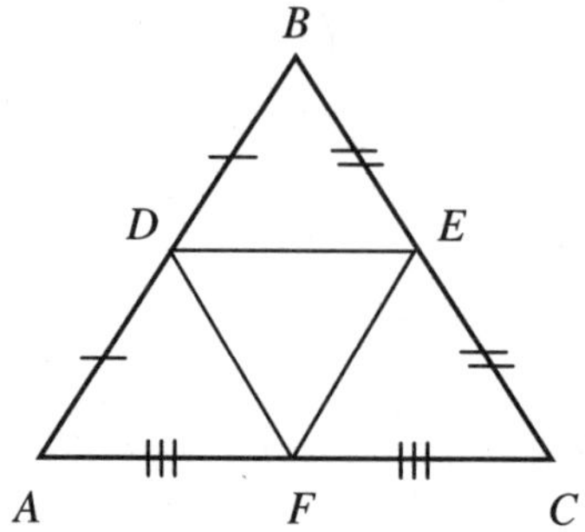

Properties of Middle Lines

1. A middle line is parallel to one of the triangle's sides:
$DE \| AC; DF \| BC; FE \| AB$.

2. The length of a middle line is equal to half of its corresponding parallel side of the triangles.

For example, $DE = \frac{1}{2} AC$

3. The triangles *DBE*, *ADF*, and *FEC* are similar to triangle *ABC*.

The Area of a Triangle

There are several ways to determine the area of a triangle:

$$A = \frac{1}{2} ah_a = \frac{1}{2} bh_b = \frac{1}{2} ch_c$$

$$A = \sqrt{p(p-a)(p-b)(p-c)}, \text{ where } p = \frac{a+b+c}{2}$$

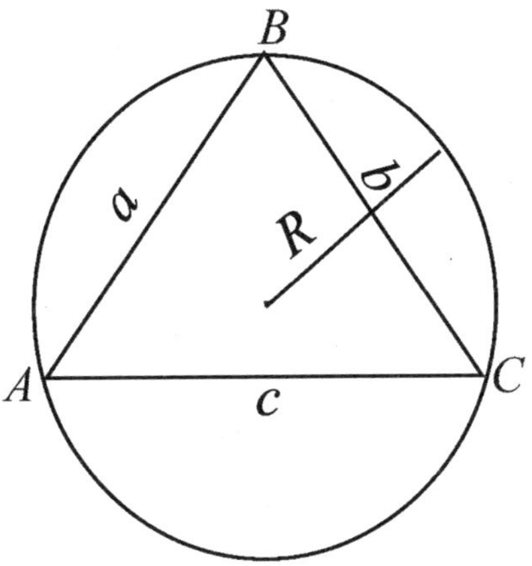

$A = \dfrac{abc}{4R}$, where R is the radius of a circle that circumscribes the triangle.

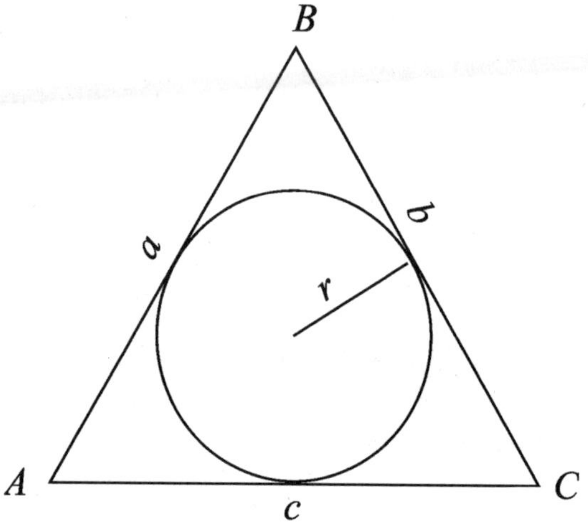

$A = pr$, where r is the radius of the inscribed circle and $p = \dfrac{a+b+c}{2}$

3.5.3 Right Triangles

The sides of a right triangle are related to each other in the following way (the Pythagorean Theorem):

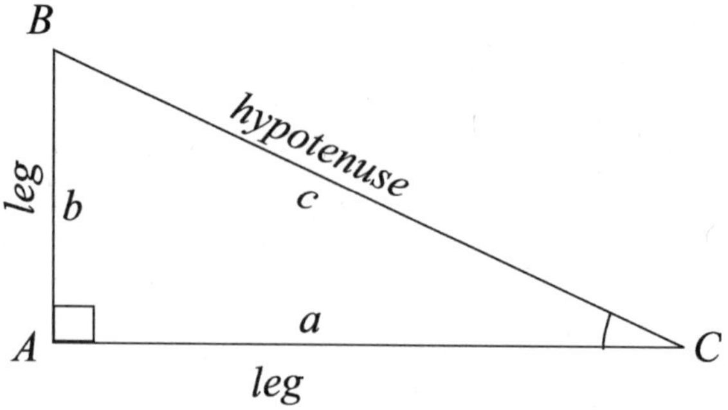

$c^2 = a^2 + b^2$, or $c = \sqrt{a^2 + b^2}$

The square of the length of the hypotenuse is equal to the sum of the squares of the lengths of the other two sides (the legs). (See **3.5.6** for a proof of this theorem).

The Area of a Right Triangle:

$$A = \frac{1}{2}ab$$

If $\angle ACB = 30°$, then $AB = \frac{1}{2}BC$

If $\angle ACB = 60°$, then $AC = \frac{\sqrt{3}}{2}BC$

For the right triangle $ABC, m\angle B + m\angle C = 90°$

3.5.4 Congruent Triangles

Two triangles (ABC and $A^1B^1C^1$) are congruent if any of the following is true:

1. All three pairs of corresponding sides are congruent (sss):

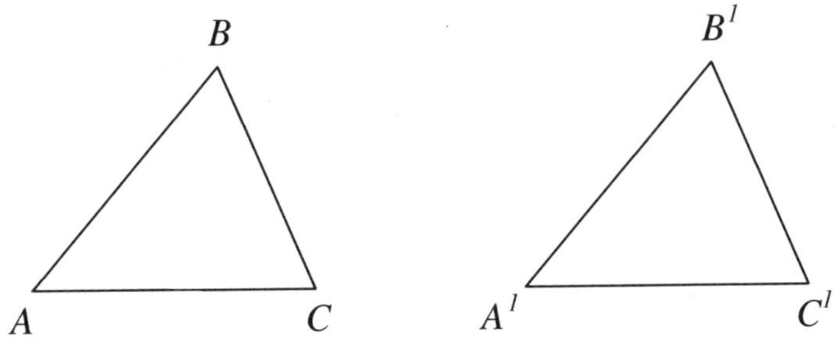

$$\overline{AB} \cong \overline{A^1B^1}, \overline{BC} \cong \overline{B^1C^1}, \overline{AC} \cong \overline{A^1C^1}$$

2. Two pairs of corresponding sides and the included pair of corresponding angles are congruent (sas):

$$\overline{AB} \cong \overline{A^1B^1}, \overline{AC} \cong \overline{A^1C^1}, \text{ and}$$

$$\angle A \cong \angle A^1.$$

3. Two pairs of corresponding angles and any pair of corresponding sides are congruent:

$$\overline{AC} \cong \overline{A^1C^1}, \angle A \cong \angle A^1, \text{ and } \angle C \cong \angle C^1, \text{ (asa).}$$

or $$\overline{AC} \cong \overline{A^1C^1}, \angle A \cong \angle A^1, \text{ and } \angle B \cong \angle B^1, \text{ (aas).}$$

3.5.5 Similarity of Triangles

Two triangles are similar if their corresponding angles are congruent and their corresponding sides are in proportion. The symbol for similarity is "~".

Example 1 of similar triangles:

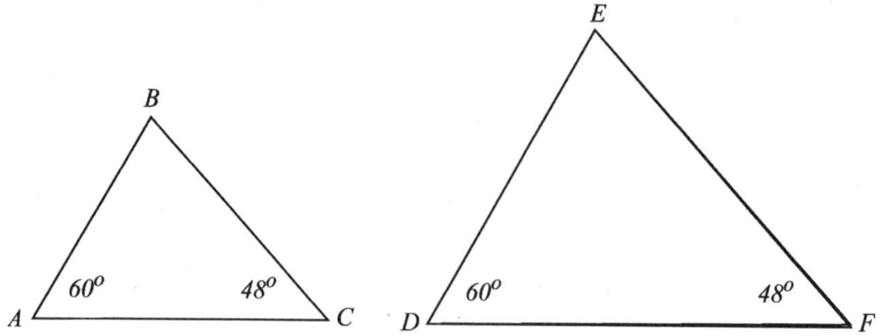

For these triangles the following ratios hold: $\frac{AB}{DE} = \frac{BC}{EF}$;

$\frac{EF}{BC} = \frac{DF}{AC}$

Example 2: The measures of the sides of ΔDEF are 15cm, 20cm, and 25cm. In ΔPQR $PQ = 3$cm, and $PR = 4$cm. $\Delta PQR \sim \Delta DEF$. Find QR.

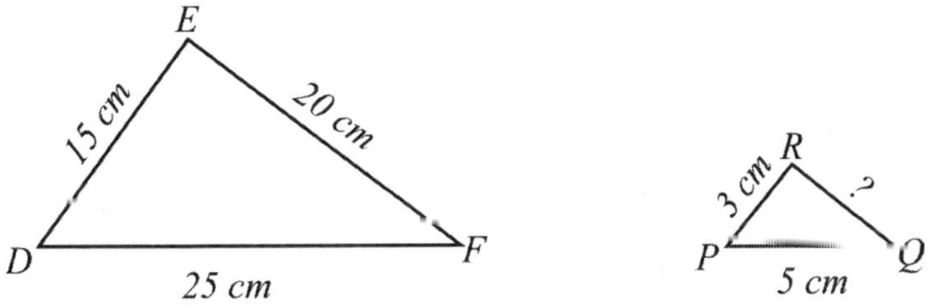

From the proportion $\frac{15}{3} = \frac{20}{QR}$, find QR. $QR = \frac{3 \cdot 20}{15} = 4$ cm.

3.5.6. The Pythagorean Theorem

The well-known Pythagorean Theorem is often used in mathematics. Therefore we will consider this theorem in detail.

Theorem: In any right triangle, the square of the length of the hypotenuse is equal to the sum of the squares of the lengths of the other two sides (the legs).

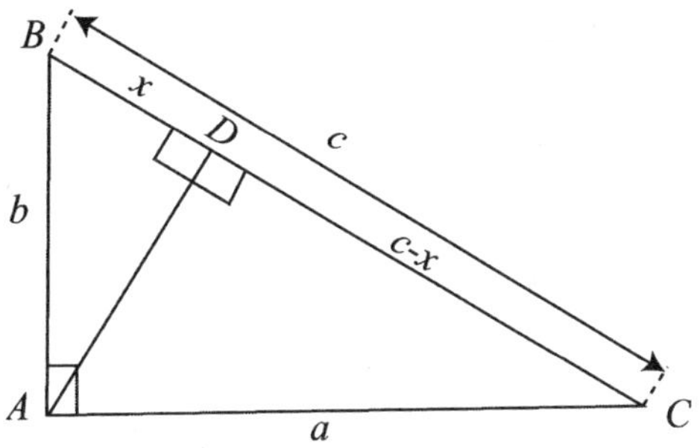

Proof:

Given: The right triangle ΔABC.

Draw AD, the altitude to hypotenuse BC.

$$\text{Let } BD = x \text{ and } DC = c - x.$$

The triangles ΔABC *and* ΔADC are similar.

$$\text{Then } \frac{c}{a} = \frac{a}{c-x} \text{ and } \frac{c}{b} = \frac{b}{x},$$

$$c^2 - cx = a^2, \; cx = b^2,$$

$$\boxed{c^2 = a^2 + b^2} \text{ which was to be proven.}$$

3.5.7 Typical Problems Involving Triangles

1) ΔABC is a right triangle with $\angle C = 30°$ and the hypotenuse $BC = 6$ inches.

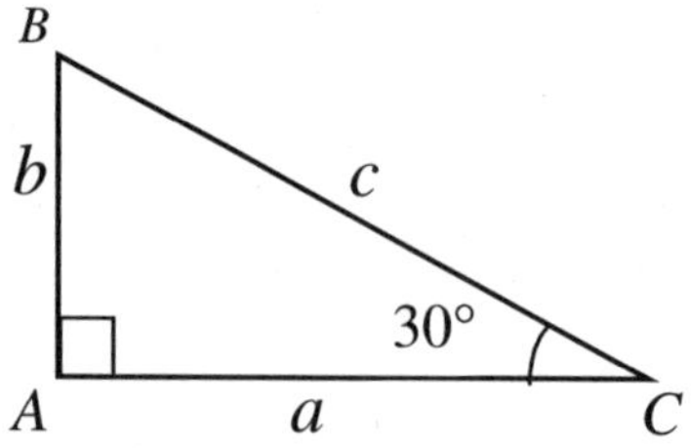

Find the legs AB and AC, and thus the area of the triangle.

Solution:

If $\angle ACB = 30°$ then $AB = \frac{1}{2}BC$ or $b = \frac{1}{2} \cdot 6 = 3$ inches.

$c^2 = a^2 + b^2$

$a = \sqrt{c^2 - b^2} = \sqrt{6^2 - 3^2} = \sqrt{27} \approx 5$ inches.

$AC = a \approx 5$ inches.

Area: $A = \frac{1}{2}ab \approx \frac{1}{2} \cdot 5 \cdot 3 \approx 7.5$ square inches

2) In $\Delta ABC\ DE \| AC$. If $DE = 10$ feet, $AC = 20$ feet, $BD = 6$ feet, and $EC = 8$ feet, find AB and BE.

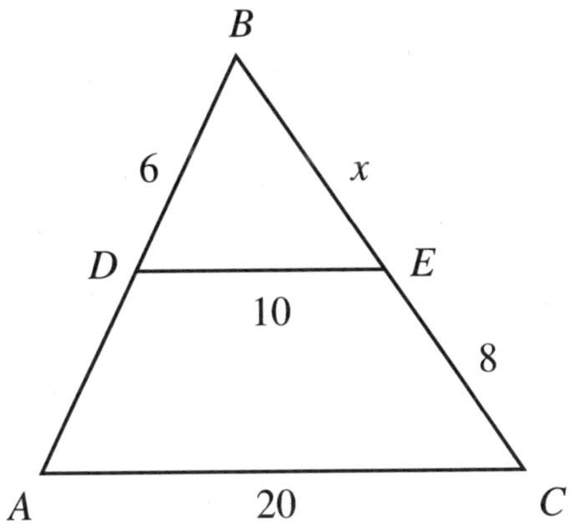

Solution:

Since $\overline{DE} \| \overline{AC}$ and $\overline{DE}$ intersects sides $\overline{AB}$ and

$\overline{BC}$, $\Delta DBE \sim \Delta ABC$

First Proportion:

$$\frac{DE}{AC} = \frac{BD}{AB}$$

$$AB = \frac{AC \cdot BD}{DE} = \frac{20 \cdot 6}{10} = 12 \text{ feet.}$$

AB = 12 feet.

Second Proportion:

$$\frac{BE}{DE} = \frac{BC}{AC}$$

Let $BE = x.$

Then $BC = x + 8.$

$$\frac{x}{10} = \frac{x+8}{20}$$

$$20x = 10(x+8) = 10x + 80$$

$$10x = 80$$

$$x = 8$$

$BE = 8$ feet

3) ΔABC is an isosceles triangle. The base $AC = 30$ cm. The altitude $BD = 20$ cm. Find the altitude AE.

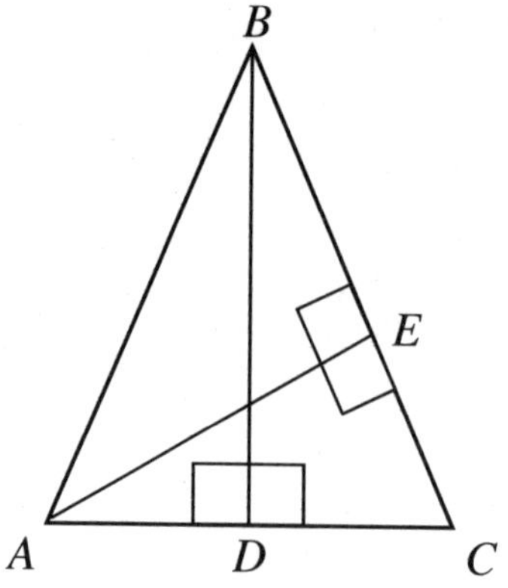

Solution:

Find the area of ΔABC using the altitudes:

First: $A = \frac{1}{2} AC \cdot BD$

Second: $A = \frac{1}{2} BC \cdot AE$

Both areas are equal. Therefore

$$AC \cdot BD = BC \cdot AE$$

$$AE = \frac{AC \cdot BD}{BC} = \frac{30 \cdot 20}{BC}$$

Since ΔABC is isosceles, the altitude BD divides ΔABC into congruent right triangles ΔADB and ΔCDB. Thus $AD = DC$ and $AD + DC = AC = 30$cm so AD=15 cm and DC=15cm.
Applying the Pythagorean Theorem to the right triangle ΔCDB, we can find BC:

$$BC = \sqrt{20^2 + 15^2} = \sqrt{625} = 25$$

$$AE = \frac{AC \cdot BD}{BC} = \frac{30 \cdot 20}{25} = 24\text{cm.}$$

4) In the triangle ΔABC the base AC is 60 feet, the altitude BD is 12 feet, and the median BE is 13 feet. Find sides AB and BC.

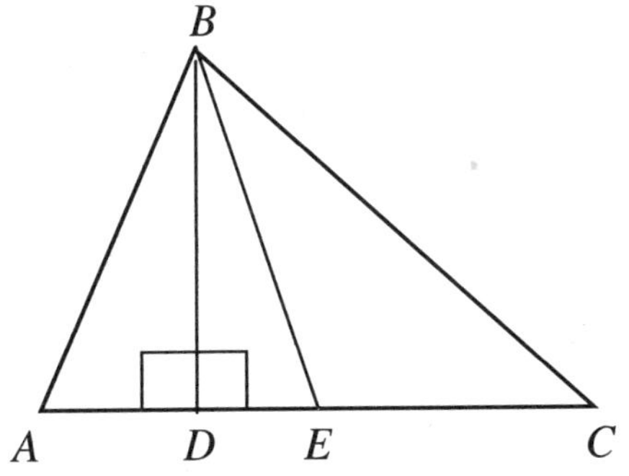

Solution:

Find from the right triangle *BDE*:

$DE = \sqrt{13^2 - 12^2} = \sqrt{169 - 144} = \sqrt{25} = 5$ feet

Therefore $AD = AE - DE = \frac{1}{2}AC - DE = \frac{1}{2} \cdot 60 - 5 = 25$ feet,

and $DC = DE + EC = 35$ feet.

Side

$AB = \sqrt{(BD)^2 + (AD)^2} = \sqrt{12^2 + 25^2} = \sqrt{769} \approx 27.7$ feet.

Side $BC = \sqrt{(BD)^2 + (DC)^2} = \sqrt{12^2 + 35^2} = \sqrt{144 + 1225} =$

$= \sqrt{1369} = 37$ feet

$AB \approx 27.7$ feet
$BC = 37$ feet

5. In a triangle ΔABT, the length of the line segment *MN* that connects the midpoints of two sides of a triangle is one half the length of the third side of the triangle with $AT = 3x + 12$.

Find *x*.

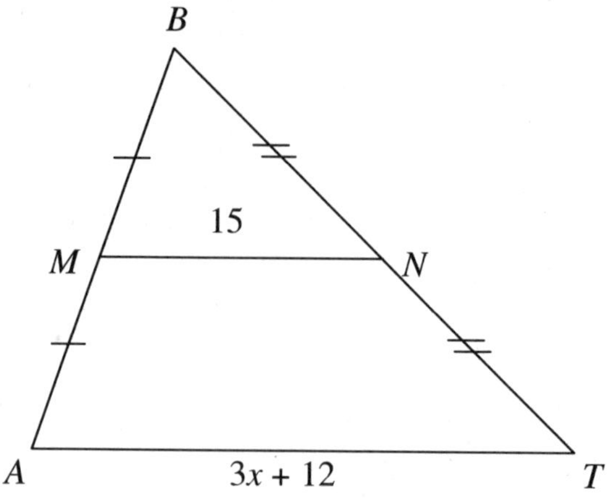

Solution:

$MN = \frac{1}{2}AT$

$15 = \frac{1}{2}(3x + 12)$

$30 = 3x + 12$

$18 = 3x$

$x = 6$

3.6 Quadrilaterals

A quadrilateral has four sides and four angles. The sum of the inside angles of a quadrilateral is $180°(4-2)=360°$.

3.6.1 Parallelograms

In a parallelogram both pairs of opposite sides are parallel and congruent.

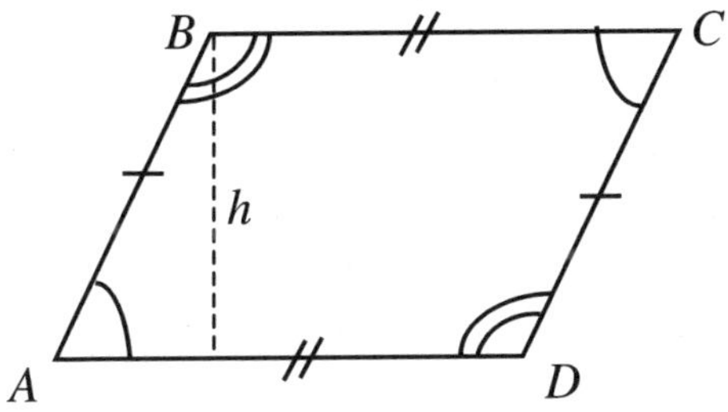

If $m\angle A = x$, then $m\angle B = 180° - x$.

Properties of Parallelograms

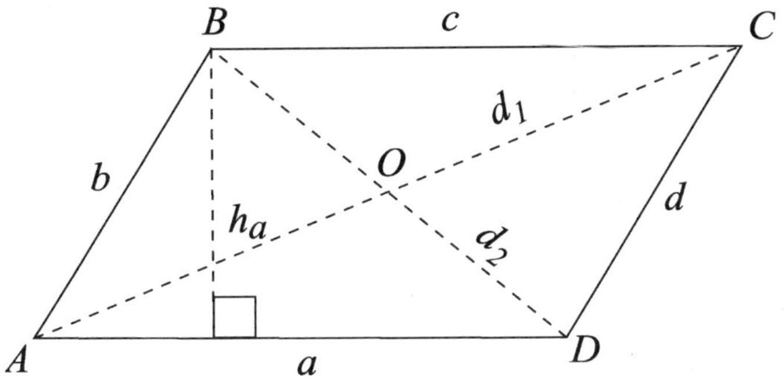

1. Opposite sides of a parallelogram are equal.
2. Opposite angles of a parallelogram are equal.
3. Each diagonal (d_1 and d_2) divides the parallelogram into two congruent triangles.

4. The diagonals of a parallelogram intersect each other at the middle point.

5. The sum of squares of the diagonals equals the sum of the squares of all the sides:

$$d_1^{\,2} + d_2^{\,2} = 2(a^2 + b^2)$$

Area of a Parallelogram:

$A = a \cdot h$, where h is the altitude.

3.6.2 Rectangles

A rectangle is a parallelogram where all four angles are right angles.

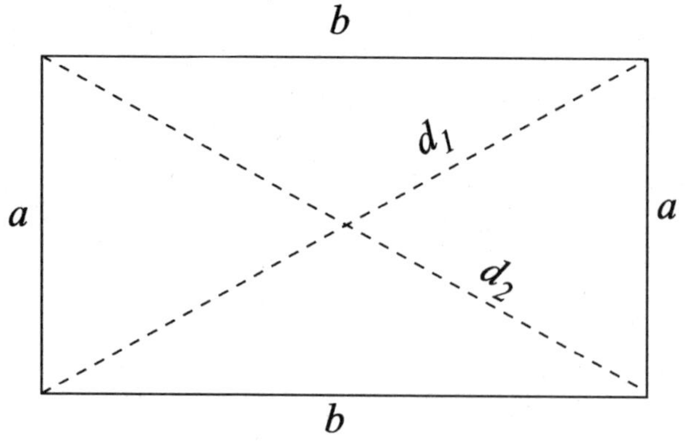

Perimeter: $p = 2(a + b)$

Diagonals are equal: $d_1 = d_2$

Area of a rectangle: $A = a \cdot b$

3.6.3 Rhombuses

In a rhombus both pairs of opposite sides are parallel. All four sides are congruent. The diagonals of a rhombus are the bisectors of the inside angles. $d_1 \perp d_2$

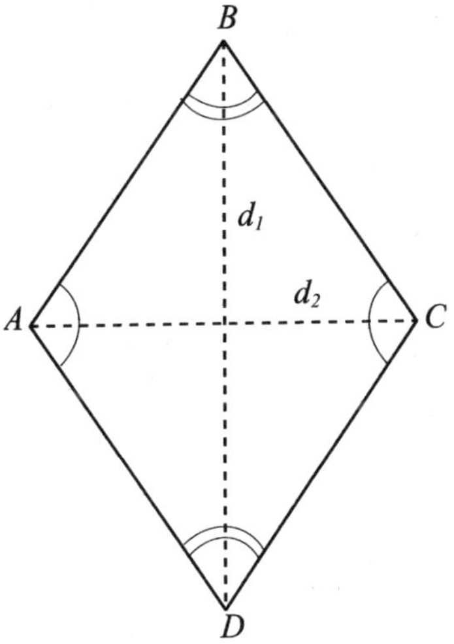

Area of a rhombus: $A = \frac{1}{2} d_1 d_2$

3.6.4 Squares

A square is a rectangle where all sides are congruent.

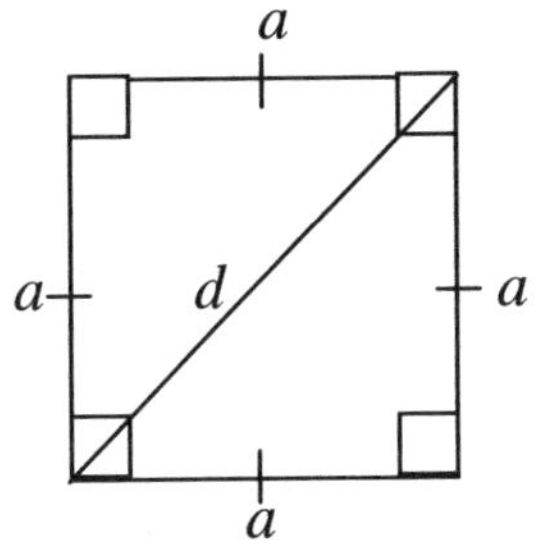

Area of a square: $A = a^2$

A square has all the properties of a parallelogram, a rectangle, and a rhombus.

The length of the diagonal d, given lengths of sides = a:
$d = a\sqrt{2}$
This formula follows from the Pythagorean Theorem:

$$d^2 = a^2 + a^2 = 2a^2 \qquad d = \sqrt{2a^2} = a\sqrt{2}$$

3.6.5 Trapezoids

In a trapezoid only one pair of opposite sides is parallel.

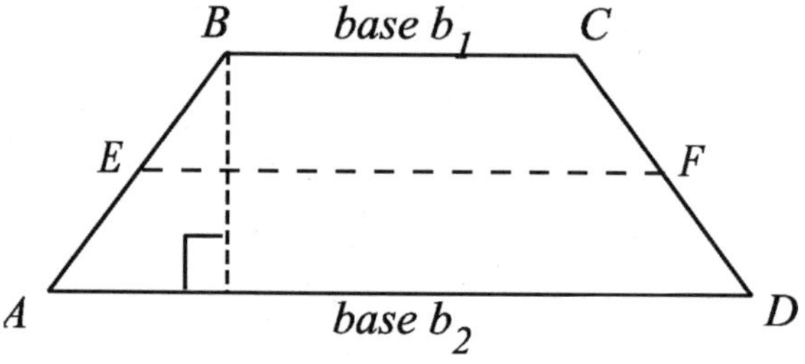

If $\overline{AB} = \overline{CD}$, the trapezoid is called an isosceles trapezoid.

A line segment EF that connects the middle points of the legs is called the **middle line** of the trapezoid.

Length of middle line:

$$\text{EF} = \frac{1}{2}(b_1 + b_2)$$

If a trapezoid is isosceles, then the base angles are congruent and conversely $\angle A \cong \angle D$, also the diagonals are congruent and conversely.

Area of a trapezoid:

$$A = \frac{1}{2}(b_1 + b_2)h$$

3.6.6 Typical Problems Involving Quadrilaterals

1. Given a trapezoid where $a = 250$ cm, $b = 100$ cm, $m\angle A = 45°$, and $m\angle D = 30°$, find the area of the trapezoid.

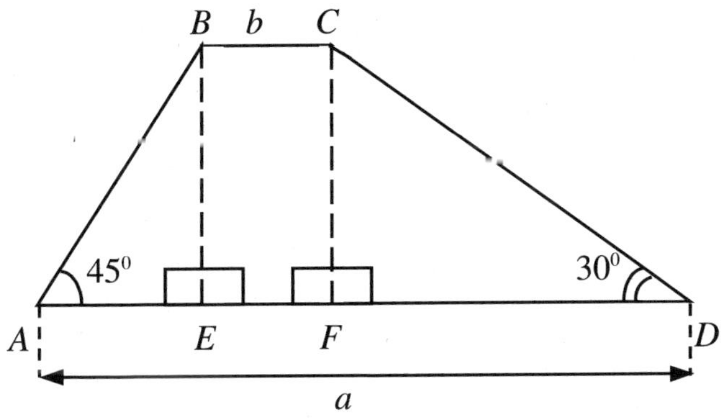

Solution:

$$\text{Let } BE = CF = x$$

If $m\angle D = 30°$, then $CF = \frac{1}{2}CD$

$CD = 2CF = 2x$

In ΔABE, $m\angle B = 45^\circ$ $(45 + 45 + 90 = 180°)$

Therefore $AE = BE = x$

$(CD)^2 = (CF)^2 + (FD)^2$ [The Pythagorean Theorem]

$(FD)^2 = (CD)^2 - (CF)^2$

$(FD)^2 = (2x)^2 - x^2 = 4x^2 - x^2 = 3x^2$

$FD = \sqrt{3x^2} = x\sqrt{3}$

$$a = AE + EF + FD = x + b + x\sqrt{3}$$

Find x.

$$x = \frac{a-b}{\sqrt{3}+1} = \frac{250-100}{\sqrt{3}+1} \approx 67.5\,\text{cm}^2$$

Area: $A = \frac{1}{2}(a+b)h = \frac{1}{2}(250+100)\cdot 67.5 \approx 11{,}812.5\,\text{cm}^2$

2. Given the rhombus *ABCD* with a perimeter 2*p* (in.) and two diagonals, which sum to $m = d_1 + d_2$, find the area of the rhombus.

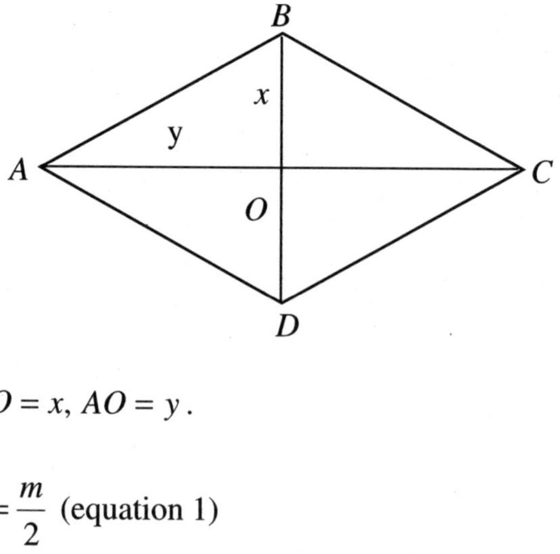

Solution:

Let $BO = x, AO = y$.

$$x + y = \frac{m}{2} \text{ (equation 1)}$$

Area of a rhombus:

$$A = \frac{1}{2}d_1 d_2 = \frac{2x \cdot 2y}{2} = 2xy$$

For ΔABO, $x^2 + y^2 = (AB)^2 = \left(\frac{2p}{4}\right)^2 = \left(\frac{p}{2}\right)^2$ (equation 2)

Square equation 1 and subtract equation 2 from it:

$$(x+y)^2 = \left(\frac{m}{2}\right)^2 = x^2 + 2xy + y^2 = \frac{m^2}{4}$$

$$x^2 + 2xy + y^2 - x^2 - y^2 = \frac{m^2}{4} - \frac{p^2}{4}$$

$$2xy = \frac{m^2 - p^2}{4}$$

Answer: $A = \dfrac{m^2 - p^2}{4}$ (in^2)

3.7 Circles

A circle is a set of points forming a curved figure in a plane, where all points in the set are the same distance from one point called the center.

The distance around a circle (the perimeter of a circle) is called the **circumference**.

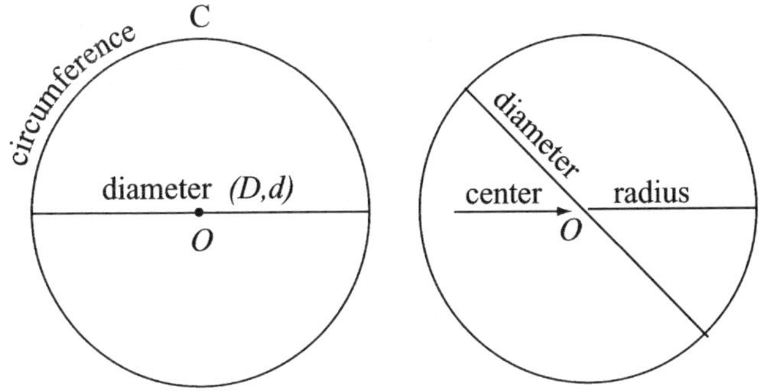

A line segment that passes through the center of a circle and has its endpoints on the circle is called the **diameter**.

A length that is half the diameter of a circle, i.e. the distance from the center of the circle to the circle itself, is called the **radius**.

Diameter: D, d

Radius: R, r

$D = 2R \qquad d = 2r$

$$R = \frac{D}{2} \qquad r = \frac{d}{2}$$

The ratio of the circumference to the diameter of a circle is always the same. The value of this constant ratio is represented by the Greek letter pi: π. The approximate value of π is $\frac{22}{7} = 3.142... \approx 3.14$

Circumference: $C = 2\pi \cdot R$

Since diameter $D = 2R$, $C = \pi D$

(remember, $\pi = \frac{C}{D}$ by definition)

Area of a circle: $A = \pi r^2$, or $A = \pi(\frac{D}{2})^2 = \frac{\pi D^2}{4}$

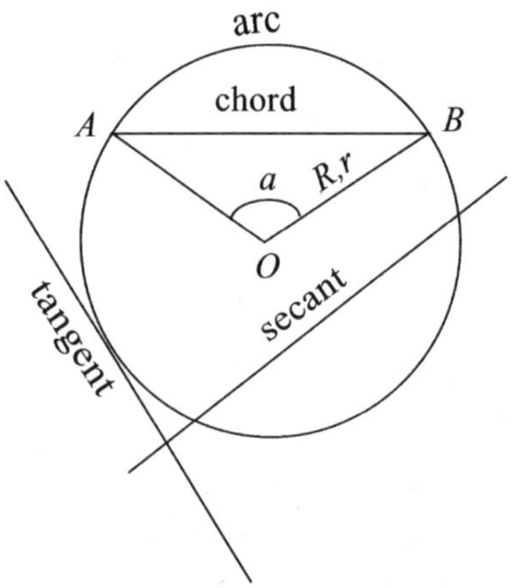

Any line segment that passes through a circle and has endpoints on the circle is called a **chord**.

The part of a circle between the points of a chord is called an **arc**.

The length of an arc: $l = \dfrac{\pi r\alpha}{180}$

An angle with a vertex in the center of a circle is called a **central angle** ($\angle AOB$).

A **tangent** is a line in the same plane as the circle that intersects the circle in exactly one point.

A **secant** is a line that intersects the circle in two points.

Problem:

Inside a circle with a radius of 13 cm there exists a point M.

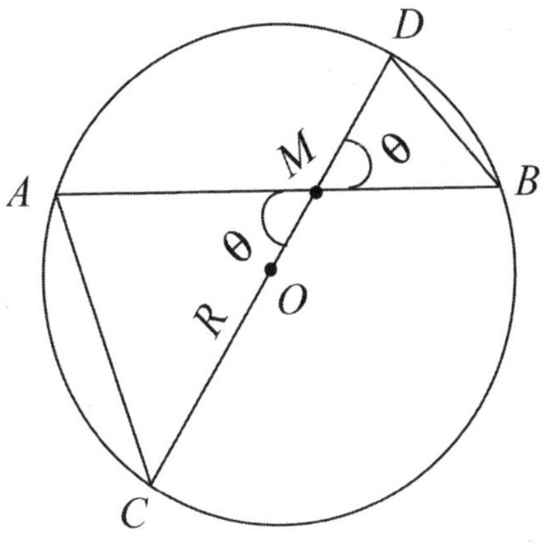

$$OM = 5 \text{ cm}$$

$$\text{Chord } AB = 25 \text{ cm}$$

Find the length of AM and MB.

Solution:

Since $R = 13$ cm and $OM = 5$ cm,

$MD = 8$ cm and $MC = 18$ cm.

Let $MB = x$. Then $AM = 25 - x$.

$\Delta AMC \cong \Delta MDB$ therefore,

$$\frac{AM}{MD} = \frac{MC}{MB}$$

or $AM \cdot MB = MD \cdot MC$

Since $AM \cdot MB = MD \cdot MC$,

$$(25 - x)x = 18 \cdot 8 = 144$$

$$-x^2 + 25x - 144 = 0 \quad x_1 = 16; x_2 = 9$$

Answer: $AM = 16$ cm; $MB = 9$ cm

3.7.1 Circumscribed and Inscribed Circles

A circle is* circumscribed *about a polygon when all the vertices of the polygon are on the circle. That polygon is* inscribed *in the circle.

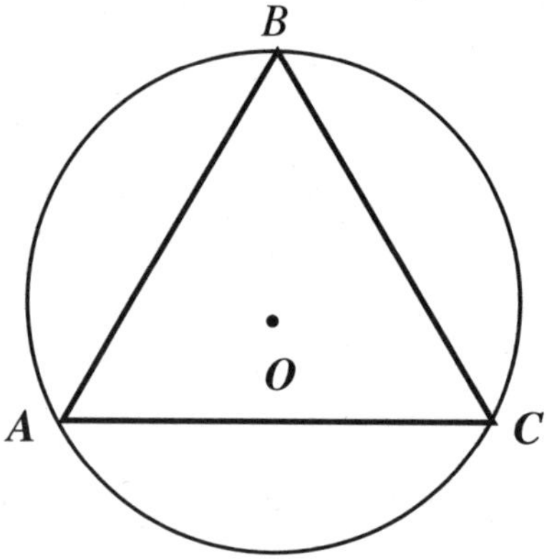

ΔABC is inscribed in circle O.

When a square is inscribed in a circle, the diagonals of the square are also diameters of the circle

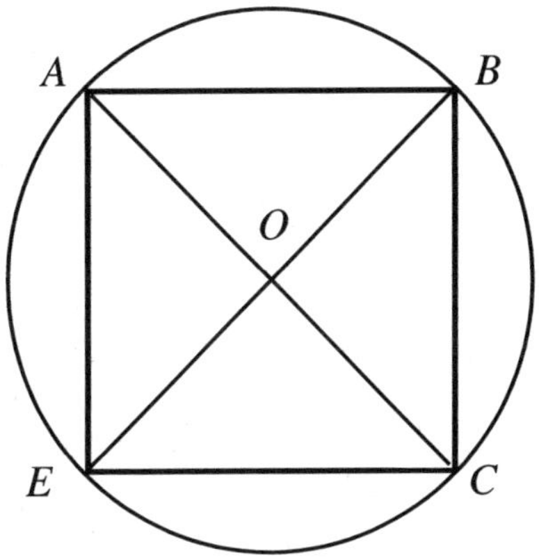

$AC = D$; $BE = D$.

When a circle is inscribed in a square, the sides of the square have the same length as the diameter of the circle.

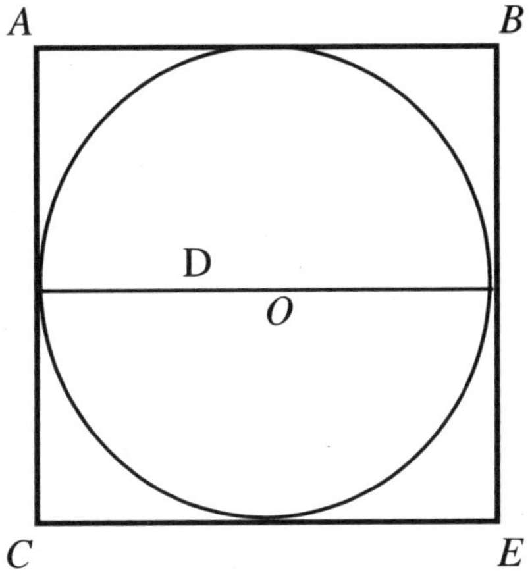

$AB = D$; $AC = D$

3.8 Regular Polygons

Regular polygons have equal sides and equal angles.

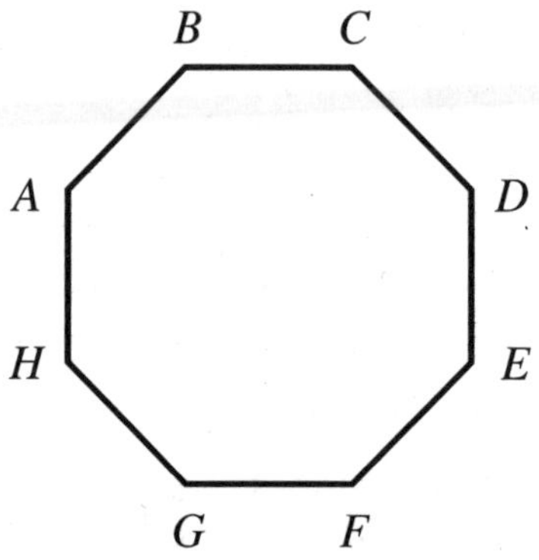

Each angle of a regular polygon equals $\frac{180°(n-2)}{n}$, where n is the number of sides of the polygon.

Area of a regular polygon: $A = p \cdot h$, where

$$p = \frac{1}{2}(AB + BC + CD + ...)$$

Side b_n of a circumscribed regular polygon relates to side a_n of an inscribed regular polygon in the formula $b_n = R \div \sqrt{R^2 - \frac{1}{4}a_n}$, where R is the radius of the circle.

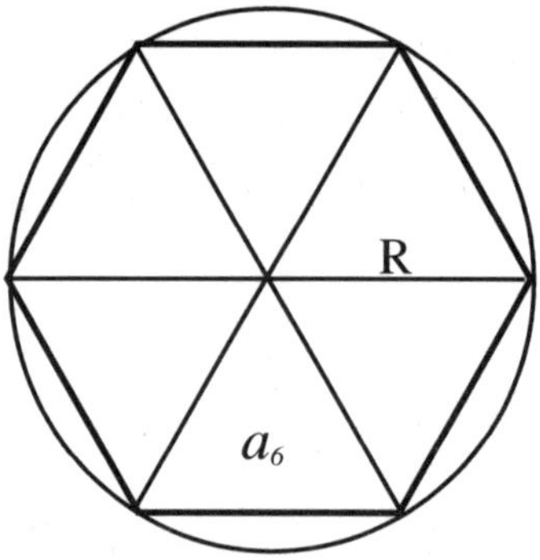

The following formulas are used in solving problems (a_n is the length of a side of a polygon with number of sides *n* inscribed in a circle of radius R):

$$a_3 = R\sqrt{3} \approx 1.7321R$$

$$a_4 = R\sqrt{2} \approx 1.4142R$$

$$a_5 = R\sqrt{\frac{5-\sqrt{5}}{2}} \approx 1.1755R$$

$$a_6 = R$$

$$a_8 = R\sqrt{2-\sqrt{2}} \approx 0.7654R$$

$$a_{10} = R\frac{\sqrt{5}-1}{2} \approx 0.6180R$$

Examples:

1) We have a circular log with a diameter of 40 cm. Can we use it to make a square post that measures 36 cm by 36 cm

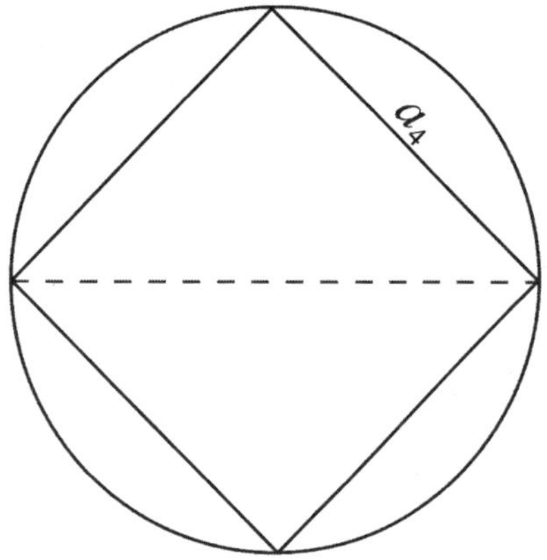

Solution:

The radius of the log $R = \frac{D}{2} = \frac{40}{2} = 20\,\text{cm}$

$$a_4 = R\sqrt{2} = 20 \cdot 1.4142 \approx 28\,\text{cm}$$

28 cm < 36 cm, therefore we cannot make that thick of a post.

2) A circle is inscribed in an isosceles triangle. (It can be shown that the altitude *BD* passes through the center of the circle). $\angle EOB = 60°$. $OE \perp AB$.

Find the lengths of *AB* and *AC*.

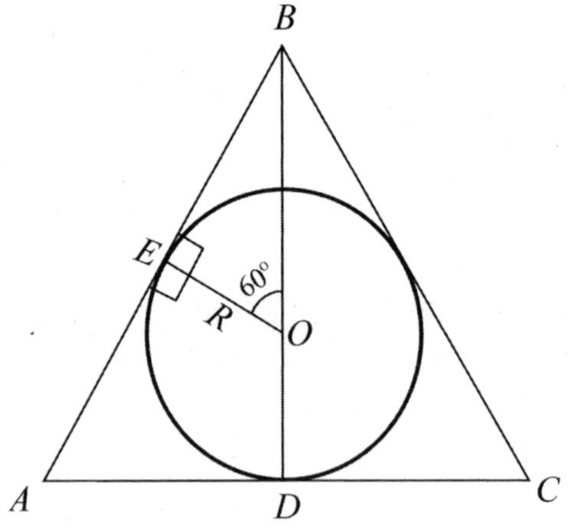

Solution:

Since $\angle EOB = 60°$, $BO = EO\frac{2}{\sqrt{3}} = \frac{2R}{\sqrt{3}}$

Therefore $BD = R + BO = R + \frac{2R}{\sqrt{3}} = \frac{R(\sqrt{3}+2)}{\sqrt{3}}$

From ΔABD we find:

$$AB = \frac{2R(\sqrt{3}+2)}{\sqrt{3}} \text{ and } AD = R(\sqrt{3}+2) \text{ because } \angle ABD = 30^\circ$$

Therefore $AC = 2(AD) = 2R(\sqrt{3}+2)$

Answer: $AB = BC = \dfrac{2R(\sqrt{3}+2)}{\sqrt{3}}$; $AC = 2R(\sqrt{3}+2)$

3.9 Three-Dimensional Figures

A spatial figure that has length, width, and height is called a three-dimensional figure.

3.9.1 Prisms

A prism is a three-dimensional figure with bases that are the same polygons, and sides that are parallelograms. A right prism has sides perpendicular to its base.

Side area of prism: $S_s = p \cdot H$, where *p* is the perimeter of the base of the prism, and *H* is altitude.

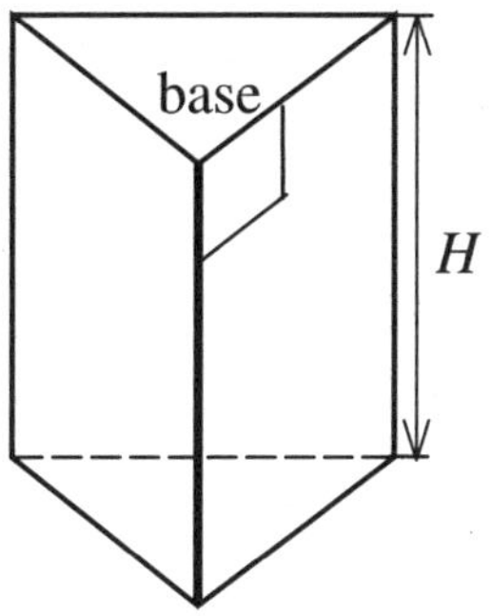

Volume of a prism: $V = S_{base} \cdot H$

3.9.2 Parallelepipeds

A parallelepiped is a prism in which the bases are parallelograms.

A rectangular parallelepiped that has a square base will have a diagonal d: $d^2 = a^2 + b^2 + c^2$

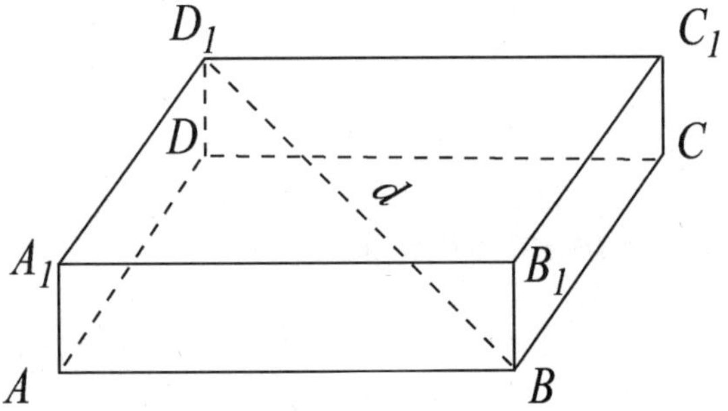

All diagonals in a rectangular parallelepiped are equal.

The volume of a rectangular parallelepiped: $V = a \cdot b \cdot c$

If all sides of a rectangular parallelepiped are equal, then it is called a **cube**.

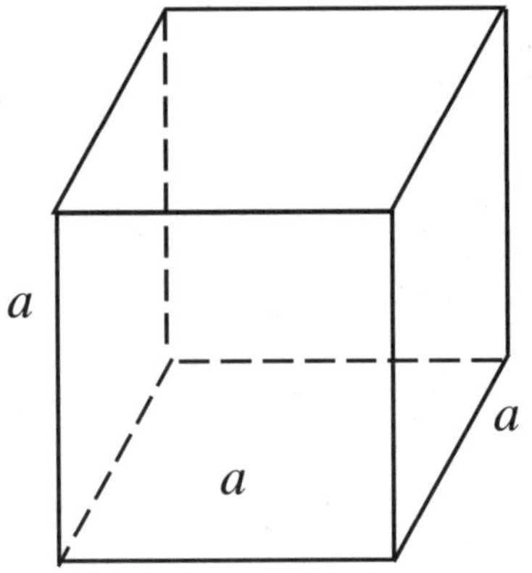

Volume of a cube: $V = a^3$, where $a = b = c$

3.9.3 Pyramids

A pyramid is a polyhedron where one side can be any polygon and the rest of the sides are triangles.

A pyramid is called regular when the base is a regular polygon and a perpendicular projection from the vertex to the base intersects with the center of the base.

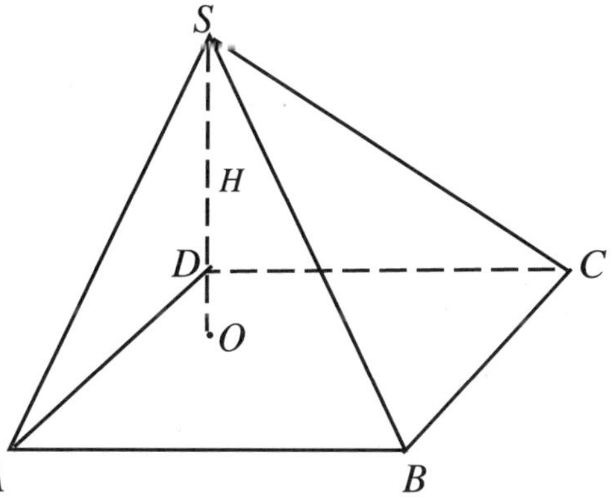

- The volume of a pyramid is found by using the formula: $V = \frac{1}{3} S \cdot H$, where S is the area of a base.
- The volume of a truncated pyramid:

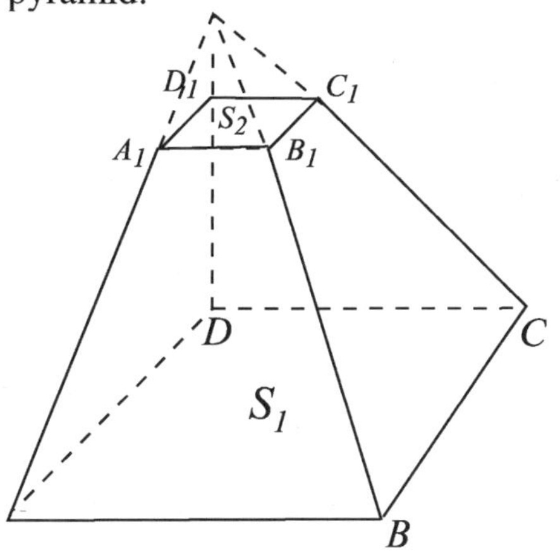

- $V = \frac{1}{3} H(S_1 + \sqrt{S_1 S_2} + S_2)$, where S_1 is the area of upper base and S_2 is the area of the lower base.

3.9.4 Cylinders

A cylinder is a figure with one curved surface and two circular bases.

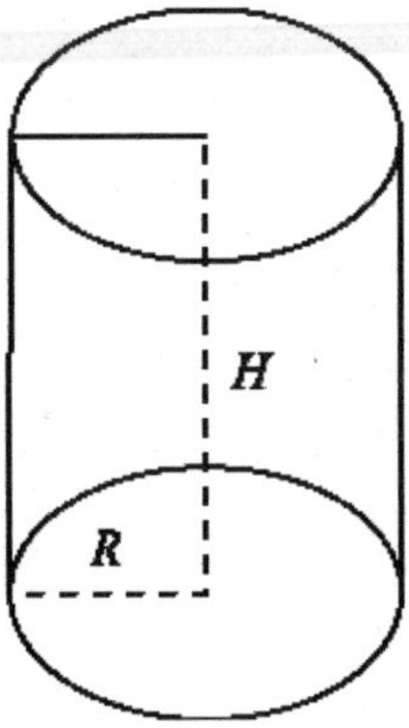

Side area of a cylinder: $S = 2\pi RH$

Full surface area: $S_f = 2\pi RH + 2\pi R^2$

Volume of a cylinder: $V = \pi R^2 H$

3.9.5 Cones

A cone is a figure with one curved surface, one vertex, and one circular base.

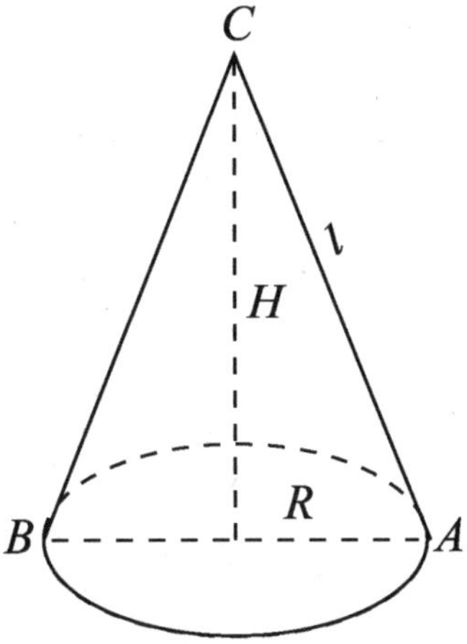

Side area of a cone: $S = \pi R l$, where R is the radius of the base of the cone and $l = AC$

Full surface area of a cone:

$$S_{(f)} = \pi R l + \pi R^2 = \pi R(l + R)$$

Volume of a cone: $V = \frac{1}{3}\pi R^2 H$

Truncated Cones

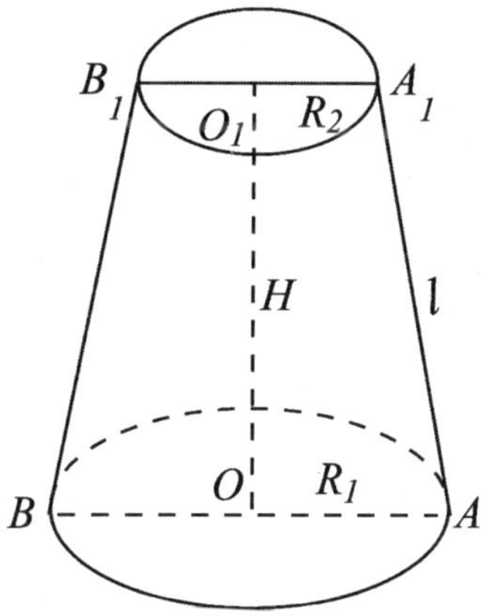

Side area of a cone:

$S = \pi(R_1 + R_2)l$, where

R_1 is the radius of the base,

R_2 is the radius of the truncated part, and $l = A_1A_2$

Volume of a truncated cone:

$$V = \frac{1}{3}\pi H(R_1^{\ 2} + R_1R_2 + R_2^{\ 2}),$$

where $H = OO_1$.

3.9.6 Spheres

A sphere is the set of all points that are a given distance from a fixed point.

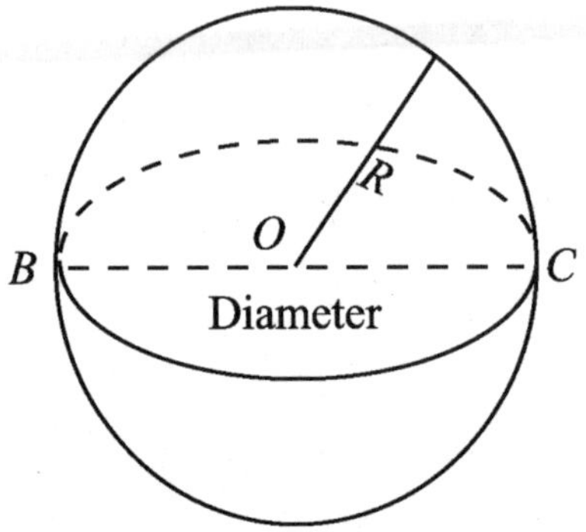

Area of a sphere: $S = 4\pi R^2$, where R is the radius of the sphere.

Volume of a sphere: $V = \frac{4}{3}\pi R^3$

3.10 Transformations

A transformation moves each point of a plane figure according to some rule, mapping the original figure onto an image.

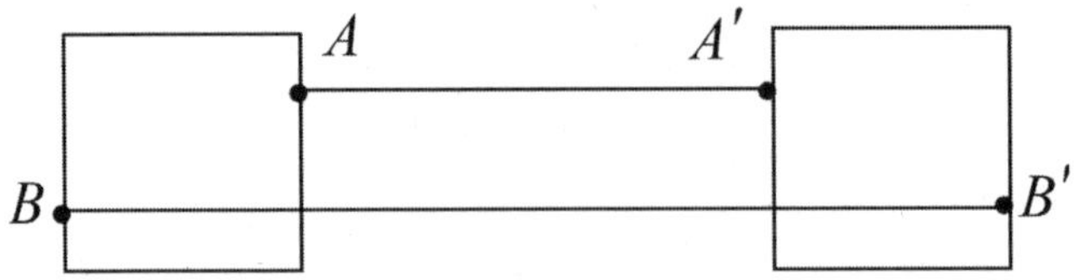

There is a 1:1 correspondence between points

In symbols	In words
$A \longrightarrow A'$	The image of A is A'
$B \longrightarrow B'$	The image of B is B'

3.10.1 Reflection in a Line (Mirror Image)

In this figure the letter *E* is reflected in line *k*.

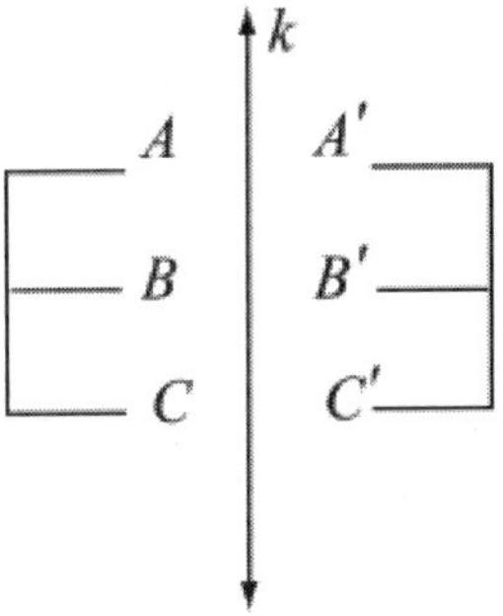

A reflection in line *k* is a transformation of the plane such that:
If A^1 is the image of *A* and point *A* is not on line *k*, then line *k* is the perpendicular bisector AA^1.
If point *A* is on line *k* the image of *A* is *A*.

3.10.2 Point Reflections and Point Symmetry

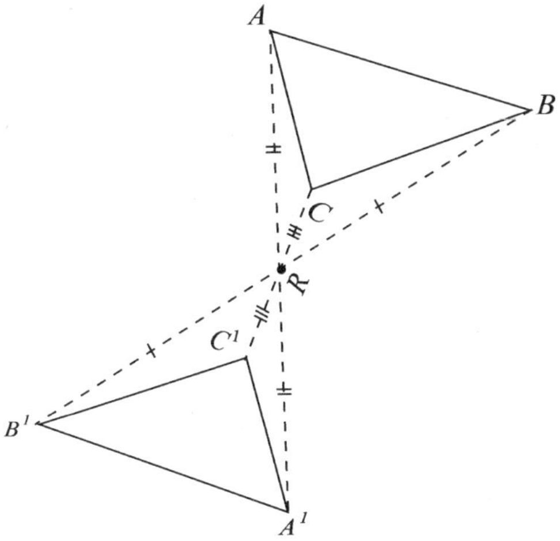

Point *R* is the point of reflection of triangles *ABC* and $A^1B^1C^1$.
For this point reflection, we can state that the image of *A* is A^1 by writing *B* and B^1.

Point symmetry occurs in a figure when the figure is its own image as reflected around a certain point.
P — the point of symmetry.

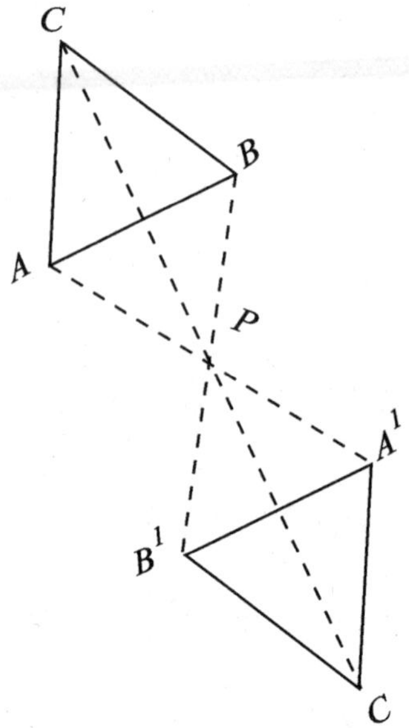

3.10.3 Line Symmetry

In the figure below there is a line k on which the figure could be folded so that the parts of the figure on opposite sides of the line would coincide.

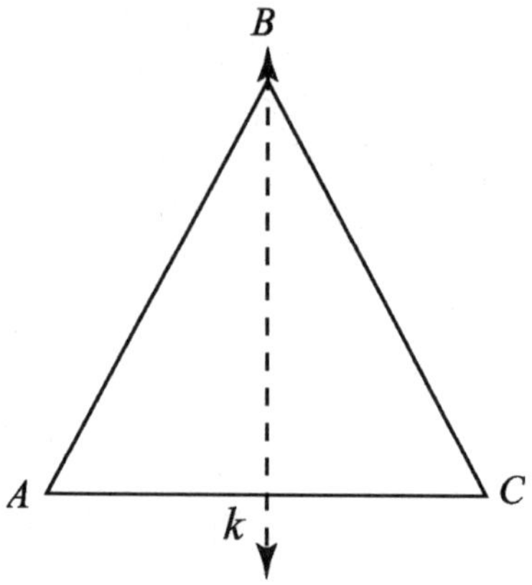

That line is a line of reflection, and each point of the figure has as its image another point of the figure. This line of reflection is a line of symmetry, and the figure has the line of symmetry *k*.

3.10.4 Rotations

A simple example of rotation is turning a figure about a fixed point. In this figure the letter E is rotated 90° clockwise around point *O*.

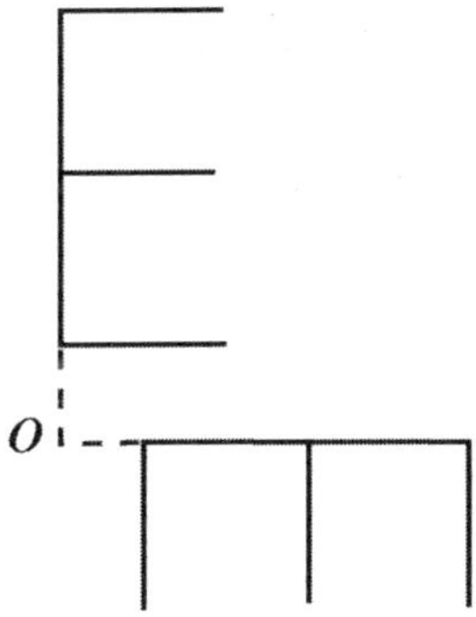

In general, a rotation preserves distance and angle measure. In a rotation, a figure is congruent to its image.

3.10.5 Translations

A translation moves every point in the plane the same distance in the same direction.

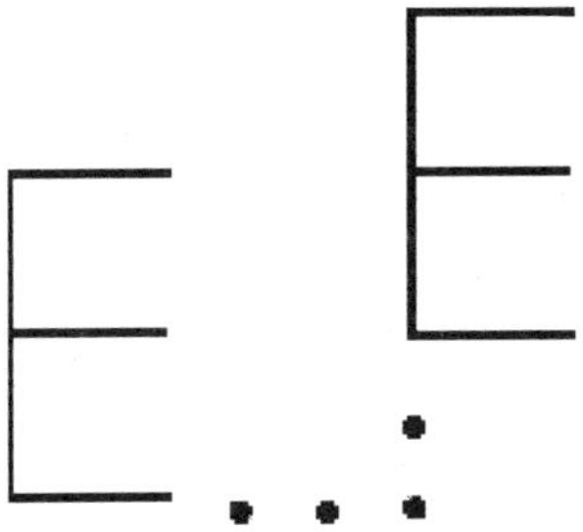

In the figure the letter E is translated 3 units right and 2 units up.

In this figure ΔABC is translated by moving every point 5 units to the right and 6 units down.

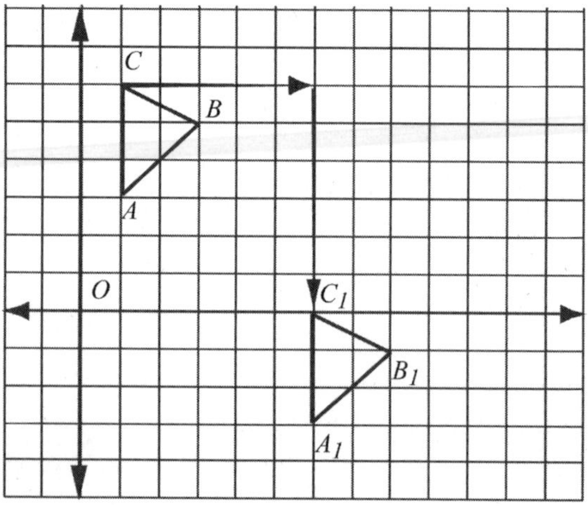

From the figure: A (1,3)→ A^1(6,-3)
B (3,5)→ B^1(8,-1)
C (1,6)→ C^1(6, 0)

Under a translation of a units in the horizontal direction and b units in the vertical direction, the image of any point $P\ (x, y)$ is $P^1(x+a,\ y+b)$.

3.10.6 Dilations

In this figure there is a constant ratio of the distances between points in the original figure and the enlargement or reduction. This kind of transformation is called dilation.

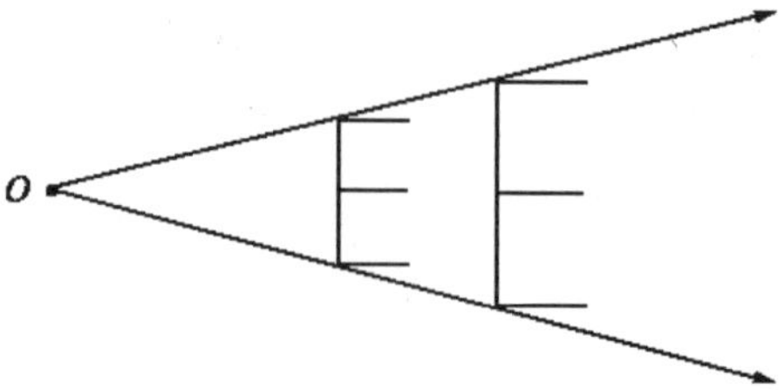

Here the letter E is dilated from center O.

3.11 Commonly Asked Questions: Geometry

1) **Q:** What is the difference between a line and a segment?

A: A line is theoretically infinite. A segment is a finite part of a line.

2) **Q:** Can a figure with two angles be a closed figure?

A: No, the smallest number of angles a closed figure made up of straight lines can have is three.

3) **Q:** What is the connection between the altitude, median, and the bisector in a triangle?

A: The altitude, median and bisector are all different, except in the special case of isosceles and equilateral triangles.

3) **Q:** What is a $1°$ angle?

A: A $1°$ angle, when drawn as a central angle of a circle between two neighboring radii, equals $\frac{1}{360}$ of the perimeter of the circle (a full sweep of the radius equals $360°$).

4) **Q:** I know I can solve many problems involving right triangles by using the Pythagorean Theorem. Are there other methods of solving such problems?

A: Yes, but other methods not only use the sides, but also the angles of a triangle. These methods are studied in part of mathematics called trigonometry.

5) **Q:** What is the difference between the symbols $\angle$ and $m\angle$?

A: The $\angle$ symbol is the symbol of an angle, but it has no actual measure associated with it. The $m\angle$ symbol, on the other hand, shows that the angle has a dimension. This measure could be a result of some calculations or of physically measuring the angle with a protractor.

6) **Q:** What is the relationship between algebra and geometry?

A: The relationship is very close. Solving geometric problems requires the use of formulas and calculations. Without algebra, solving geometric problems would be impossible.

7) **Q:** Can only triangles be similar, or can other figures be similar too?

A: Any two figures can be similar as long as they are the same shape and their dimensions are related proportionally.

4 CHAPTER

TRIGONOMETRY

Trigonometry is the science of solving problems that involve triangles.

4.1 Basic Trigonometric Functions

In a right-angled ΔABC,

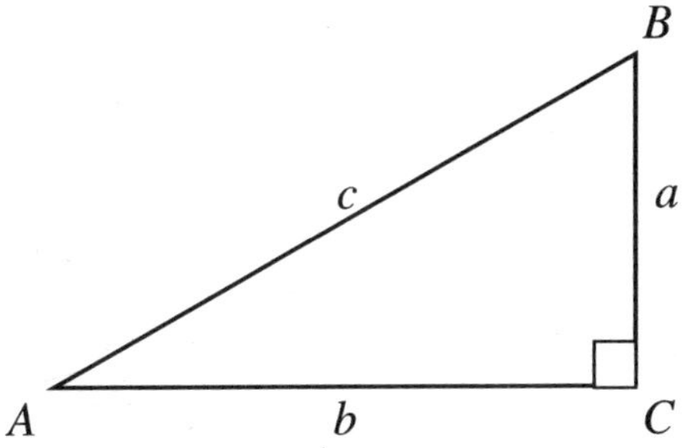

leg $\overline{BC}$ is opposite $\angle A$; leg $\overline{AC}$ is adjacent to $\angle A$.

The ratio $\frac{\overline{BC}}{\overline{AB}} = \frac{a}{c}$ is called the **sine** of angle A.

The sine of angle A ($\sin A$) is the ratio of the length of the side opposite $\angle A$ to the length of the hypotenuse.

The ratio $\frac{\overline{AC}}{\overline{AB}} = \frac{b}{c}$ is called the **cosine** of angle A.

The cosine of angle A ($\cos A$) is the ratio of the length of the side adjacent to $\angle A$ to the length of the hypotenuse.

The ratio $\dfrac{\overline{BC}}{\overline{AC}} = \dfrac{a}{b}$ is called the **tangent** of angle A.

The tangent of angle A ($\tan A$) is the ratio of the length of the side opposite $\angle A$ to the length of the side adjacent to $\angle A$.

The functions $\sin A$, $\cos A$, and $\tan A$ are the basic functions of trigonometry. There are also derived functions:

The ratio $\dfrac{\overline{AC}}{\overline{BC}} = \dfrac{b}{a}$ is called the **cotangent** of angle A ($\cot A$).

The cotangent of $\angle A$ is the ratio of the length of the side adjacent to $\angle A$ to the side opposite $\angle A$.

$$\tan A = \frac{a}{b}$$

$$\cot A = \frac{b}{a}$$

$$\text{therefore } \cot A = \frac{1}{\tan A}$$

The ratio $\dfrac{\overline{AB}}{\overline{AC}} = \dfrac{c}{b}$ is called the **secant** of angle A.

The secant of $\angle A$ (sec A) is the ratio of the length of the hypotenuse to the length of the side adjacent to $\angle A$.

$$\cos A = \frac{b}{c}$$

$$\sec A = \frac{c}{b}$$

$$\text{Therefore } \sec A = \frac{1}{\cos A} \quad (\cos A \neq 0)$$

The ratio $\frac{\overline{AB}}{\overline{BC}} = \frac{c}{a}$ is called the **cosecant** of angle A.

The cosecant of $\angle A$ ($\csc A$) is the ratio of the length of the hypotenuse to the length of the side opposite $\angle A$.

$$\sin A = \frac{\overline{BC}}{\overline{AB}} = \frac{a}{c}$$

$$\csc A = \frac{\overline{AB}}{\overline{BC}} = \frac{c}{a}$$

$$\text{Therefore } \csc A = \frac{1}{\sin A} \quad (A \neq 0).$$

It is very important to note that the values of

$$\sin\theta, \cos\theta, \tan\theta, \sec\theta, \csc\theta$$

depend only on the value of the angle θ and not on the size of the triangle.

4.1.1. Angles as Rotations

A circle can be divided into a rectangular coordinate system using a pair of perpendicular axes.

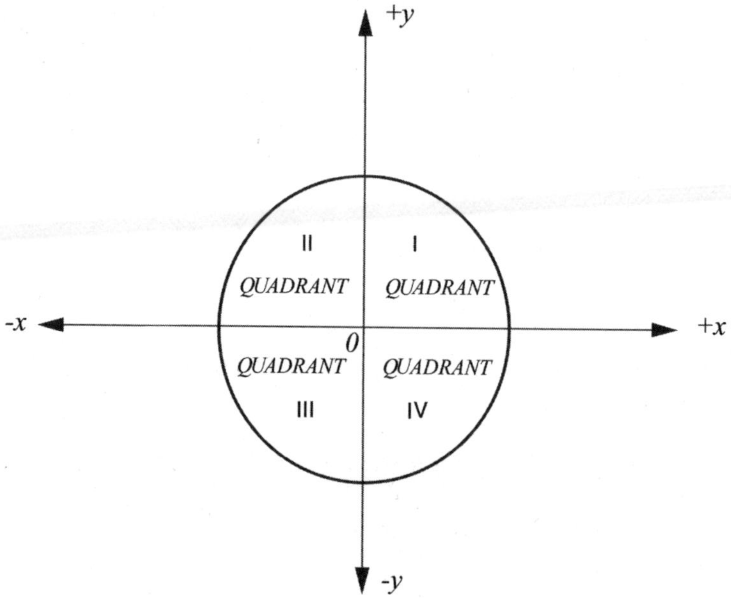

The axes divide the plane into **quadrants** I, II, III, and IV.

In this figure, the hypotenuse *OA* of the right triangle *OAB* is the radius *R* of the circle. Let $R = 1$. This is called the unit radius.

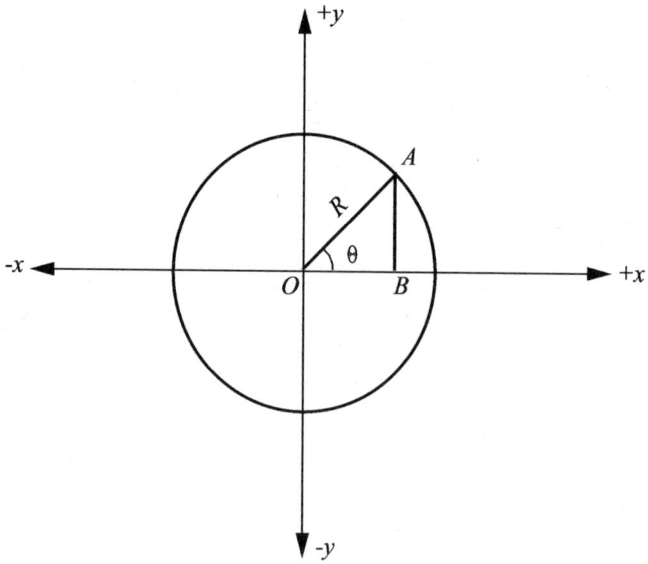

The radius R can swing all the way around the center O.

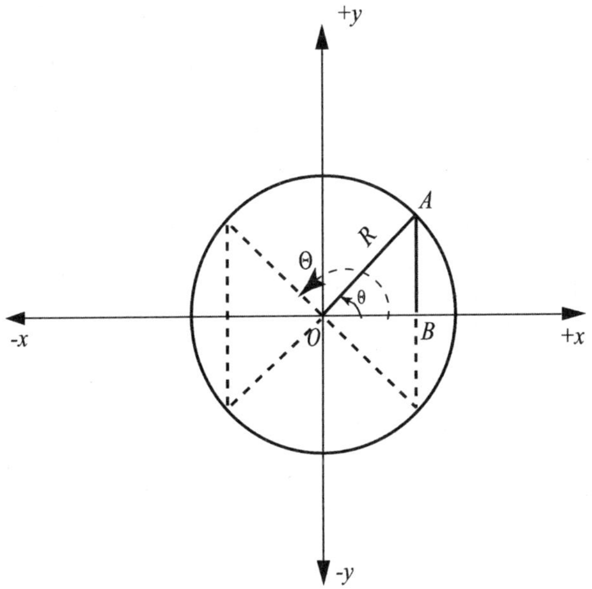

The angle θ has a sign that shows the direction of rotation:

if the radius turns counterclockwise, θ is positive ($+\theta$).

If the radius turns clockwise, then θ is negative ($-\theta$).

$$\sin\theta = \frac{AB}{OA} = \frac{AB}{R} = \frac{AB}{1} = AB$$

The length of the line segment $\overline{AB}$ is equal to the sine.

If $\theta = 0$, $OB = R$, $AB = 0$, and $\sin 0° = \frac{AB}{R} = \frac{0}{R} = 0$.

If the radius turns in a positive direction, the angle θ increases, so sine θ (=AB) increases too.

If $\theta = 90°$, $AB = R$ and $\sin 90° = \frac{AB}{R} = \frac{R}{R} = 1$.

Therefore $\sin\theta$ can vary within the following range:
$0 \le \sin\theta \le 1$.

In the *first quadrant*, $\sin\theta$ has a positive sign.

When the radius *R* is in the *second quadrant* ($90° \le \theta \le 180°$) and the angle θ increases, $\sin\theta$ decreases from 1 to 0. In the second quadrant, $\sin\theta$ also has a positive sign.

When the radius *R* is in the *third quadrant* ($180° \le \theta \le 270°$) and the angle θ increases, $\sin\theta$ increases from 0 to 1 and has a negative sign.

When the radius *R* is in the *fourth quadrant* ($270° \le \theta \le 360°$) and the angle θ increases, $\sin\theta$ decreases from 1 to 0 and has a negative sign.

Therefore the sign of $\sin\theta$ changes according to which quadrant it is in.

Quadrant	I	II	III	IV
Sign of $\sin\theta$	+	+	-	-

In ΔOAB $\cos\theta = \dfrac{OB}{OA} = \dfrac{OB}{R} = \dfrac{OB}{1} = OB$

The length of the line segment $\overline{OB}$ is equal to the cosine.
When $\theta = 0$ $OA = OB = 1$ and $\cos 0° = 1$. In the first quadrant, $\cos\theta$ has a positive sign.

If $\theta = 90°$ the line OB disappears and $\cos 90° = 0$.

When the radius moves in the second quadrant, the line segment *OB* and $\cos\theta$ increase. In the second quadrant, $\cos\theta$ has a negative sign, because *OB* is negative.

If $\theta = 180°$ the line segment $OB = R$ and $\cos\theta = -1$.

When the radius moves in the third quadrant, $\cos\theta$ has a negative sign, and when $\theta = 270°$, $\cos\theta = 0$.

In the fourth quadrant, the line segment OB increases and $\cos\theta$ increases too. When $\theta = 360°$ (0°), $\cos\theta = 1$.

Therefore the sign of $\cos\theta$ also changes according to which quadrant it is in.

Quadrant	I	II	III	IV
Sign of $\cos\theta$	+	-	-	+

From the figure we see that:

$$\sin\theta = \frac{AB}{OA}; \cos\theta = \frac{OB}{OA}$$

$$\frac{\sin\theta}{\cos\theta} = \frac{AB}{OA} \div \frac{OB}{OA} = \frac{AB}{OB} = \tan\theta$$

Therefore $\tan\theta = \dfrac{\sin\theta}{\cos\theta}$

If $\theta = 0°$ $\tan 0° = \dfrac{\sin 0°}{\cos 0°} = \dfrac{0}{1} = 0$

In the first quadrant, $\sin\theta$ and $\cos\theta$ have positive signs, so $\tan 0°$ will also have a positive sign.

If $\theta = 90°$ $\tan 90° = \dfrac{\sin 90°}{\cos 90°} = \dfrac{1}{0}$, which is undefined.

In the second quadrant the sine is positive and the cosine is negative, so the tangent will be negative.

If $\theta = 180°$ $\tan 180° = \dfrac{\sin 180°}{\cos 180°} = \dfrac{0}{-1} = 0$.

In the third quadrant the sine and cosine are negative, so the tangent is positive.

If $\theta = 270°$ $\tan 270° = \dfrac{\sin 270°}{\cos 270°} = \dfrac{1}{0}$, which is undefined.

In the fourth quadrant the tangent is negative. $\tan 360° = 0$.

Therefore the sign of $\tan\theta$ changes according to which quadrant it is in.

Quadrant	I	II	III	IV
Sign of $\tan\theta$	+	-	+	-

Consolidated Table

	I	II	III	IV
$\sin\theta$	+	+	-	-
$\cos\theta$	+	-	-	+
$\tan\theta$	+	-	+	-
$\cot\theta$	+	-	+	-

4.2 Trigonometric Functions for Angles of More than 90°

In the following figure we have drawn two right triangles, *OAB* and OA_1B_1. To find the measure of the reference angle, let us study the figure.

Since $\angle BOA$ and $\angle B_1OA_1$ are supplementary,

$m\angle B_1OA_1 = 180° - m\angle BOA = 180° - \theta$.

Because angle measure is preserved with a line reflection,

$m\angle BOA = m\angle B_1OA_1 = 180° - \theta$.

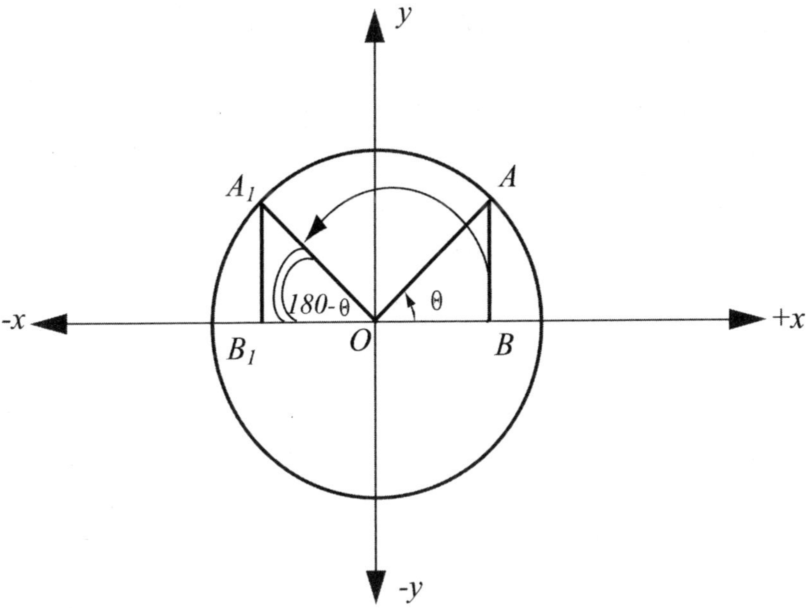

Therefore: for every angle in the second quadrant whose degree measure is $180° - \theta$, there is a reference angle in the first quadrant whose measure is θ .

$\sin(180° - \theta) = \sin\theta$; $\cos(180° - \theta) = -\cos\theta$

$\tan(180° - \theta) = -\tan\theta$; $\cot(180° - \theta) = -\cot\theta$

$\sec(180° - \theta) = -\sec\theta$; $\csc(180° - \theta) = \csc\theta$

Similar operations allow us to construct a table for the major angles:

Functio n	$-\theta$	$90° - \theta$	$90° + \theta$	$180° - \theta$	$180° + \theta$
sin	$-\sin\theta$	$+\cos\theta$	$+\cos\theta$	$+\sin\theta$	$-\sin\theta$
cos	$+\cos\theta$	$+\sin\theta$	$-\sin\theta$	$-\cos\theta$	$-\cos\theta$
tan	$-\tan\theta$	$+\cot\theta$	$-\cot\theta$	$-\tan\theta$	$+\tan\theta$
cot	$-\cot\theta$	$+\tan\theta$	$-\tan\theta$	$-\cot\theta$	$+\cot\theta$
sec	$+\sec\theta$	$+\csc\theta$	$-\csc\theta$	$-\sec\theta$	$-\sec\theta$
csc	$-\csc\theta$	$+\sec\theta$	$+\sec\theta$	$+\csc\theta$	$-\csc\theta$

Function	$270° - \theta$	$270° + \theta$	$360° - \theta$	$360° + \theta$
sin	$-\cos\theta$	$-\cos\theta$	$-\sin\theta$	$+\sin\theta$
cos	$-\sin\theta$	$+\sin\theta$	$+\cos\theta$	$+\cos\theta$
tan	$+\cot\theta$	$-\cot\theta$	$-\tan\theta$	$+\tan\theta$
cot	$+\tan\theta$	$-\tan\theta$	$-\cot\theta$	$+\cot\theta$
sec	$-\csc\theta$	$+\csc\theta$	$+\sec\theta$	$+\sec\theta$
csc	$-\sec\theta$	$-\sec\theta$	$-\csc\theta$	$+\csc\theta$

4.3 Radian Measure

In addition to the unit degree, there is another unit of measurement called the **radian**.

An angle drawn as the central angle of a circle that intercepts an arc of that circle equal to the radius of the circle has a measure of one radian.

The circumference of a circle:

$$C = 2\pi R$$

$$2\pi \text{ radians} = 360°$$

$$1 \text{ radian} = \left(\frac{180}{\pi}\right)^{\circ} \approx 57°$$

$$1° = \frac{\pi}{180} \text{ radians} \approx 0.017534 \text{ radians}$$

$$1' = \frac{\pi}{180 \cdot 60} \text{ radians} \approx 0.000291 \text{ radians}$$

It may be useful to memorize the following table of degree and radian measures of some important angles:

Angles in degree	360°	180°	90°	60°	45°	30°
Angles in radians	2π	π	$\frac{\pi}{2}$	$\frac{\pi}{3}$	$\frac{\pi}{4}$	$\frac{\pi}{6}$

To convert between radian and degree measure, multiply by the appropriate conversion factor.

Conversion from radians to degrees: multiply by $\dfrac{180}{\pi \text{ radians}}$

Conversion from degrees to radians: multiply by $\dfrac{\pi}{180 \text{ degrees}}$

Table of Conversion - Radians into Degrees

Radians	Degrees and Minutes	Radians	Degrees and Minutes	Radians	Degrees and Minutes
1	57°18′	0.1	5°44′	0.01	0°34′
2	114°35′	0.2	11°28′	0.02	1°09′
3	171°53′	0.3	17°11′	0.03	1°43′
4	229°11′	0.4	22°55′	0.04	2°18′
5	280°29′	0.5	28°39′	0.05	2°52′
6	343°40′	0.6	34°23′	0.06	3°26′
7	401°04′	0.7	40°06′	0.07	4°01′
8	458°22′	0.8	45°50′	0.08	4°35′
9	515°40′	0.9	51°34′	0.09	5°09′

Radians	Minutes	Radians	Minutes
0.001	0°03′	0.0001	0°00′
0.002	0°07′	0.0002	0°01′
0.003	0°10′	0.0003	0°01′
0.004	0°14′	0.0004	0°01′
0.005	0°17′	0.0005	0°02′
0.006	0°21′	0.0006	0°02′
0.007	0°24′	0.0007	0°02′
0.008	0°28′	0.0008	0°03′
0.009	0°31′	0.0009	0°03′

Example: Convert 1.360 radians into degrees

1 radian = 57°18′
0.3 radians = 17°11′
0.060 radians = 3°26′

$$\begin{array}{r} 57°18' \\ 17°11' \\ +\ 3°26' \\ \hline 77°55' \end{array}$$

Table of Conversion – Degrees into Radians

Degrees	*Radians*	*Degrees*	*Radians*	*Degrees*	*Radians*
0	0.0000	35	0.6109	70	1.2217
1	0.0175	36	0.6283	71	1.2392
2	0.0349	37	0.6458	72	1.2566
3	0.0524	38	0.6632	73	1.2741
4	0.0698	39	0.6807	74	1.2915
5	0.0873	40	0.6981	75	1.3090
6	0.1047	41	0.7156	76	1.3265
7	0.1222	42	0.7330	77	1.3439
8	0.1396	43	0.7505	78	1.3614
9	0.1571	44	0.7679	79	1.3788
10	0.1745	45	0.7854	80	1.3963
11	0.1920	46	0.8029	81	1.4137
12	0.2094	47	0.8203	82	1.4312
13	0.2269	48	0.8378	83	1.4486
14	0.2443	49	0.8552	84	1.4661
15	0.2618	50	0.8727	85	1.4835
16	0.2793	51	0.8901	86	1.5010
17	0.2967	52	0.9076	87	1.5184
18	0.3142	53	0.9250	88	1.5359
19	0.3316	54	0.9425	89	1.5533
20	0.3491	55	0.9599	90	1.5708
21	0.3665	56	0.9774	91	1.5882
22	0.3840	57	0.9948	92	1.6057
23	0.4014	58	1.0123	93	1.6239
24	0.4189	59	1.0297	94	1.6406
25	0.4363	60	1.0472	95	1.6581
26	0.4538	61	1.0647	96	1.6755
27	0.4712	62	1.0821	97	1.6930
28	0.4887	63	1.0996	98	1.7104
29	0.5061	64	1.1170	99	1.7279
30	0.5236	65	1.1345	100	1.7453
31	0.5411	66	1.1519	180	3.1416
32	0.5585	67	1.1694	200	3.4907
33	0.5760	68	1.1868	300	5.2360
34	0.5934	69	1.2043	360	6.2832

Minutes	*Radians*	*Minutes*	*Radians*
0	0.0000	30	0.0087
1	0.0003	31	0.0090
2	0.0006	32	0.0093
3	0.0009	33	0.0096
4	0.0012	34	0.0099
5	0.0015	35	0.0102
6	0.0017	36	0.0105
7	0.0020	37	0.0108
8	0.0023	38	0.0111
9	0.0026	39	0.0113
10	0.0029	40	0.0116
11	0.0032	41	0.0119
12	0.0035	42	0.0122
13	0.0038	43	0.0125
14	0.0041	44	0.0128
15	0.0044	45	0.0131
16	0.0047	46	0.0134
17	0.0049	47	0.0137
18	0.0052	48	0.0140
19	0.0055	49	0.0143
20	0.0058	50	0.0145
21	0.0061	51	0.0148
22	0.0064	52	0.0151
23	0.0067	53	0.0154
24	0.0070	54	0.0157
25	0.0073	55	0.0160
26	0.0076	56	0.0163
27	0.0079	57	0.0166
28	0.0081	58	0.0169
29	0.0084	59	0.0172

Examples: Convert 12°30’

- In the degrees column find 12 and the corresponding radian measure of .2094

- In the minutes column find 30 and the corresponding radian measure of 0.0087

$$\begin{array}{r} 0.2094 \\ +\ \underline{0.0087} \\ 0.2181 \end{array} \qquad \text{Answer - } .2181$$

4.4 Correlations among the Trigonometric Functions

$$\sin^2\alpha + \cos^2\alpha = 1$$

$$\tan\alpha \cdot \cot\alpha = 1$$

$$\tan\alpha = \frac{\sin\alpha}{\cos\alpha}$$

$$\cot\alpha = \frac{\cos\alpha}{\sin\alpha}$$

$$\sin\alpha \cdot \csc\alpha = 1$$

$$\cos\alpha \cdot \sec\alpha = 1$$

$$\sec^2\alpha = 1 + \tan^2\alpha$$

$$\csc^2\alpha = 1 + \cot^2\alpha$$

$$\cos^2\alpha = \frac{1}{1+\tan^2\alpha} = \frac{\cot^2\alpha}{1+\cot^2\alpha}$$

$$\sin^2\alpha = \frac{1}{1+\cot^2\alpha} = \frac{\tan^2\alpha}{1+\tan^2\alpha}$$

$$\csc\alpha = \frac{1}{\sin\alpha}$$

$$\sec\alpha = \frac{1}{\cos\alpha}$$

$$\cot\alpha = \frac{1}{\tan\alpha}$$

Example: Simplify $\dfrac{1}{1+\tan^2\alpha}+\sin^2\alpha$

$$\tan^2\alpha = \frac{\sin^2\alpha}{\cos^2\alpha}; \quad 1+\tan^2\alpha = 1+\frac{\sin^2\alpha}{\cos^2\alpha}$$

$$\frac{1}{1+\dfrac{\sin^2\alpha}{\cos^2\alpha}} = \frac{1}{\dfrac{\cos^2\alpha+\sin^2\alpha}{\cos^2\alpha}} = \cos^2\alpha$$

$$\cos^2\alpha+\sin^2\alpha = 1$$

Answer $\dfrac{1}{1+\tan^2\alpha}+\sin^2\alpha = 1$

How to express trigonometric functions by way of other functions

	Sin X	**Cos X**	**Tan X**
Sin X		$\pm\sqrt{1-\cos^2 x}$	$\dfrac{\tan x}{\pm\sqrt{1+\cot x}}$
Cos X	$\pm\sqrt{1-\sin^2 x}$		$\dfrac{1}{\pm\sqrt{1+\tan^2 x}}$
Tan X	$\dfrac{\sin x}{\pm\sqrt{1-\sin^2 x}}$	$\dfrac{\pm\sqrt{1-\cos^2 x}}{\cos x}$	
Cot X	$\dfrac{\pm\sqrt{1-\sin^2 x}}{\sin x}$	$\dfrac{\cos x}{\pm\sqrt{1-\cos^2 x}}$	$\dfrac{1}{\tan x}$
Sec X	$\dfrac{1}{\pm\sqrt{1-\sin^2 x}}$	$\dfrac{1}{\cos x}$	$\pm\sqrt{1+\tan^2 x}$
Csc X	$\dfrac{1}{\sin x}$	$\dfrac{1}{\pm\sqrt{1-\cos^2 x}}$	$\dfrac{\pm\sqrt{1+\tan^2 x}}{\tan x}$

	Cot X	**Sec X**	**Csc X**
Sin X	$\frac{1}{\pm\sqrt{1+\cot^2 x}}$	$\frac{\pm\sqrt{\sec^2 x}}{\sec x}$	$\frac{1}{\csc x}$
Cos X	$\frac{\cot x}{\pm\sqrt{1+\cot^2 x}}$	$\frac{1}{\sec x}$	$\frac{\pm\sqrt{\csc^2 x-1}}{\csc x}$
Tan X	$\frac{1}{\cot x}$	$\pm\sqrt{\sec^2 x-1}$	$\frac{1}{\pm\sqrt{\csc^2 x-1}}$
Cot X		$\frac{1}{\pm\sqrt{\sec^2 x-1}}$	$\pm\sqrt{\csc^2 x-1}$
Sec X	$\frac{\pm\sqrt{1+\cot^2 x}}{\cot x}$		$\frac{\csc x}{\pm\sqrt{\csc^2 x-1}}$
Csc X	$\pm\sqrt{1+\cot^2 x}$	$\frac{\sec x}{\pm\sqrt{\sec^2 x-1}}$	

4.5 Formulas for Addition and Subtraction

$$\sin(\alpha + \beta) = \sin\alpha\cos\beta + \cos\alpha\sin\beta$$

$$\sin(\alpha - \beta) = \sin\alpha\cos\beta - \cos\alpha\sin\beta$$

$$\cos(\alpha + \beta) = \cos\alpha\cos\beta - \sin\alpha\sin\beta$$

$$\cos(\alpha - \beta) = \cos\alpha\cos\beta + \sin\alpha\sin\beta$$

$$\tan(\alpha + \beta) = \frac{\tan\alpha + \tan\beta}{1 - \tan\alpha\tan\beta}$$

$$\tan(\alpha - \beta) = \frac{\tan\alpha - \tan\beta}{1 + \tan\alpha\tan\beta}$$

4.6 Formulas for Double, Triple, and Half Angles

$$\sin 2\alpha = 2\sin\alpha\cos\alpha$$

$$\cos 2\alpha = \cos^2\alpha - \sin^2\alpha = 1 - 2\sin^2\alpha = 2\cos^2\alpha - 1$$

$$\tan 2\alpha = \frac{2\tan\alpha}{1-\tan^2\alpha}$$

$$\cot 2\alpha = \frac{\cot^2\alpha - 1}{2\cot\alpha}$$

$$\sin 3\alpha = 3\sin\alpha - 4\sin^3\alpha$$

$$\cos 3\alpha = 4\cos^3\alpha - 3\cos\alpha$$

$$\tan 3\alpha = \frac{3\tan\alpha - \tan^3\alpha}{1-3\tan^2\alpha}$$

$$\cot 3\alpha = \frac{\cot^3\alpha - 3\cot\alpha}{3\cot^3\alpha - 1}$$

$$\sin\frac{\alpha}{2} = \pm\sqrt{\frac{1-\cos\alpha}{2}}$$

$$\cos\frac{\alpha}{2} = \pm\sqrt{\frac{1+\cos\alpha}{2}}$$

$$\tan\frac{\alpha}{2} = \pm\sqrt{\frac{1-\cos\alpha}{1+\cos\alpha}} = \frac{\sin\alpha}{1+\cos\alpha} = \frac{1-\cos\alpha}{\sin\alpha}$$

$$\cot\frac{\alpha}{2} = \pm\sqrt{\frac{1+\cos\alpha}{1-\cos\alpha}} = \frac{\sin\alpha}{1-\cos\alpha} = \frac{1+\cos\alpha}{\sin\alpha}$$

4.7 Some Important Formulas

$$\sin\alpha\sin\beta = \frac{1}{2}[\cos(\alpha-\beta)-\cos(\alpha+\beta)]$$

$$\cos\alpha\cos\beta = \frac{1}{2}[\cos(\alpha-\beta)+\cos(\alpha+\beta)]$$

$$\sin\alpha\cos\beta = \frac{1}{2}[\sin(\alpha+\beta)+\sin(\alpha-\beta)]$$

$$\sin\alpha = \frac{2\tan\frac{\alpha}{2}}{1+\tan^2\frac{\alpha}{2}}$$

$$\cos\alpha = \frac{1-\tan^2\frac{\alpha}{2}}{1+\tan^2\frac{\alpha}{2}}$$

$$\tan\alpha = \frac{2\tan\frac{\alpha}{2}}{1-\tan^2\frac{\alpha}{2}}$$

$$\sin\alpha+\sin 2\alpha+\sin 3\alpha+....+\sin n\alpha = \frac{\cos\frac{\alpha}{2}-\cos\frac{(2n+1)\alpha}{2}}{2\sin\frac{\alpha}{2}}$$

$$\cos\alpha+\cos 2\alpha+\cos 3\alpha+....+\cos n\alpha = \frac{\sin\frac{(2n+1)\alpha}{2}-\sin\frac{\alpha}{2}}{2\sin\frac{\alpha}{2}}$$

4.8 Proving The Trigonometric Identities

Examples:

1) Prove $\sec\left(\frac{\pi}{4}+\alpha\right)\sec\left(\frac{\pi}{4}-\alpha\right)=2\sec 2\alpha$

$$\sec\left(\frac{\pi}{4}+\alpha\right)\sec\left(\frac{\pi}{4}-\alpha\right)=\frac{1}{\cos\left(\frac{\pi}{4}+\alpha\right)\cos\left(\frac{\pi}{4}-\alpha\right)}$$

Since $\cos\left(\frac{\pi}{4}+\alpha\right)=\sin\left[\frac{\pi}{2}-\left(\frac{\pi}{4}+\alpha\right)\right]=\sin\left(\frac{\pi}{4}-\alpha\right)$

Therefore

$$\frac{2}{2\sin\left(\frac{\pi}{4}-\alpha\right)\cos\left(\frac{\pi}{4}-\alpha\right)}=\frac{2}{\sin\left(\frac{\pi}{2}-2\alpha\right)}=\frac{2}{\cos 2\alpha}=2\sec 2\alpha$$

2) Prove $\frac{\cos\alpha+\sin\alpha}{\cos\alpha-\sin\alpha}=\tan 2\alpha+\sec 2\alpha$

(Hint: multiply the numerator and denominator of the left side by cos α+ sinα)

$$\frac{(\cos\alpha+\sin\alpha)^2}{(\cos\alpha+\sin\alpha)(\cos\alpha-\sin\alpha)}=\frac{\cos^2\alpha+2\cos\alpha\sin\alpha+\sin^2\alpha}{\cos^2\alpha-\sin^2\alpha}=$$

$$=\frac{1+\sin 2\alpha}{\cos 2\alpha}\quad \textit{or}$$

$$\frac{1}{\cos 2\alpha}+\frac{\sin 2\alpha}{\cos 2\alpha}= \quad \sec 2\alpha+\tan 2\alpha$$

3) Prove $\dfrac{1+\sin 2\alpha}{\cos 2\alpha}=\dfrac{1+\tan\alpha}{1-\tan\alpha}$

Since $1=\sin^2\alpha+\cos^2\alpha$

$$\frac{\sin^2\alpha+\cos^2\alpha+\sin 2\alpha}{\cos 2\alpha}=\frac{\sin^2\alpha+\cos^2\alpha+2\sin\alpha\cos\alpha}{\cos^2\alpha-\sin^2\alpha}=$$

$$=\frac{(\sin\alpha+\cos\alpha)^{\cancel{2}}}{(\cancel{\cos\alpha+\sin\alpha})(\cos\alpha-\sin\alpha)} \quad [\textit{divide by } \cos\alpha]$$

$$\frac{\dfrac{\sin\alpha}{\cos\alpha}+1}{1-\dfrac{\sin\alpha}{\cos\alpha}}=\frac{1+\tan\alpha}{1-\tan\alpha}$$

4) Prove $\dfrac{\cos\alpha+\sin\alpha}{\cos\alpha-\sin\alpha}=\tan(45^\circ+\alpha)$

(Hint: divide the numerator and denominator of the fraction by cos α)

$$\frac{\cos\alpha+\sin\alpha}{\cos\alpha-\sin\alpha}=\frac{1+\tan\alpha}{1-\tan\alpha}$$

Since 1= tan 45° $\dfrac{1+\tan\alpha}{1-\tan\alpha}=\dfrac{\tan 45^\circ+\tan\alpha}{1-\tan\alpha\cdot\tan 45^\circ}=\tan(45^\circ+\alpha)$

5) Simplify the expression $\cos 2\alpha + \sin 2\alpha \tan\alpha$

$$\cos 2\alpha = \cos^2\alpha - \sin^2\alpha$$

$$\sin 2\alpha = 2\sin\alpha\cos\alpha$$

$$\cos^2\alpha - \sin^2\alpha + (2\sin\alpha\cos\alpha)\frac{\sin\alpha}{\cos\alpha}$$

$$\cos^2\alpha - \sin^2\alpha + \frac{2\sin^2\alpha\,\cancel{\cos\alpha}}{\cancel{\cos\alpha}}$$

$$\cos^2\alpha - \sin^2\alpha + 2\sin^2\alpha = \cos^2\alpha - \cancel{\sin^2\alpha} + \sin^2\alpha + \cancel{\sin^2\alpha}$$

$$\cos^2\alpha + \sin^2\alpha = 1$$

$$\cos 2\alpha + \sin 2\alpha \tan\alpha = 1$$

4.9 Calculations Involving Right Triangles

Given two sides of a right triangle, the third side can be calculated using the Pythagorean Theorem.

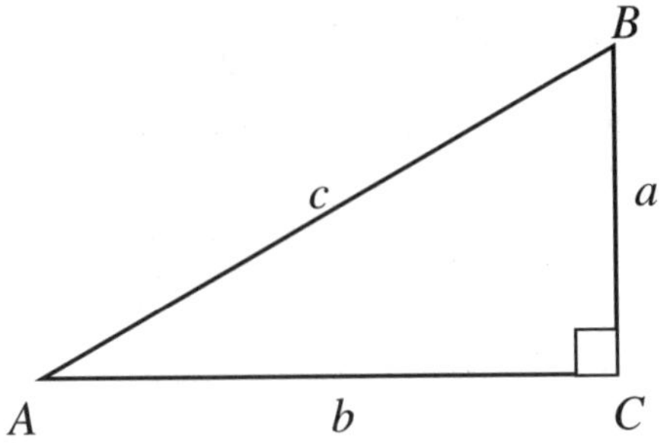

The acute angles: A= 90°- B

B = 90°-A

Example 1:

Given leg $a = 0.528$ and hypotenuse $c= 0.697$,

find angles A and B.

$$Step1:\ b = \sqrt{c^2 - a^2} = \sqrt{0.697^2 - 0.528^2} \approx 0.455m$$

$$Step2: \quad \sin A = \frac{a}{c} = \frac{0.528}{0.697} \approx 0.757$$

You can use the table of trigonometric functions or the calculator to find angles A and B.

$$m\angle A \approx 49^\circ 10'$$

$$m\angle B = 90^\circ - A \approx 90 - 49^\circ 10' \approx 40^\circ 50'$$

Example 2:

Given legs a=8.3 cm and b=12.4cm,

find leg c and angles A and B

Step1: Find the hypotenuse c

$$c = \sqrt{a^2 + b^2} = \sqrt{8.3^2 + 12.4^2} \approx 14.9cm$$

Step2: Find angle A

$$\tan A = \frac{a}{b} = \frac{8.3}{12.4} \approx 0.67 \quad m\angle A \approx 34^\circ$$

Step3: Find angle B

$$m\angle B = 90^\circ - A \approx 90^\circ - 34^\circ \approx 56^\circ$$

When given a side and an acute angle

Example 3:

Given hypotenuse c=79.79cm and $m\angle A = 66^\circ 36'$

Find angle B, and legs a and b

Step1: Find angle B

$$m\angle B = 90^\circ - m\angle A = 90^\circ - 66^\circ 36' = 23^\circ 24'$$

Step 2: Find leg a

$$a = c \sin A = 79.79 \cdot \sin 66^\circ 36'$$

$$a \approx 79.79 \cdot 0.9178 \approx 73.23cm$$

Step3: Find leg b

$$b = c \cos A \approx 79.79 \cdot 0.3971 \approx 31.68cm$$

Example 4:

Given leg a =12.3m and acute angle $m\angle A = 63^\circ 00'$.

Find angle B, leg b, and hypotenuse c.

Step1: Find angle B

$$m\angle B = 90^\circ - 63^\circ 00' = 27^\circ 00'$$

Step2: Find leg b

$$b = a \tan B = 12.3 \tan 27^\circ 00' \approx 12.3 \cdot 0.509 \approx 6.23m$$

Step3: Find hypotenuse c

$$c = \frac{a}{\sin A} = \frac{12.3}{\sin 63^\circ 00'} \approx \frac{12.3}{0.891} \approx 13.8m$$

4.10 Fundamental Correlations among Elements of Triangles

The Law of Sines- in any triangle, the ratio between the sine of an angle and the length of a side opposite that angle is constant.

$$\boxed{\frac{\sin A}{a}=\frac{\sin B}{b}=\frac{\sin C}{c}}$$

In any Δ ABC , the sides *a, b*, and *c* correspond to the opposite angles *A, B,* and *C.*

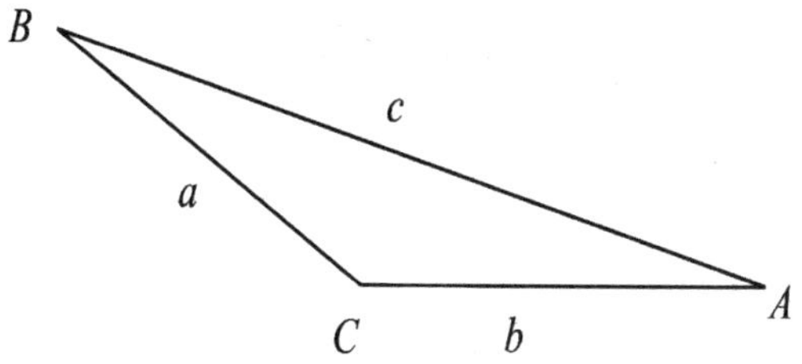

From the Law of Sines, we can derive two formulas.

$$\frac{a+b}{a-b}=\frac{\tan\dfrac{A+B}{2}}{\tan\dfrac{A-B}{2}}=\frac{\cot\dfrac{c}{2}}{\tan\dfrac{A-B}{2}} \quad \textit{and}$$

$$\frac{a+b}{c}=\frac{\cos\dfrac{A-B}{2}}{\sin\dfrac{C}{2}};\quad \frac{a-b}{c}=\frac{\sin\dfrac{A-B}{2}}{\cos\dfrac{C}{2}}$$

The Law of Cosines- in any Δ ABC

$$c^2 = a^2 + b^2 - 2ab \cos C$$

4.11 Calculations on Oblique Triangles

Example 1: Given ΔABC, $\angle C = 40°$, a=10 and b=20;
Find side c

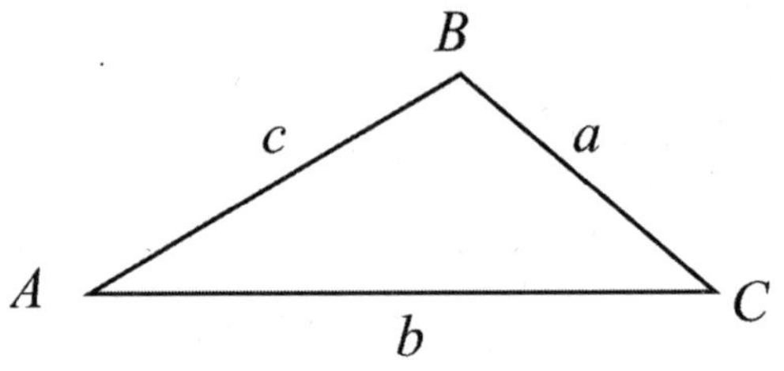

Solution: Apply the Law of Cosines

$c^2 = a^2 + b^2 - 2ab \cos C$

$= 10^2 + 20^2 - 2(10)(20) \cos 40°$

$= 100 + 400 - 400(0.7660) \approx 500 - 306.40 \approx 193.60$

$c^2 \approx 193.60 \qquad c = \sqrt{193.60} \approx 13.91$

Example 2:

Given Δ ABC, a=74, b=130, c=186;

Find: m$\angle A$, m$\angle B$, m$\angle C$

Solution: Apply the Law of Cosines and the Law of Sines

$$\cos A = \frac{b^2 + c^2 - a^2}{2bc} = \frac{130^2 + 186^2 - 74^2}{2(130)(186)} =$$

$$= \frac{16{,}900 + 34{,}596 - 5{,}476}{48{,}360} = \frac{46{,}020}{48{,}360} = 0.95 \qquad \cos A = 0.95 \quad m\angle A \approx 18^\circ$$

$$\frac{a}{\sin A} = \frac{b}{\sin B} \qquad \sin B = \frac{b \cdot \sin A}{a} \approx \frac{130\,(\sin 18^\circ)}{74} \approx \frac{130 \cdot 0.3}{74} \approx 0.53$$

$$\sin B \approx 0.53 \qquad m\angle B \approx 32^\circ \qquad m\angle C = 180^\circ - (18^\circ + 32^\circ) \approx 130^\circ$$

Example 3:

Given ΔABC, $m\angle A = 60^\circ$, $m\angle B = 45^\circ$;

Find the ratio $\frac{a}{b}$

Solution: Apply the Law of Sines

$$\frac{a}{\sin A} = \frac{b}{\sin B} \qquad \sin 60^\circ = \frac{\sqrt{3}}{2}, \qquad \sin 45^\circ = \frac{\sqrt{2}}{2}$$

$$\frac{a}{\frac{\sqrt{3}}{2}} = \frac{b}{\frac{\sqrt{2}}{2}} \qquad \frac{a}{\sqrt{3}} = \frac{b}{\sqrt{2}}$$

$$\frac{a}{b} = \frac{\sqrt{3}}{\sqrt{2}} = \sqrt{\frac{3}{2}}$$

Result: $\sqrt{\frac{3}{2}}$

4.12 Inverse Trigonometric Functions

The expression $x = \sin y$ makes it possible to find the value x by the value of angle y using the calculator or the table of trigonometric functions. We can also find y by the value of x. This operation is written as **y=arc sin x**. This is read as "y is an angle whose sine is x" or "y equals the arc sine of x."

Example:

Instead of writing $\frac{1}{2} = \sin 30^\circ$, we can write $30^\circ = \text{arc}\sin\frac{1}{2}$

The inverse of $\cos x$ *is* $\text{arc}\cos x$

The inverse of $\tan x$ *is* $\text{arc}\tan x$

For example,

$\text{arc}\sin\frac{1}{2}$ equals 30°, 150°(180°-30°),

390 (360°+30°) etc.

$\text{arc}\cos\frac{1}{2} = 60°, 300°, 420°$ etc.

arc sin θ has its primary domain between $-\frac{\pi}{2}$ *and* $+\frac{\pi}{2}$; that is, between -90° and +90°.

arc cos θ has its primary domain between 0 *and* π; that is, between 0° and 180°.

arc tan θ has its primary domain between $-\frac{\pi}{2}$ *and* $+\frac{\pi}{2}$.

arc cot θ has its primary domain between 0 *and* π.

Example 1:

$$\text{arc sin}\frac{1}{2} = k\pi + (-1)^k \frac{\pi}{6}$$

If k=0 $$\text{arc sin}\frac{1}{2} = 0\cdot\pi + (-1)^0 \frac{\pi}{6} = \frac{\pi}{6} \ or\ 30^\circ$$

If k=1 $$1\cdot\pi + (-1)^1 \frac{\pi}{6} = \pi - \frac{\pi}{6} = \frac{5\pi}{6} \ or\ 150^\circ$$

If k=2 $$2\cdot\pi + (-1)^2 \frac{\pi}{6} = 2\frac{1}{6}\pi \ \ or\ 390^\circ$$

If k= -1 $$-\pi + (-1)^{-1} \frac{\pi}{6} = -\pi - \frac{\pi}{6} = -1\frac{1}{6}\pi \ or\ -210^\circ$$

Example 2:

$$\text{arc cos}\frac{1}{2} = 2k\pi \pm \frac{\pi}{3}$$

If k=0 $$\frac{\pi}{3} \ or\ 60^\circ \ and\ -\frac{\pi}{3} \ or -60^\circ$$

If k=1 $$2\pi + \frac{\pi}{3} = 2\frac{1}{3}\pi \ \ or\ 420^\circ \ and\ 1\frac{2}{3}\pi \ or\ \ 300^\circ$$

4.13 Simple Correlations between Inverse Trigonometric Functions

$$\text{arc}\sin\alpha = -\text{ arc}\sin(-\alpha) = \frac{\pi}{2} - \text{arc}\cos\alpha = \text{arc}\tan\frac{\alpha}{\sqrt{1-\alpha^2}}$$

$$\text{arc}\cos\alpha = \pi - \text{arc}\cos(-\alpha) = \frac{\pi}{2} - \text{arc}\sin\alpha = \text{arc}\cot\frac{\alpha}{\sqrt{1-\alpha^2}}$$

$$\text{arc}\tan\alpha = \pi - \text{arc}\cot(-\alpha) = \frac{\pi}{2} - \text{arc}\tan\alpha = \text{arc}\sin\frac{\alpha}{\sqrt{1+\alpha^2}}$$

$$\text{arc}\cot\alpha = \pi - \text{arc}\cot(-\alpha) = \frac{\pi}{2} - \text{arc}\tan\alpha = \text{arc}\cos\frac{\alpha}{\sqrt{1+\alpha^2}}$$

4.14 Trigonometric Equations

A **trigonometric equation** is an equation in which the variable is expressed in terms of a trigonometric function value.

The expression $\sin\ y = \frac{1}{2}$ is a trigonometric equation.

Its roots are:

$$y = 30^\circ;\ y = 180^\circ - 30^\circ = 150^\circ;$$

$$y = 2 \cdot 180^\circ + 30^\circ = 390^\circ;$$

$$y = 3 \cdot 180^\circ - 30^\circ = 510^\circ$$

Also,

$$y = -180^\circ - 30^\circ = -210^\circ;$$

$$y = -2 \cdot 180^\circ + 30^\circ = -330^\circ \; etc.$$

We can write the general solution $y = k \cdot 180^\circ + (-1)^k \cdot 30^\circ$ where k is any whole number (positive, negative, or zero).

4.15 Solving Trigonometric Equations

Example 1:

$$3 + 2\cos\alpha = 4\sin^2\alpha$$

Solving $\sin^2\alpha = 1 - \cos^2\alpha$

$$3 + 2\cos\alpha = 4(1 - \cos^2\alpha) \text{ or } 4\cos^2\alpha + 2\cos\alpha - 1 = 0$$

This is a quadratic equation.

$$(\cos\alpha)_1 = \frac{-1+\sqrt{5}}{4} = 0.3090$$

$$(\cos\alpha)_2 = \frac{-1-\sqrt{5}}{4} = -0.8090$$

From which: $\alpha = 360°k \pm 72°00'$ and $\alpha = 360°k \pm 144°00'$

Or $\alpha = 2\pi \cdot k \pm \frac{2\pi}{5}$ $\qquad \alpha = 2\pi \cdot k \pm \frac{4\pi}{5}$

Example 2:

$$\sin\frac{5x}{2} \cdot \cos\frac{x}{2} \cdot \cos x = 0$$

We have three equations:

$$\sin\frac{5x}{2}=0; \qquad \cos\frac{x}{2}=0; \qquad \cos x=0$$

$$\text{Roots: } x=72^\circ\cdot k \quad \left(\frac{5x}{2}=k\cdot 180^\circ,\ x=72^\circ\cdot k\right)$$

$$x=180^\circ(2k+1) \qquad x=90^\circ(2k+1)$$

Example 3:

$$4\sin^2 x=3$$

Solution

$$\sin^2 x=\frac{3}{4}$$

$$\sqrt{\sin^2 x}=\sqrt{\frac{3}{4}}$$

$$\sin x=\pm\frac{\sqrt{3}}{2}$$

$$x=\pm 60^\circ+180^\circ\cdot k \ \ or\ \frac{\pi}{3}+\pi k$$

Example 4:

$$\sin x+7\cos x=5$$

Since $\sin x=\pm\sqrt{1-\cos^2 x}$ *then* $\pm\sqrt{1-\cos^2 x}+7\cos x=5$

$$\pm\sqrt{1-\cos^2 x}=5-7\cos x$$

Square both parts of the equation and simplify

$$50\cos^2 x - 70\cos x + 24 = 0$$

Find:

$$(\cos x)_1 = 0.8 \qquad (\cos x)_2 = 0.6$$

Roots: $x = \pm 36°52' + 360°\,k$

and $\quad x = \pm 53°07' + 360°\,k$

Example 5:

$$3\tan^2 x - 8\tan x + 5 = 0$$

Solution

$$3\tan^2 x - 8\tan x + 5 = (3\tan x - 5)(\tan x - 1)$$

$$(\tan x)_1 = 1; \quad (\tan x)_2 = \frac{5}{3}$$

$$x = 180°k + 45° \quad \text{and} \quad x = 180°k + 59°$$

Example 6:

$$\sin^2 x - 5\sin x\cos x - 6\cos^2 x = 0$$

Solution

Divide both parts of the equation by $\cos^2 x$

$$\tan^2 x - 5\tan x - 6 = 0$$

$$(\tan x)_1 = 6 \quad \text{and} \quad (\tan x)_2 = -1$$

The roots of this equation are:

$x = 80°32' + 180°k$ and

$x = -45° + 180°k$

4.16 Values of the Trigonometric Ratios

Angle	*Sine*	*Cosine*	*Tangent*
0°	.0000	1.0000	
1°	.0175	.9998	.0175
2°	.0349	.9994	.0349
3°	.0523	.9986	.0524
4°	.0698	.9976	.0699
5°	.0872	.9962	.0875
6°	.1045	.9945	.1051
7°	.1219	.9925	.1228
8°	.1392	.9903	.1405
9°	.1564	.9877	.1584
10°	.1736	.9848	.1763
11°	.1908	.9816	.1944
12°	.2079	.9781	.2126
13°	.2250	.9744	.2309
14°	.2419	.9703	.2493
15°	.2588	.9659	.2679
16°	.2756	.9613	.2867
17°	.2924	.9563	.3057
18°	.3090	.9511	.3249
19°	.3256	.9455	.3443
20°	.3420	.9397	.3640
21°	.3584	.9336	.3839
22°	.3746	.9272	.4040
23°	.3907	.9205	.4245
24°	.4067	.9135	.4452
25°	.4226	.9063	.4663
26°	.4384	.8988	.4877
27°	.4540	.8910	.5095
28°	.4695	.8829	.5317
29°	.4848	.8746	.5543
30°	.5000	.8660	.5774

Angle	*Sine*	*Cosine*	*Tangent*
31°	.5150	.8572	.6009
32°	.5299	.8480	.6249
33°	.5446	.8387	.6494
34°	.5592	.8290	.6745
35°	.5736	.8192	.7002
36°	.5878	.8090	.7265
37°	.6018	.7986	.7536
38°	.6157	.7880	.7813
39°	.6293	.7771	.8098
40°	.6428	.7660	.8391
41°	.6561	.7547	.8693
42°	.6691	.7431	.9004
43°	.6820	.7314	.9325
44°	.6947	.7193	.9657
45°	.7071	.7071	1.0000
46°	.7193	.6947	1.0355
47°	.7314	.6820	1.0724
48°	.7431	.6691	1.1106
49°	.7547	.6561	1.1504
50°	.7660	.6428	1.1918
51°	.7771	.6293	1.2349
52°	.7880	.6157	1.2799
53°	.7986	.6018	1.3270
54°	.8090	.5878	1.3764
55°	.8192	.5736	1.4281
56°	.8290	.5592	1.4826
57°	.8387	.5446	1.5399
58°	.8480	.5299	1.6003
59°	.8572	.5150	1.6643
60°	.8660	.5000	1.7320
61°	.8746	.4848	1.8040
62°	.8829	.4695	1.8807

Angle	*Sine*	*Cosine*	*Tangent*
63°	.8910	.4540	1.9616
64°	.8988	.4384	2.0503
65°	.9063	.4226	2.1445
66°	.9135	.4067	2.2460
67°	.9205	.3907	2.3559
68°	.9272	.3746	2.4751
69°	.9336	.3584	2.6051
70°	.9397	.3420	2.7475
71°	.9455	.3256	2.9042
72°	.9511	.3090	3.0777
73°	.9563	.2924	3.2709
74°	.9613	.2756	3.4874
75°	.9659	.2588	3.7321
76°	.9703	.2419	4.0108
77°	.9744	.2250	4.3315
78°	.9781	.2079	4.7046
79°	.9816	.1908	5.1446
80°	.9848	.1736	5.6713
81°	.9877	.1564	6.3138
82°	.9903	.1392	7.1154
83°	.9925	.1219	8.1443
84°	.9945	.1045	9.5144
85°	.9969	.0872	11.4301
86°	.9976	.0698	14.3007
87°	.9986	.0523	19.0811
88°	.9994	.0349	28.6363
89°	.9998	.0175	57.2900
90°	1.0000	.0000	

4.17 Applying Trigonometry to Solve Problems in Geometry

Problem 1:

The sides of the base of a rectangular parallelepiped are *a* and *b*.

Between the diagonal of the parallelepiped and the base, an angle α is formed.

Find the side area of the parallelepiped.

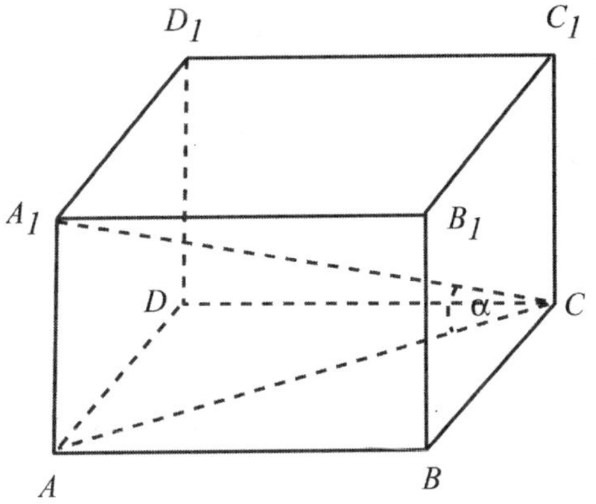

Solution:

The projection of diagonal A_1C onto the plane of base ABCD is AC.

Therefore, angle α between A_1C and the plane ABCD conforms to the $\angle A_1CA$.

From the triangle ΔAA_1C we know the following:

$$AA_1 = AC\tan\alpha = \sqrt{a^2+b^2}\ \tan\alpha .$$

Substitute in the formula $S_s=(2a+2b)\,AA_1$

Find $S_s = 2(a+b)\cdot\sqrt{a^2+b^2}\ \tan\alpha$ ← Answer

Problem 2:

The angle at the vertex of the axis section of a cone is equal to 2α and the sum of the lengths of altitude *h* and the generatrix *l* is equal to *m*.

Find the volume and the complete surface area of the cone.

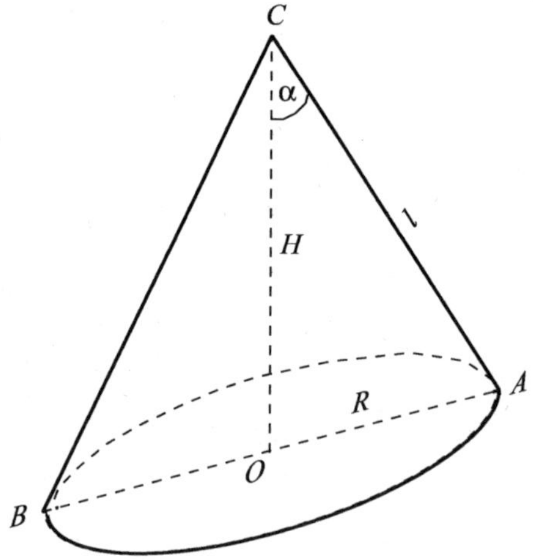

Solution:

The radius of the base $R = l\sin\alpha$, the altitude of the cone is $H = l\cos\alpha$

Volume $V = \dfrac{\pi r^2 H}{3} = \dfrac{\pi l^3 \sin^2\alpha\cos\alpha}{3}$

Complete surface $S_c = \pi r(l+r) = \pi l^2 \sin\alpha\,(1+\sin\alpha)$.

$l + H = m$ therefore, $l = m - H = m - l\cos\alpha = \dfrac{m}{1+\cos\alpha}$

$$Since\ \cos\frac{\alpha}{2} = \pm\sqrt{\frac{1+\cos\alpha}{2}} \qquad 1+\cos\alpha = 2\cos^2\frac{\alpha}{2}$$

$$therefore\ l = \frac{m}{2\cos^2\dfrac{\alpha}{2}}$$

Substituting for l:

$$\text{Volume}\ \ V = \frac{\pi\, m^3 \sin^2\alpha\cos\alpha}{24\cos^6\dfrac{\alpha}{2}}$$

$$\text{Complete surface}\ \ S_c = \frac{\pi\, m^2 \sin\alpha\,(1+\sin\alpha)}{4\cos^4\dfrac{\alpha}{2}}$$

Answer:

$$\text{Volume}\ \ V = \frac{\pi\, m^3 \sin^2\alpha\cos\alpha}{24\cos^6\dfrac{\alpha}{2}} \qquad S_c = \frac{\pi\, m^2 \sin\alpha\,(1+\sin\alpha)}{4\cos^4\dfrac{\alpha}{2}}$$

Problem 3:

A sphere is inscribed in a cone. The ratio of the surface of the sphere to the area of the base of a cone is equal to 4:3 respectively.

Find the angle at the vertex of a cone (2α).

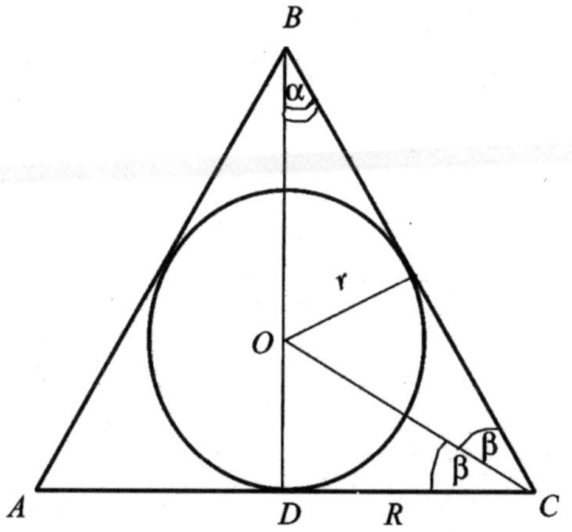

Solution:

Let R = the radius of the base of the cone

α = the angle between the axis of the cone and the surface

r = the radius of the sphere

$\angle OAC = \beta$

The axis cross section of the cone is an isosceles triangle ABC.

Then $\tan\beta = \dfrac{r}{R}$. The surface of the sphere $S_s = 4\pi r^2$.

The area of the base of the cone $S_c = \pi R^2$

We know that

$$\frac{S_s}{S_c} = 4:3 = \frac{4}{3} \quad or \quad \frac{4\pi\, r^2}{\pi\, R^2} = 4\left(\frac{r}{R}\right)^2 = \frac{4}{3};\ \left(\frac{r}{R}\right)^2 = \frac{1}{3}$$

$$\frac{r}{R}=\frac{1}{\sqrt{3}} \qquad \frac{r}{R}=\tan\beta=\frac{1}{\sqrt{3}} \qquad \textit{therefore} \qquad \beta=\frac{\pi}{6}(30^\circ)$$

From ΔCBD

$$\alpha+2\beta=\frac{\pi}{2}(or\ 90^\circ) \qquad \alpha=\frac{\pi}{2}-2\beta=\frac{\pi}{2}-\frac{\pi}{3}=\frac{\pi}{6}$$

Result: $2\alpha=\frac{2\pi}{6}=\frac{\pi}{3}(or\ 60^\circ)$

Problem 4:

The volume of a given right pyramid equals V.

The angle at the edge of a slope, which meets the side of the base, is equal to α.

Find the length of the edge EB of the pyramid.

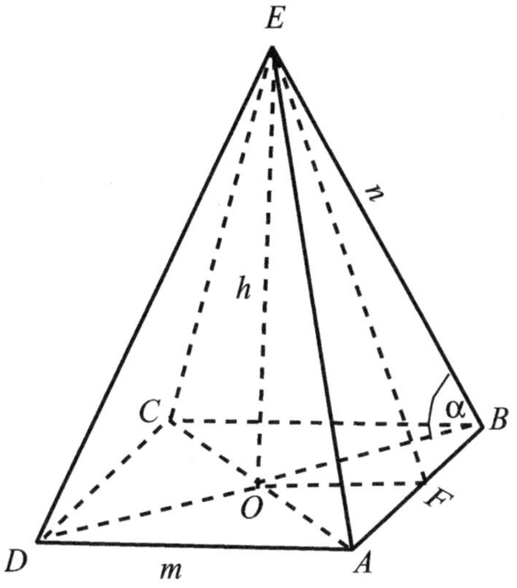

Solution: Let length $EB = n$

The volume of a regular pyramid is $V = \frac{1}{3} S \cdot h$

Where S = the area of the base ($s = m^2$)

h= the altitude of a pyramid

From ΔEBO: $h = n \sin \alpha$.

In ΔOAB, $(AB)^2 = (OB)^2 + (OA)^2$ [The Pythagorean Theorem]

Since $OB = OA$ then

$$(AB)^2 = (OB)^2 + (OA)^2 = 2\,(OB)^2$$

$$AB = m = \sqrt{2(OB)^2} = OB\sqrt{2}$$

From ΔEBO: $OB = n \cos\alpha$

Therefore, $m = OB\sqrt{2} = n\sqrt{2}\cos\alpha$ $\qquad n = \dfrac{m}{\sqrt{2}\cos\alpha}$

The value

$$V = \frac{Sh}{3} = \frac{m^2 \cdot n\sin\alpha}{3} = \frac{2n^2\cos^2\alpha \cdot n\sin\alpha}{3} = \frac{2}{3}n^3\cos^2\alpha\sin\alpha$$

Since $2 \cos \alpha \sin \alpha = \sin 2\alpha$

therefore,

$$V = \frac{1}{3}n^3 \sin 2\alpha\cos\alpha \qquad n = \sqrt[3]{\frac{3V}{\sin 2\alpha\cos\alpha}}$$

Answer: $B = n = \sqrt[3]{\dfrac{3V}{\sin 2\alpha\cos\alpha}}$

4.18 Commonly Asked Questions: Trigonometry

1) Q: Why are trigonometric functions called periodical?

A: During the continuous rotation of the radius of a unit circle we see that all trigonometric functions repeat their value. For the majority of functions, the period of repetition equals 360°(a complete turn of the radius).

2) Q: How is the sign of an angle determined?

A: The angle is positive (+θ) if the ray forming the angle turns counter clockwise; if the ray turns clockwise it is negative (-θ).

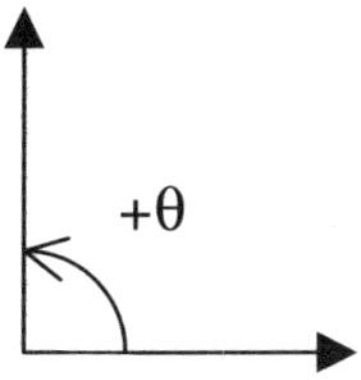

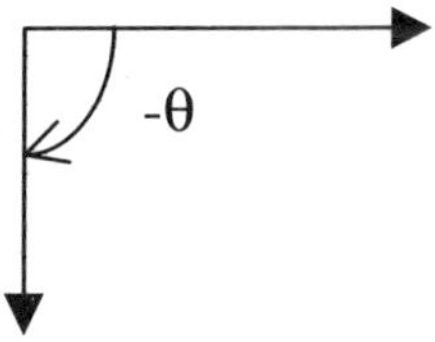

3) Q: Are there any tricks that can be used to solve trigonometric problems?

A: Yes. For example, many problems are easier to solve if you use the following identities.

$$\sin 90° = 1$$

$$\cos 0° = 1$$

$$\sin^2 \theta + \cos^2 \theta = 1$$

$$\tan \theta \cdot \cot \theta = 1$$

$$\sin \theta \cdot \csc \theta = 1$$

$$\cos \theta \cdot \sec \theta = 1$$

$$2\cos^2\frac{\theta}{2} - \cos\theta = 1$$

$$2\sin^2\frac{\theta}{2} + \cos\theta = 1$$

Any of these can be substituted for 1 in an equation. Or, because they equal 1, you can multiply or divide by them without changing the equation.

4) Q: Which special parameters does a trigonometric function have if the argument of this function is time, as in $y = \sin t$?

A: Time is an independent variable. In this case, some important parameters are present:

Period (T) – time it takes to complete a single cycle.

Frequency (f) – number of periods per second. (See 5.7)

5) Q: What is the practical application of an inverse trigonometric function?

A: In the process of problem solving, there is often a trigonometric function involved.

When solving everyday problems, one has to be able to determine the measure of the angle that corresponds to a particular functional value. The inverse function allows us to calculate that measure.

6) Q: When solving trigonometric equations, why is it necessary to determine periodicity?

A: The basic trigonometric functions repeat every 360° or 2π radians.

For example, if $\sin\theta = \frac{1}{2}$, we know that θ can be 30°.

But if $\theta = 30° + 360° = 390°$, we also have a value of $\frac{1}{2}$ for $\sin\theta$.

Because $\sin\theta$ has this value every 360°, we can write

$$\theta = 30° + 360° \cdot k, \text{ where k is a whole number.}$$

For a more general solution of $\sin\theta = \frac{1}{2}$, see section 4.14.

7) Q: When are radian and degree measures of an angle used?

A: It is not a question of principal. You can use either in most cases. In practice, using radian measure in solving trigonometric equations and graphing functions is recommended.

8) Q: We know that in a circle with a unit radius there are lines equal to the sine and cosine. Is there a line which is equal to the value of the tangent?

A: Yes, in the figure below a tangent line is represented by line m. Line m is a line in the plane of the circle that intersects the circle in exactly one point, B.

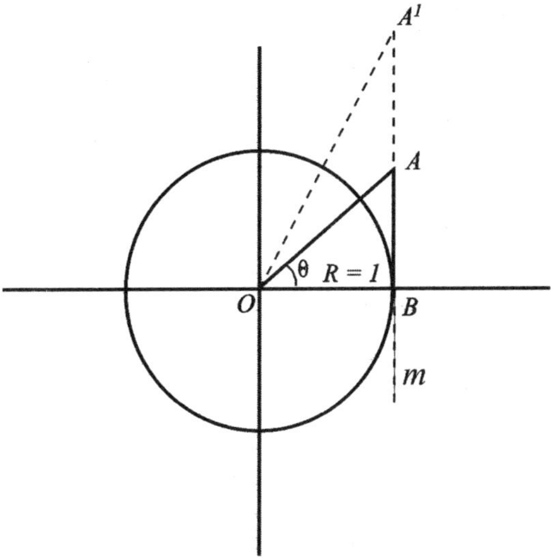

$$\tan\theta = \frac{AB}{OB} = \frac{AB}{R} = AB$$

5 CHAPTER

FUNCTIONS AND GRAPHS

5.1 Functions

A **function** is a relation in which each element of the domain corresponds to one and only one element in the range. It is symbolized by $y = f(x)$ or $y = f(x,y,z...)$ Where y is a function and x,y,z are the arguments.

For example: the size of a metal (Y_m) depends on the temperature (t°) $Y_m = f(t^\circ)$.

There are many ways in which a function may be represented: a set, a table, a graph, etc. The most obvious method is a graph.

A graph on a plane has a horizontal line called the **x-axis** and a vertical line called the **y-axis.**

These two number lines have the same scale and are drawn perpendicular to each other. They are known as **coordinate axes**.

In a coordinate plane, the intersection of the two lines is called the **origin.** It is indicated by point 0. At this point of intersection, both x and y are equal to 0.

The x-axis and the y-axis separate the plane into four regions called **quadrants**. These quadrants are numbered I, II, III and IV in a counterclockwise direction. The rotation begins from the upper right quadrant (I) as shown on the graph.

Every point on the plane can be described by two numbers or the **coordinates of a point**. They are usually written as an **ordered pair** or a set of two.

The first number in the pair is the **x-coordinate** or the **abscissa.** The second number is the **y-coordinate** or the **ordinate.**

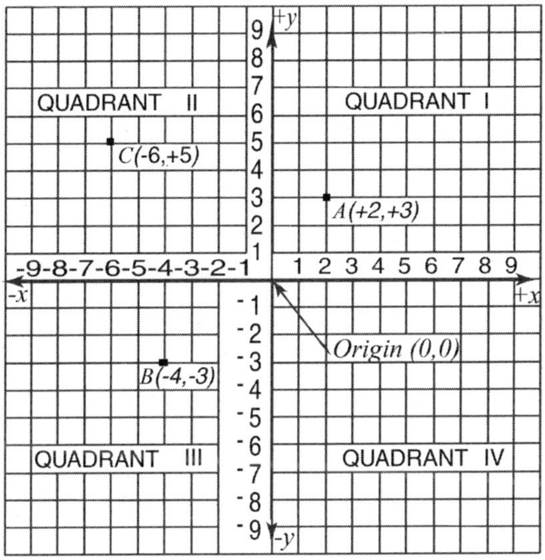

5.2 Linear Functions

Every first-degree, linear equation is a function whose domain is the set of real numbers.

Equation	Graph
y* = *kx k = the coefficient of slope $k = \frac{y_2 - y_1}{x_2 - x_1}$	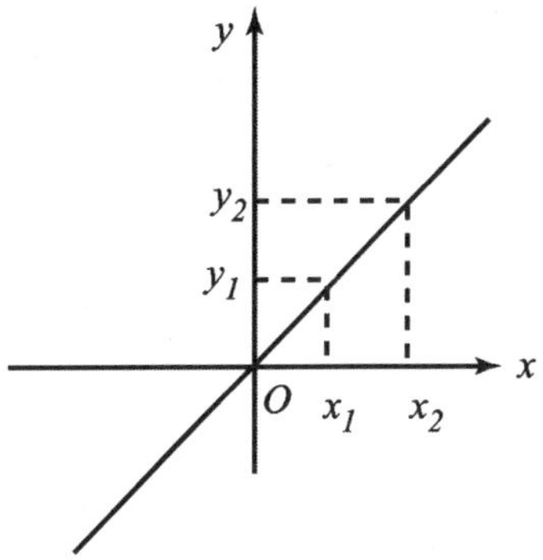

Equation	Graph
$y = kx + b$	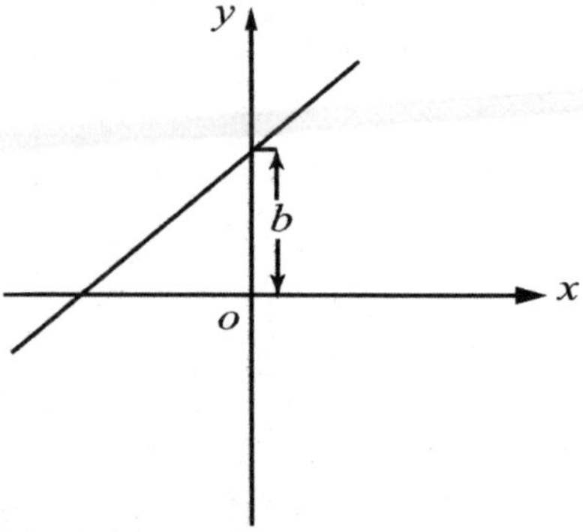
$y = a$	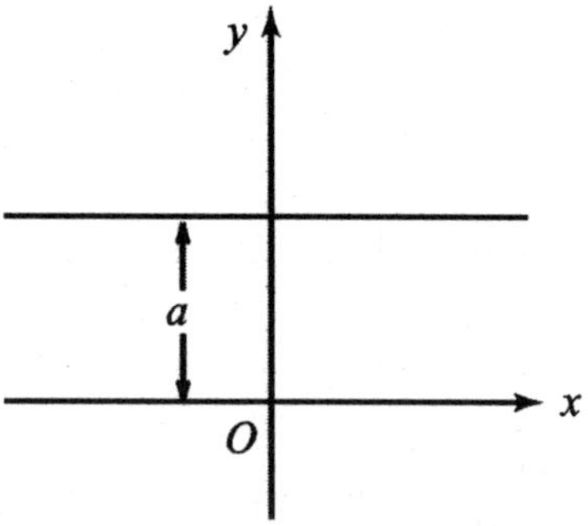
$x = a$	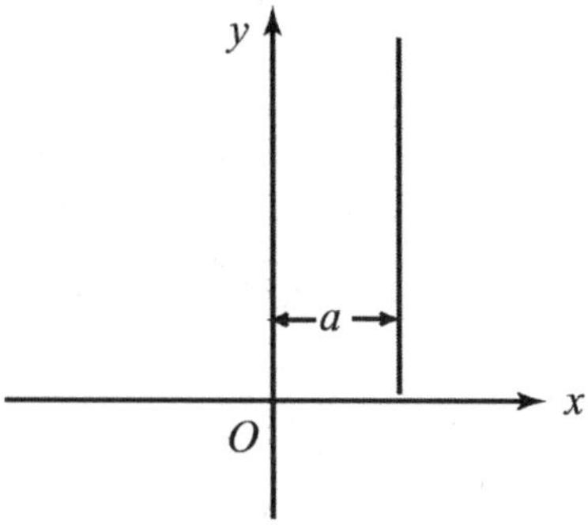

The distance (d) between the two points (x_1, y_1) and (x_2, y_2) is given by the formula: $d = \sqrt{(x_2 - x_1)^2 + (y_2 - y_1)^2}$

5.3 Circles and Ellipses

The equation of a circle whose center is the origin (0,0) and whose radius is r is : $x^2 + y^2 = r^2$

A **circle** is a locus of points in a plane equidistant from a fixed point as a center.

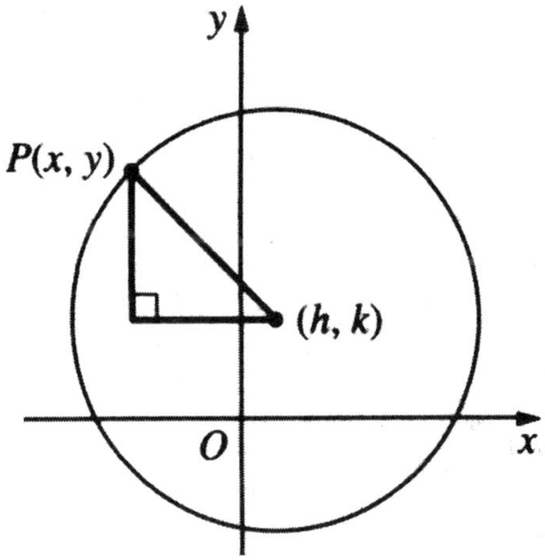

From the above graph, the center of a circle is at (h, k). We let P (x, y) represent any point on a circle and use the distance formula.

$$d = \sqrt{(x_1 - x_2)^2 + (y_1 - y_2)^2}$$

$$r = \sqrt{(x - h)^2 + (y - k)^2} \qquad or \qquad r^2 = (x - h)^2 + (y - k)^2$$

In the equation $ax^2 + by^2 = c$, $a \neq b$ and a, b, c have the same sign. This is an equation for an ellipse.

The figure below is called an ellipse. An **ellipse** is the locus of points such that the sum of the distances of any point on the locus from the two fixed points is constant. Each of the fixed points is a focus of the ellipse.

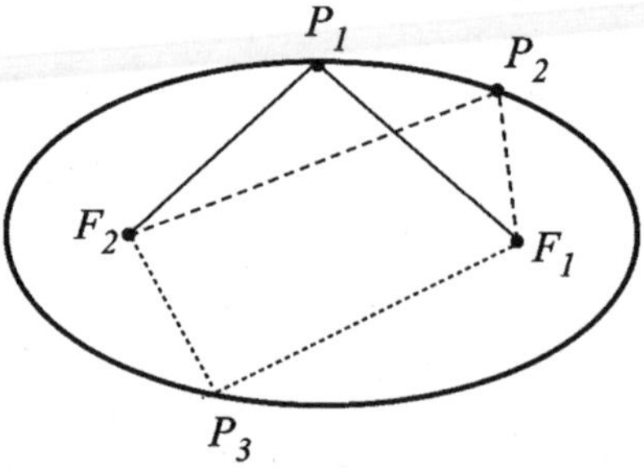

For example, if F_1 and F_2 are the foci and P_1, P_2, and

P_3 are points on the ellipse then

$$F_1P_1 + F_2P_1 = F_1P_2 + F_2P_2 = F_1P_3 + F_2P_3$$

Equation: $\dfrac{x^2}{b^2} + \dfrac{y^2}{a^2} = 1$

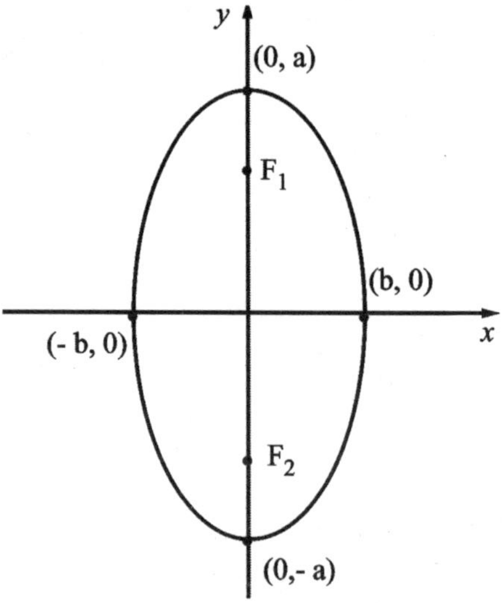

Equation: $\frac{x^2}{a^2} + \frac{y^2}{b^2} = 1$

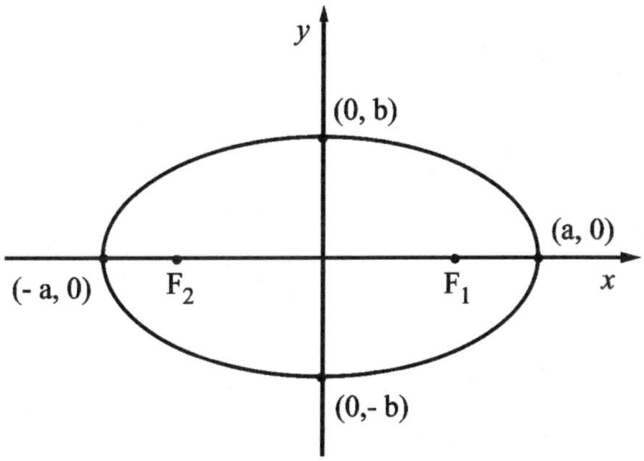

5.4 Parabolas

A **parabola** is the locus of points equidistant from a fixed point and a fixed line. The fixed point is called a **focus,** and the fixed line is the **directrix.**

The general equation of a parabola is $y = ax^2 + bx + c$

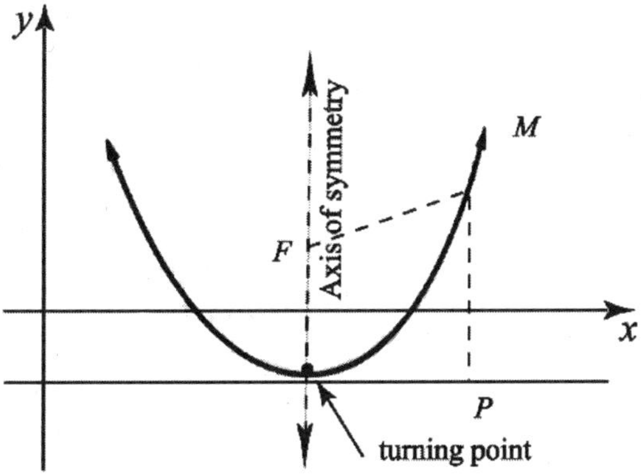

The equation of the Axis of symmetry is: $x = \frac{-b}{2a}$

If we change the variables x and y: $x = ay^2 + by + c$ Then the graph is turned 90°.

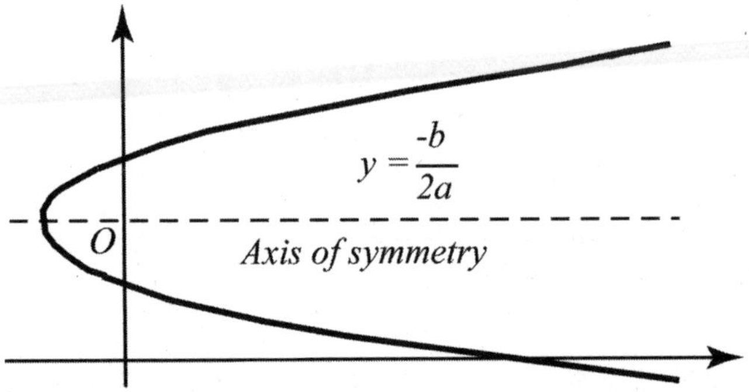

If the parabola equation is $ax^2 + bx + c = 0$, and it intersects the x-axis in two distinct points, then the roots of the equation are real and unequal ($b^2 - 4ac > 0$).

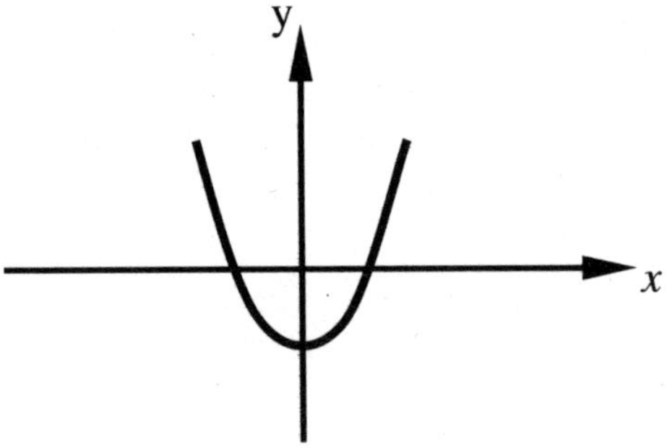

If the parabola touches the x-axis in exactly one point, its roots are real and equal ($b^2 - 4ac = 0$).

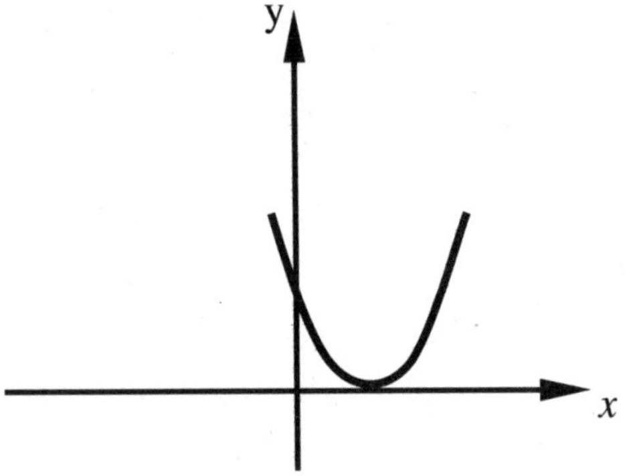

If the parabola does not intersect the x-axis, the roots are imaginary ($b^2 - 4ac < 0$).

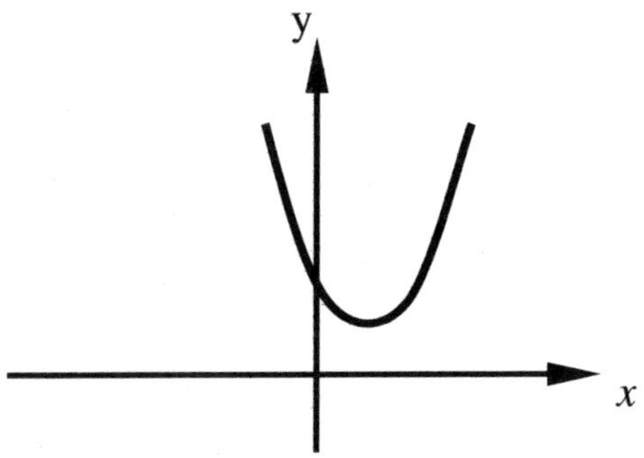

5.5 Hyperbolas

When a and b have different signs, the graph of the equation $ax^2 + by^2 = c$ is called a **hyperbola.**

For example: $4x^2 - y^2 = 16$ is the equation of a hyperbola

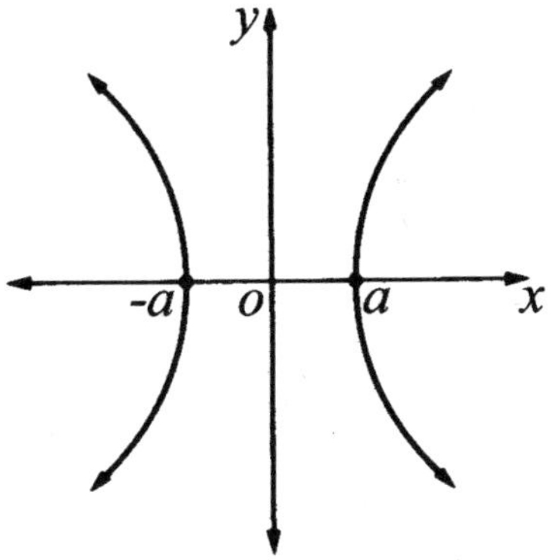

This hyperbola has two x-intercepts, but no y-intercepts.

Alternatively, a hyperbola may have y-intercepts but no x-intercepts, for example, if x and y are exchanged in the equation.

5.6 Inversely Proportional Functions

The general equation of an inversely proportional function is $y = \frac{k}{x} \quad (x \neq 0)$ $k =$ the constant of variation

To draw the graph of $y = \frac{k}{x}$ we find the ordered pairs that are elements of the solution set.

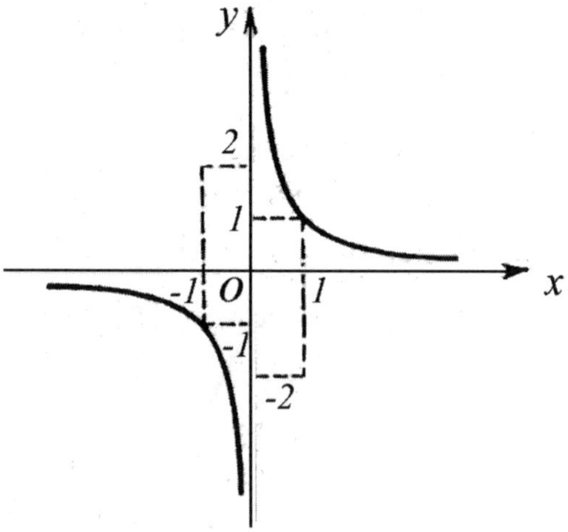

In this graph, the hyperbola has two parts in Quadrant I and Quadrant III.

- The graph has line symmetry.
- The x and y axes serve as the lines of symmetry.
- The origin (0,0) is a point of symmetry.

5.7 Graphs of the Trigonometric Functions

If we divide the interval from 0 to 2π (from 0 to 360°) into four equal parts, the curve of the graph of function y = sin x increases from 0 to 1 in the first quarter, and decreases from 1 to 0 in the second quarter. Then, decreases from 0 to –1 in the third quarter, and finally increases from –1 to 0 in the fourth quarter. In the unit circle, we observe the same pattern for y = sin x.

y = sin x

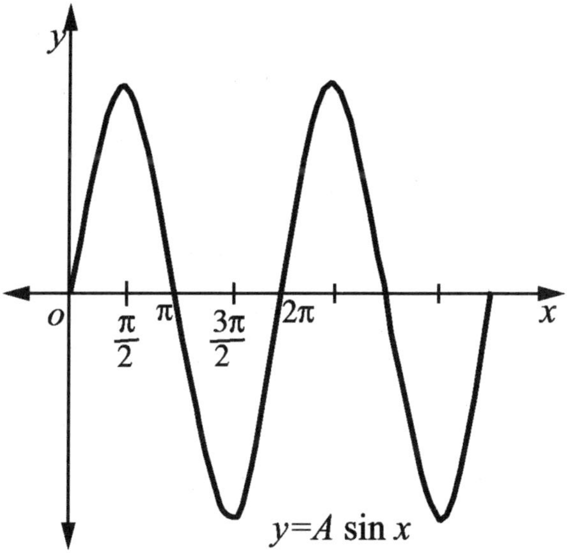

In quadrant I, as θ increases from 0 to 90°, sin θ increases from 0 to A.

In quadrant II, as θ increases from 90° to 180°, sin θ decreases from A to 0.

The same patterns apply to quadrants III and IV.

The maximum value of the function y =A sin x is called the **amplitude**.

The amplitude of the function y =A sin x is the absolute value of A or $|A|$. A complete cycle change of the periodic function is called a **period**.

The period of the function y = sin x is equal to 2π (360°).

The period of the function y = sin kx is $\frac{2\pi}{k}$ $\left(\frac{360^\circ}{k}\right)$.

The figure below shows the graph of the function y = cos x. In the unit circle we can see the same pattern of values for cos θ.

- As θ increases from 0 to 90°in quadrant I, cos θ decreases from 1 to 0.
- In quadrant II, as θ increases from 90° to 180°, cos θ decreases from 0 to –1.
- In quadrant III, as θ increases from 180° to 270°, cos θ increases from –1 to 0.
- In quadrant IV, as θ increases from 270° to 360°, cos θ increases from 0 to 1.

y = cos x

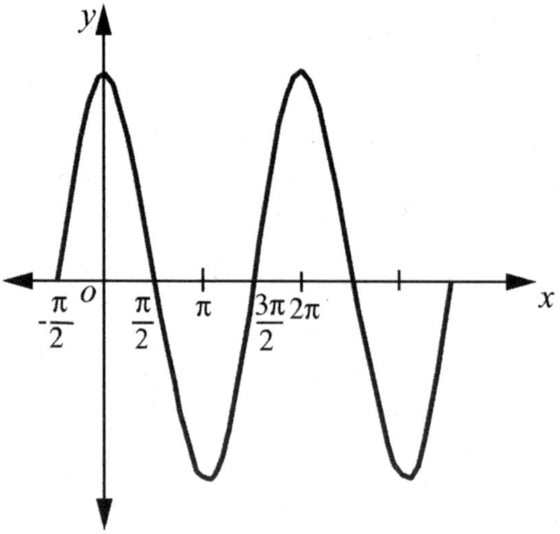

The period of the function y = cos x is equal to 2π (360°).

The period of the function y = cos kx is equal to $\frac{2\pi}{k}$ $\left(\frac{360^\circ}{k}\right)$.

The figure below shows the graph of the function y = tan x

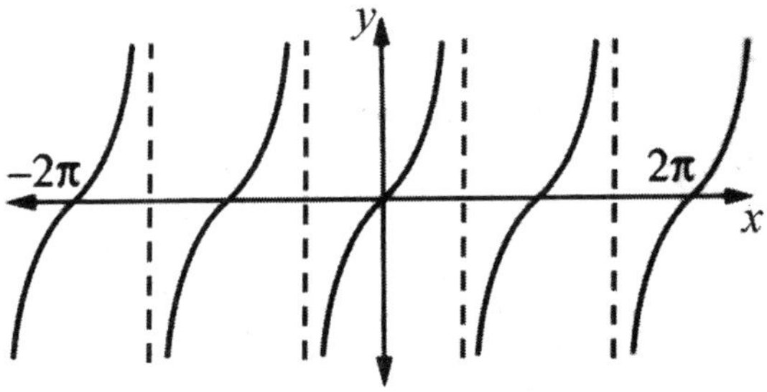

$y = tan x$

The function y = tan x has no maximum or minimum.
The tangent function does not have amplitude.
The period of this function is 180°.

The period of the function y = tan kx is $\frac{180°}{k}$.

5.8 Graphs of Exponential Functions

$y = n^x$ is a simple exponential function.

The following figures represent the graphs of three functions:

$$y = 3^x, y = 2^x, y = \left(\frac{1}{2}\right)^x$$

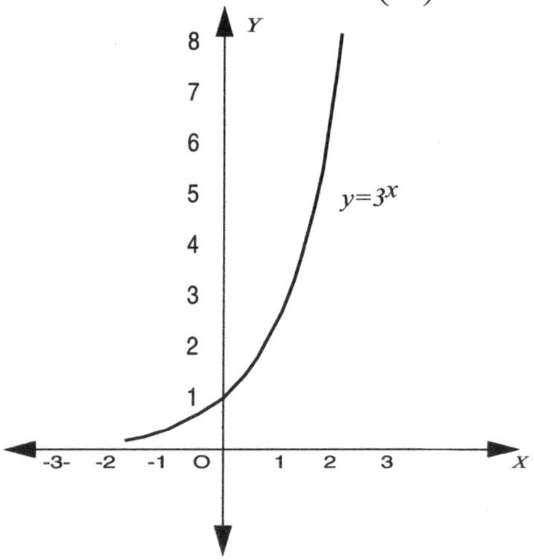

The graph of $y=\left(\dfrac{1}{2}\right)^x$ is a reflection of the graph $y=2^x$.

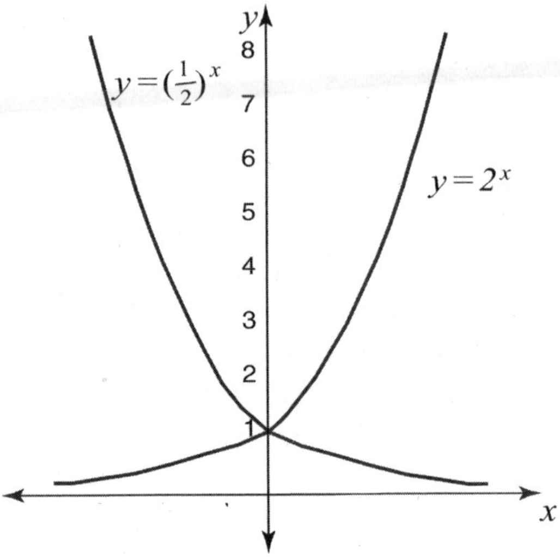

5.9 Graphs of Logarithmic Functions

$y=\log_n x$ is a simple logarithmic function.

The figure represents the graphs of three functions:

$$y=x,\ \ y=2^x,\ \ y=\log_2 x$$

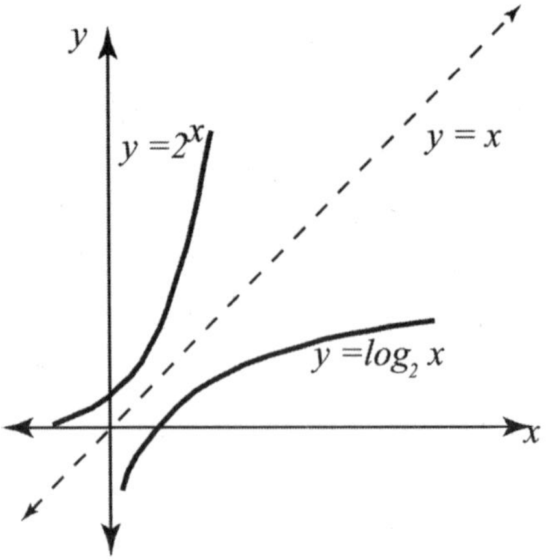

5.10 Commonly Asked Questions: Functions and Graphs

1) **Q:** In graphing functions, what is usually represented by the vertical axis, and what by the horizontal axis?

A: The dependent value is usually represented by the vertical axis, while the value on which it depends is represented by the horizontal axis. For example, in graphing a function where the speed of some object varies with time, the vertical axis would represent the speed while the horizontal axis would represent time.

2) **Q:** Are the graphs of first-degree equations always straight lines?

A: Yes, always. In order to construct the graph of a first-degree equation it is sufficient to have two points in the coordinate plane and to draw a straight line through them. In order to determine those two points one can simply allow first one of the coordinates (for example x) be equal to zero and calculate the other coordinate from the equation, then allow the other coordinate to equal zero and calculate the value of the first coordinate.

For example, the equation:

$$y = 2x + 4$$

Step 1 $x = 0, y = 4$

Step 2 $y = 0, x = -2$

The coordinate points are A (0, 4), B (-2, 0)

3) **Q:** How does one graph equations of the second or higher degree?

A: By assigning a series of values to the independent variable and calculating the value of the function for each one. In this way one creates a table of values that can be used to graph the function.

For example, the graph of the equation

$$y = 2x^2 + 4x + 10$$

can be constructed from the following table:

x	0	1	2	3	4
y	10	16	26	40	58

4) **Q:** Which special parameters does a trigonometric function have if the argument of this function is time, as in $y = \sin t$?

A: Time is an independent variable. In this case, some important parameters are present:

Period (T) – time it takes to complete a single cycle.

Frequency (f) – number of periods per second.

5) **Q:** What kind of practical applications do graphs of functions have?

A: The practical applications are so numerous and broad that it would be impossible to list them. For the sake of an example, let us take the parabola. A radio antenna whose surface has the form of a parabola has the ability to concentrate the radio waves and ensure quality reception. Satellite "dishes" have parabolic surfaces.

6 CHAPTER

LOGIC

Logic is that branch of mathematics that tells whether an argument is valid or invalid.

A sentence that can be true or false is called a statement. Each statement is designated by a letter (P, Q, etc.) and is assigned a truth value (T for true and F for false). For example, $7 \cdot 7 = 49$ is T, and $7 \cdot 7 = 50$ is F.

6.1 Basic Logical Operations

6.1.1 Negations

The **negation** of a statement, ~p (read "not p") always has a truth value that is the opposite of the truth value of the original statement.

P	~P
F	T
T	F

Example:

Let P = "It is raining." ~P then means "it is not raining."

6.1.2 Conjunction

A conjunction is true only when both P and Q are true. Its symbol is $\wedge$, which is read "and."

P	Q	$P \wedge Q$
T	T	T
T	F	F
F	T	F
F	F	F

Example: Let P = the existence of oxygen, and let Q = the existence of hydrogen. Then $P \wedge Q$ = the formation of water.

The formation of water requires the existence of both oxygen and hydrogen.

6.1.3 Disjunction

A disjunction is false only when both P and Q are false. Its symbol is $\vee$, which is read "or."

P	Q	$P \vee Q$
T	T	T
T	F	T
F	T	T
F	F	F

Example: If it is a weekend *or* a holiday, most people have the day off.

Let P = a weekend
Let Q = a holiday.

Then $P \vee Q$ = an off day.

6.1.4 Conditionals

A conditional is false only when P is true and Q is false. It is written P→Q and is read "if P then Q."

P	Q	P→Q
T	T	T
T	F	F
F	T	T
F	F	T

Example: If snow falls then Bob goes skiing.

Let P = snowfall
Let Q = Bob goes skiing

This statement is false if snow falls and Bob doesn't go skiing. Otherwise, it is true.

6.1.5 Biconditionals

A biconditional is true only when P and Q have the same truth value. It is written P↔Q and is read "P if and only if Q."

P	Q	P↔Q
T	T	T
T	F	F
F	T	F
F	F	T

Example: If factors have different signs the product is negative number.

Let P = "x is a positive factor"
Q = "y is a negative factor"

Then P↔Q is true when the product xy is negative.

6.1.6 Compound Statements

A truth table for a compound statement is built upon the truth values of its simple components.

Examples: $(P \wedge Q) \vee (\sim P \rightarrow Q)$

P	Q	$P \wedge Q$	$\sim P$	$\sim P \rightarrow Q$	$(P \wedge Q) \vee (\sim P \rightarrow Q)$
T	T	T	F	T	T
T	F	F	F	T	T
F	T	F	T	T	T
F	F	F	T	F	F

Which statements about P and ~Q would be correct headings for the last columns of the following two tables?

P	Q	~Q	?
T	T	F	F
T	F	T	T
F	T	F	T
F	F	T	T

P	Q	~Q	?
T	T	F	F
T	F	T	T
F	T	F	T
F	F	T	F

Answer:

P	~Q	$P \rightarrow \sim Q$
T	F	F
T	T	T
F	F	T
F	T	T

P	~Q	P↔~Q
T	F	F
T	T	T
F	F	T
F	T	F

6.2 Tautology

A compound statement that is always true is called a **tautology**.

Example: The statement (P∧Q)→P is always true, and thus is a tautology.

P	Q	P∧Q	(P∧Q)→P
T	T	T	T
T	F	F	T
F	T	F	T
F	F	F	T

6.3 Logic Terms (Terminology)

- **Logical Equivalence.** Two statements that always have the same truth values are logically equivalent. This means that the bi-conditional of two logically equivalent statements is a tautology.

- **Conditional.** Given as "if P, then Q." Symbol: P→Q

- **Converse.** Change P and Q: "if Q, then P." Symbol: Q→P

- **Inverse.** Negate P and Q: "if not P, then not Q." Symbol: ~P→~Q

- **Contrapositive.**_ Change P and Q and negate both sides: "if not Q, then not P." Symbol: ~Q→~P

P	Q	~P	~Q	P→Q	converse: Q→P	inverse: ~P→~Q	Contra-positive ~Q→~P
T	T	F	F	T	T	T	T
T	F	F	T	F	T	T	F
F	T	T	F	T	F	F	T
F	F	T	T	T	T	T	T

6.4 Laws of Logic

There are many laws of reasoning that allow us to present a convincing argument or a formal proof in logic. Before developing a formal proof in logic, we need first to understand what is meant by a convincing argument.

An argument consists of a series of statements called **premises** and a final statement called a **conclusion**.

Example:

Premise: If I play chess, then I need a set of chessmen.
Premise: I play chess.

Conclusion: I need a set of chessmen.

The Basic Laws of Logic

Laws of Inference	Symbolic Representations
1. Law of Detachment (Modus Ponens) If a conditional is true and its antecedent is true, then its consequent is true.	$[(p\to q)\wedge p]\to q$ Premise 1: $p\to q$ <u>Premise 2: p</u> Conclusion: q

2. Law of the Contrapositive If a conditional is true, then its contrapositive is true. (A conditional and its contrapositive are logically equivalent.)	$(p\to q)\leftrightarrow(\sim q\to\sim p)$ Premise: $p\to q$ Conclusion: $\sim q\to\sim p$
3. Law of Modus Tollens If a conditional is true and its consequent is false, then its antecedent is false.	$[(p\to q)\wedge\sim q]\to\sim p$ Premise 1: $p\to q$ Premise 2: $\sim q$ Conclusion: $\sim p$
4. Chain Rule (Law of Syllogism) If two given conditionals of the form $P\to Q$ and $Q\to R$ are true, a third conditional of the form $P\to R$ is true.	$[(p\to q)\wedge(q\to r)]\to(p\to r)$ Premise 1: $p\to q$ Premise 2: $q\to r$ Conclusion: $p\to r$
5. Law of Disjunctive inference If a disjunction is true and one of the disjuncts is false, then the other disjunct is true.	$[(p\vee q)\wedge\sim p]\to q$ Premise 1: $p\vee q$ Premise 2: $\sim p$ Conclusion: q $[(p\vee q)\wedge\sim q]\to p$ Premise1: $p\vee q$ Premise 2: $\sim q$ Conclusion: p
6. Law of Double Negation The negation of the negation of a statement is logically equivalent to the statement.	$\sim(\sim p)\leftrightarrow p$
7. DeMorgan's Law • *Negation of a conjunction* The negation of a conjunction of two statements is Logically equivalent to the disjunction of the negation of each one. • *Negation of a disjunction* The negation of a disjunction of two statements is logically equivalent to the conjunction of the negation of each one.	$\sim(p\wedge q)\leftrightarrow(\sim p\vee\sim q)$ $\sim(p\vee q)\leftrightarrow(\sim p\wedge\sim q)$

8. Law of Simplification If a conjunction is true, then each of the statements is true.	$(p \wedge q) \rightarrow p$ Premise: $p \wedge q$ Conclusion: p also $(p \wedge q) \rightarrow q$ Premise: $p \wedge q$ Conclusion: q
9. Law of Conjunction If two given statements are true, then the conjunction of the two statements is true.	$[(p) \wedge (q)] \rightarrow (p \wedge q)$ Premise 1: p Premise 2: q Conclusion: $p \wedge q$
10. Law of Disjunctive Addition If a given statement is true, then a disjunction involving that statement and any second statement is true.	$p \rightarrow (p \vee q)$ Premise: p Conclusion: $p \vee q$

6.5 Examples of Premises and Conclusions for the Basic Laws of Logic

1. **Law of Detachment (Modus Pones)**

   Premise 1: "If I am riding a bus, then I have paid" $(p \rightarrow q)$
   Premise 2: " I am riding the bus" (p)
   Conclusion: "I have paid" (q)

   Symbols $[(p \rightarrow q) \wedge p] \rightarrow q$

2. **Law of Contrapositive**

   Premise : "It's true that if it is raining, I open my umbrella" $(p \rightarrow q)$
   Conclusion: "It is also true that if I do not open my umbrella, it is not raining." $(\sim q \rightarrow \sim p)$

   Symbols $(p \rightarrow q) \leftrightarrow (\sim q \rightarrow \sim p)$

3. Law of Modus Tollens

Premise 1: "If Andy saves enough money, he will be able to buy a car." $(p \rightarrow q)$
Premise 2: "Andy can not buy a car " $(\sim q)$
Conclusion: "Andy didn't save enough money." $(\sim p)$

Symbols $[(p \rightarrow q) \wedge \sim q] \rightarrow \sim p$

4. Chain Rule (Law of Syllogism)

Premise 1: "If the car is at home then my father is home." $(p \rightarrow q)$
Premise 2: "If my father is home then the TV is on." $(q \rightarrow r)$
Conclusion: "If the car is at home then the TV is on." $(p \rightarrow r)$

Symbols $[(p \rightarrow q) \wedge (q \rightarrow r)] \rightarrow (p \rightarrow r)$

5. Law of Disjunctive Inference

Premise 1: "You are either for us or against us." $(p \vee q)$
Premise 2: "You are not for us." $(\sim p)$
Conclusion: "You are against us." (q)

Symbols $[(p \vee q) \wedge \sim p] \rightarrow q$

Or Premise 2: "You are not against us." $(\sim q)$
Conclusion: "You are for us." (p)

Symbols $[(p \vee q) \wedge \sim q] \rightarrow p$

6. Law of Double Negation

Premise : "I am not not going." $\sim(\sim p)$
Conclusion: "I'm going." p

Symbols $\sim(\sim p) \leftrightarrow p$

7. DeMorgan's Law

I. Negation of a conjunction:

" It's not true that Ann Studies math and physics." $\sim(p \wedge q)$
" It's true that Ann does not study math and/or* physics" $\sim p \vee \sim q$

Symbols $\sim(p \wedge q) \leftrightarrow (\sim p \vee \sim q)$

II. Negation of a disjunction:

Symbols $\sim(p \vee q) \leftrightarrow (\sim p \wedge q)$

8. Law of Simplification

Premise : "It is true that Johnny likes to read and to play chess." $(p \wedge q)$

Conclusion 1: "Johnny likes to read." (p)

Conclusion 2: "Johnny likes to play chess." (q)

Symbols $(p \wedge q) \rightarrow p$; $(p \wedge q) \rightarrow q$

9. Law of Conjunction

Premise 1: "A circle is round." (p)

Premise 2: "A square is square." (q)

Conclusion: "A circle is round and a square is square." $(p \wedge q)$

Symbols $[(p) \wedge (q)] \rightarrow (p \wedge q)$

10. Law of Disjunctive Addition

Premise : "The root of equation is x = 5." (p)

Conclusion: "The root of equation is x = 5 and/or * x = (your age)." $(p \vee q)$

(we could substitute in anything after "or" and the second state ment will still be true.)

Symbols $p \rightarrow (p \vee q)$

* Note:
"or" in logic, or disjunction, is like the conjunction and/or in normal English.

Example:

Given:
- If I receive a check for $500, then we will go on a trip.
- If the car breaks down, then we will not go on a trip.
- Either I receive a check for $500 or we will not buy souvenirs.
- The car breaks down.

Let C represent: "I receive a $500 check."

Let T represent: " We will go on a trip."

Let B represent: " The car breaks down."

Let S represent: "We will buy souvenirs."

Translate each of the given statements into symbolic form:

"If I receive a check for $500, then we will go on a trip" is the conditional that C implies T: $C \rightarrow T$

" If the car breaks down, then we will not go on a trip" is the conditional that B implies the negation of T: $B \rightarrow \sim T$

" Either I receive a check for $500 or we will not buy souvenirs" is the disjunction of C and the negation of S: $C \vee \sim S$

"The car breaks down " is the statement B: B

Prove that "the car breaks down" implies "we will not buy souvenirs."
Translate the statement of proof into symbolic form:
Prove: $B \rightarrow \sim S$:

Write a formal proof.

Statement	Reason
1. B	1. Given
2. $B \rightarrow \sim T$	2. Given
3. $\sim T$	3. Law of Detachment
4. $C \rightarrow T$	4. Given
5. $\sim C$	5. Law of Modus Tollens
6. $C \vee \sim S$	6. Given
7. $\sim S$	7. Law of Disjunctive Inference

6.6 Commonly Asked Questions: Logic

1) **Q:** What is the main usage of the mathematical system of logic in practice?

A: In studying mathematical logic, students acquire skills in demonstrating things in a logically rigorous way. This is useful not only for proving theorems in geometry, but also for sound argumentation in any field of learning.

2) **Q:** What is the connection between a logical problem expressed in words (the content of the problem) and the logical formulas (letters and symbols) used to express it?

A: The connection is not direct. As soon as a statement is marked by a letter, the content of the statement "disappears" in some sense. Logic formulizes or abstracts the problem as stated in words. Of course, the results of logical operations can be translated back into words by changing letters into statements. This abstraction is why the results of logical operations sometimes seem to contradict common sense.

3) **Q:** Are there any simple ways to memorize the tables of conjunction and disjunction?

A: Yes, there are. If the letters T and F in the table are changed to numbers 1 and 0 respectively, the table of conjunction will correspond to the table of multiplication. The table of disjunction will correspond to the table of addition. This method simplifies the process of memorization of logic and can easily be applied to other operations. This math with 1's and 0's is how computers do logical operations.

	Q	$P \wedge Q$
1	1	1
1	0	0
0	1	0
0	0	0

P	Q	$P \vee Q$
1	1	1
1	0	1
0	1	1
0	0	0

4) **Q:** How can tautology be applied in a practical sense?

A: In technical devices like computers, digital logic is applied when executing various operations. The true or false decisions are symbolized by 1's and 0's. The main controller in the computer uses a chip that determines decisions. The input and output signals, which travel through the circuit in different voltages can be either true or false. Sometimes it is necessary to use an operation that gives the same output regardless of the input.

7 CHAPTER

STATISTICS

Without statistics, no state, city, or even family can function properly.

When you are studying different ways to organize and to present your data, you are working in the branch of mathematics called statistics.

7.1 Typical Steps in a Statistical Study

There are three basic steps in a statistical study:

1) The collection of data.
2) The organization of the data tables, charts, and graphs.
3) The drawing of a conclusion from an analysis of this data.

7.1.1 Preparing a Table

In many cases, preliminary data is places into tables.

Rules for grouping data

1. The intervals must cover the complete range of values. A **range** is the difference between the highest and the lowest values.

2. The intervals must be equal in size.

3. The number of intervals should be rational (a recommended number of intervals is between 5-15)

7.2 Graphs in Statistics

There are different types of graphs.

Interval	Tally	Numbers (frequency)
60-66	////	4
67-73	//	2
74-80	//	2
81-87	/////	5

A **pictograph** is a graph that shows data by using picture symbols.

- Example: Time it takes to get to school --- Key: each square =2 students

Minutes	Symbols	
7	□ □	(4 students)
10	□ □ □ □	(8 students)
15	□ □ ▯	(5 students)
27	□ □ □ ▯	(7 students)

A **line plot** is a vertical graph that uses X's above a line to show data.

- Example: Time it takes to get to school --- Key: X = 1 student

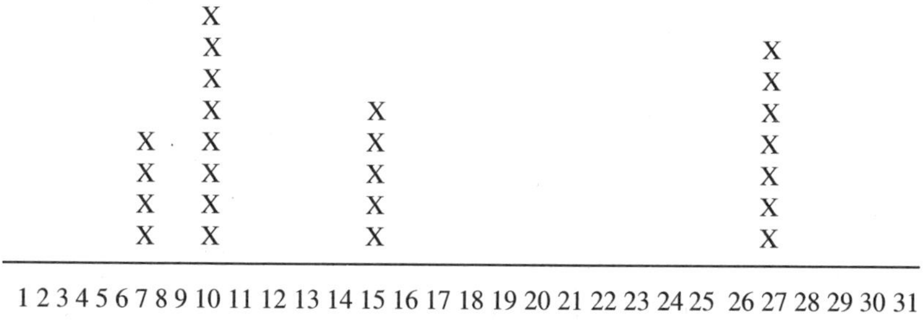

A **line graph** shows how something changes over a period of time. The dots represent data (factual information) and lines connect the dots to show increase or decrease over time.

- Example: Hundreds of dollars spent on clothing in a year.

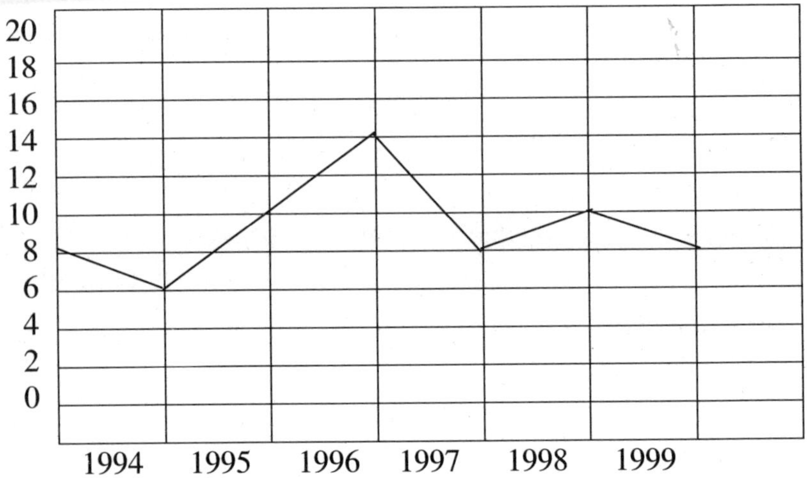

A **circle graph** shows data by dividing a circle into sections that represent the parts of a whole. The parts in a circle graph always add up to the whole.

Example: the allocation of recourses

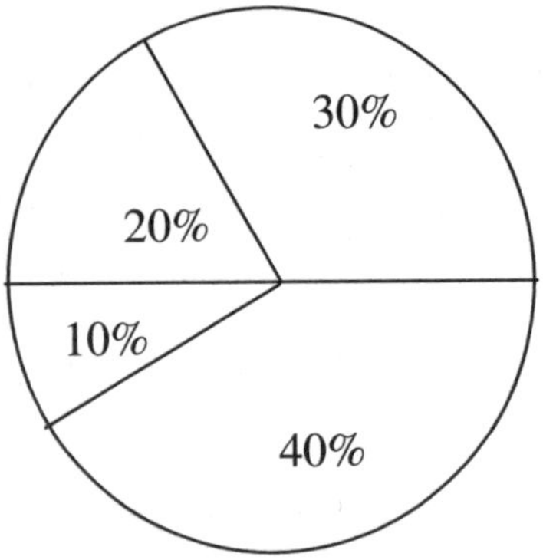

vacation........... 30%

food 40%

travel 10%

entertainment ... 20%

7.2.1 The Frequency Histogram

A **frequency histogram** is a bar graph that displays the frequencies in a series of intervals of equal length.

Example:

In January, the auto repair shop repaired a certain quantity (Q) of cars in a given amount of days. (D)

D	5	6	7	8	9	12	13	14	15	16
Q	2	8	11	6	16	20	20	9	11	20

D	19	20	21	22	23	26	27	28	29	30
Q	14	3	19	9	10	8	16	12	15	18

Histogram Interval – 5 days

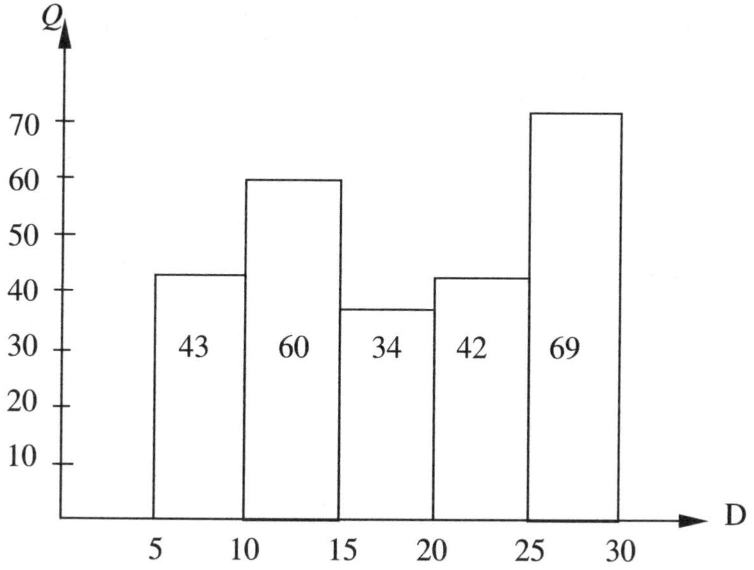

7.3 Measures of Central Tendency

7.3.1 The Mean

In a statistical study, after we have collected the data and organized it, we analyze the data and summarize our findings. One value used for analysis is the **mean.** To find the mean of a set of N numbers, add the numbers and divide the sum by N. The symbol for the mean is, $\bar{x}$ read as x-bar.

Example:

A store sold dresses for five days (N=5.) The first day, they sold 4 dresses, the second day 6, the third day 10, the fourth day 12, and the fifth day 6. Find the mean (average) number of dresses sold each day.

Step1: 4+6+10+12+6=38

Step2: mean $= \bar{x} = \frac{38}{N} = \frac{38}{5} = 7.6$ They sold an average of 7.6 dresses per day.

7.3.2 The Median

The **Median** is the value in the middle (the center of the data) after the numbers are arranged in an increasing or decreasing order.

Example:

1, 12, 14, 21, 40, 56, 71

↑

Median

If the set has an even quantity of data, then take the sum of the two middle values and divide it by two.

Example: 1, 8, 12, 20, 40, 56 $\frac{12+20}{2}=16$ ← median

7.3.3 The Mode

The **mode** is the value that occurs most frequently in a given set of data. A set of values may have more than one mode.

Examples:

1) Determine the mode for the set of values: 2, 4, 2, 3, 2, 1,
Answer: the mode is 2. It appears most often.

2) Determine the mode for the set of values: 2, 4, 1, 1, 4, 5
Answer: the modes are 4 and 1. Both values occur with the same frequency.

If the set is 1, 6, 9, 7, and 2, there is no mode since all the numbers appear only once.

7.4 Measures of Dispersion

A **measure of dispersion** measures the variability or spread in the given data. The simplest measure of dispersion is the **range**. The range is equal to the highest value minus the lowest value.

Example:

Find the range in a given set of data

12, 42, 61, 41

61-12 = 49

The range is 49

- In a set of N values, the amount by which a value x_i differs from the mean $\bar{x}$ is called the **deviation from the mean**: $x_i - \bar{x}$

- The average of the absolute values of the mean deviations is called the **mean absolute deviation.**

$$\frac{\sum_{i=1}^{n} |x_i - \bar{x}|}{n}$$

Example:

For the data set 12, 16, 54, 42

$$\text{the mean } \bar{x} = \frac{12+16+54+42}{4} = 31$$

The mean absolute deviation

$$\frac{|12-31|+|16-31|+|54-31|+|42-31|}{4} = \frac{68}{4} = 17$$

The average of the squares of the deviations from the mean is the **variance** (S^2). To compute the **standard deviation** (S), take the square root of the variance. Standard deviation is the most common measure of dispersion. It shows how data is distributed or clustered and the variation about the mean.

$$\upsilon = \frac{\sum_{i=1}^{n} (x_i - \bar{x})^2}{n}$$

Standard deviation $\sigma = \sqrt{\upsilon}$

Example:

For the set of 12, 16, 54, 42 determine the standard deviation.

$$\upsilon = \frac{(12-31)^2 + (16-31)^2 + (54-31)^2 + (42-31)^2}{4} = 309$$

standard deviation $\sigma = \sqrt{\upsilon} = \sqrt{309} \approx 17.58$

7.5 Standard Deviation and the Normal Distribution Curve

The distribution of data represented by the normal curve is called normal distribution.

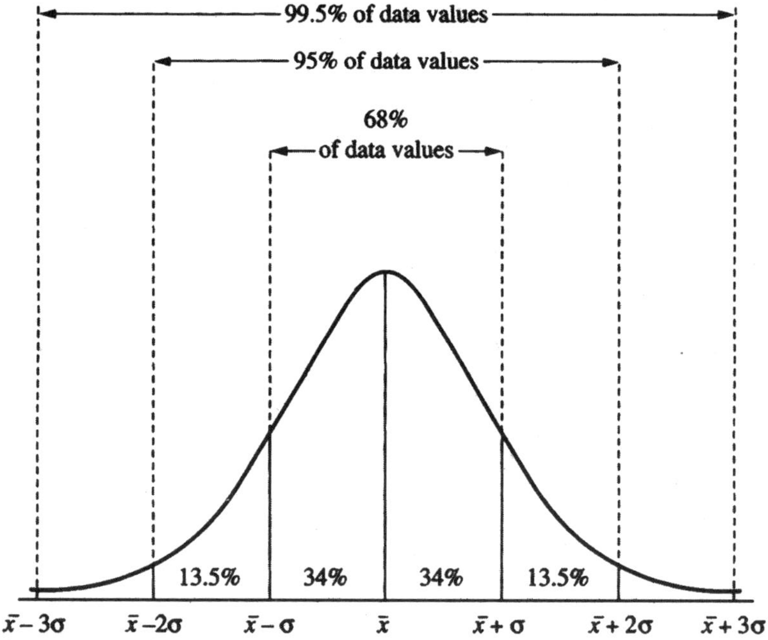

The central point on the graph is the mean $\bar{x}$.

The right and left sides reveal the amount of deviation from the mean. They are called extreme points since they are farthest from the mean. In a normal distribution, 68% of the data lie within the center of the distribution or between points $\overline{x} - \sigma$ and $\overline{x} + \sigma$, that is, within one standard deviation from the mean.

7.6 Working with Sets of Data

How to group a set of data in a frequency table and calculate the standard deviation:

1. Arrange the variables (x_i) and list them in the first column of a table. Then do the same for the frequencies (f_i) and place them in the second column.

2. Calculate the mean: $\dfrac{\sum x_i f_i}{\sum f_i}$

3. Calculate the variance.

Find:

a. The deviation of each data measure from the mean $x_i - \overline{x}$

b. The squares of the mean deviations $(x_i - \overline{x})^2$

c. The products $f_i(x_i - \overline{x})^2$ and their sum

d. Calculate the standard deviation, which is the square root of variance.

Example: Given the measures 6, 2, 6, 3, 11, 6, 0, 1, 7, 3

a) Find the standard deviation, to the nearest hundredth.

b) Determine the number of measures that are within one standard deviation of the mean.

Create a table

x_i	f_i	$x_i \cdot f_i$	$x_i - \overline{x}$	$(x_i - \overline{x})^2$	$f_i(x_i - \overline{x})^2$
0	1	0	0- 4.5 = -4.50	20.25	20.25
1	1	1	1- 4.5 = -3.50	12.25	12.25
2	1	2	2- 4.5 = -2.50	6.25	6.25
3	2	6	3- 4.5 = -1.50	2.25	4.50
6	3	18	6- 4.5 = 1.50	2.25	6.75
7	1	7	7- 4.5 = 2.50	6.25	6.25
11	1	11	11-4.5= 6.50	42.25	42.25
Total	10	45			98.50

$$\overline{x} = \frac{\sum x_i f_i}{\sum f} = \frac{45}{10} = 4.5$$

$$\upsilon = \frac{98.50}{10} = 9.85$$

$$\sigma = \sqrt{\upsilon} = \sqrt{9.85} \approx 3.14$$

We want to know how many measures are
between 4.5 +3.14 = 7.64 and 4.5- 3.14 = 1.36

Four of the measures, namely 2,3,6,7 are
between 1.36 and 7.64

The sum of their frequencies is 1+2+3+1= 7 ← Answer

7.7 Commonly Asked Questions: Statistics

1) **Q:** What is the purpose of using the Greek letter Σ (sigma) for naming the sum?

A: The letter Σ represents in Greek the first letter of the word sum. This symbol stands for any number of identical (equal) elements and therefore, the mathematical expression is significantly simplified.

For example: $\sum_{i=1}^{4} 2^i$ simply means the sum of the values of 2^i, as i increases from 1 to 4. In this case, 1 is called the lower limit or the starting value of i and 4 is called the upper limit, which is the ending value of i. (i is called the index variable.)

$$\sum_{i=1}^{4} 2^i = 2^1 + 2^2 + 2^3 + 2^4$$

2) **Q:** What is the advantage of a histogram over other types of graphs?

A: When making a statistical analysis, histograms clearly show the results in a visual form that everyone easily understands.

3) **Q:** If frequency in fact expresses quantity, why is it still referred to as frequency?

A: In many statistical problems, frequency is a number that is the same as the quantity of a given thing (*for example,* the number of students that it takes 10 minutes to get to school). However, in many other problems, the frequency of a given result, x_i , does not refer to a quantity of concrete things (*for example*: how often a horse in lane one wins the race). Frequency is therefore a better term in general for statistical problems.

5) Q: Why is the difference between x_i *and* $\overline{x}$, that is $(x_i - \overline{x})$, squared in the formulas of variance and standard deviation?

A: The difference between any given result, x_i, and the mean, $\overline{x}$, can be negative or positive. Squaring makes the result positive. This allows us to add up the sizes of the variations without being concerned with the direction, positive or negative, in which the variation occurs. If we did not square, negative and positive differences would tend to cancel each other out.

8 CHAPTER

PROBABILITY

Probability is the branch of mathematics in which a value is given to the chance of an event happening. This numerical value indicates how likely it is that the event will occur.
Probability is used every day in the most various fields, from product safety and economics to politics and insurance.

8.1 Basic Concepts

outcome — a result of a given act.

sample space — the set of all possible outcomes for a given act. For example, for the act of tossing a coin, we might define the sample space as

{*heads, tails, an invalid toss (stuck in the mud)*}.

event — a subset of the sample space for which we wish to define the probability. For example, we may wish to determine the probability of the event "heads," or perhaps, the probability of the event "a valid toss," which would be the subset {heads, tails}. In theoretical probability, however, we usually ignore things like invalid tosses and assume that the coin is fair and unbiased. In what follows, then, the *sample space* for a coin toss will be {heads, tails}, and possible *events* will be "heads," "tails," "either heads or tails" (which will have a probability of 1), and "neither heads nor tails" (which will have a probability of 0).

independent event — if the result of an action, the event B, does not affect at all the probability of the event A, the result of another action, then the event A is called independent.

For example, if we toss two coins, the results of the two tosses are independent.

compound event — the combination of two or more independent events is a compound event. For example, the events of 'rolling a four with a fair die' and 'rolling an even number with a second fair die' can be seen as a compound event, since each roll is independent of the other.

$$probability\ of\ event = \frac{number\ of\ \ favorable\ outcomes}{number\ of\ \ possible\ outcomes}$$

$$P(E) = \frac{n\,(E)}{n\,(S)}$$

Examples:

1. What is the probability that you roll an even number with a die?

A die has only 6 numbers. Only 3 of them are even (2,4,6).

$P(E) = \frac{3}{6} = \frac{1}{2}$ Answer: $P(E) = \frac{1}{2}$

2. If you toss a coin, what is the probability that it will come up heads? Answer: $P(E) = \frac{1}{2}$

8.1.1 The Probability of Certainty

Some outcomes are always certain. In this case, the number of ways that an event can occur is equal to the number of possible outcomes. Therefore, P(E) =1 and P(certainty)=1

For example, if in a box there are four apples and nothing else, if something is taken out of the box, the probability that it will be an apple is P(apple) = 1.

8.1.2 The Probability of Impossibility

Sometimes, no favorable outcomes may occur.

Therefore, P(impossibility) = 0

For example, if in the box there are only 4 plums, the probability that an apple will be taken out of the box is P(apple) = 0

8.1.3 Values for Probabilities

The probability that any event will occur is between 0 and 1 inclusive: $0 \le P(E) \le 1$

The sum of the probabilities of all possible outcomes for any sample space must always equal 1.

For example, in tossing a coin,

$$P(S) = P(\text{head}) + P(\text{tail}) = \frac{1}{2} + \frac{1}{2} = 1$$

If in a box there are three colored balls, 1 red, 1 yellow, and 1 green, and we take 3 balls out of the box,

$$P(S) = P(\text{red}) + P(\text{yellow}) + P(\text{green}) = \frac{1}{3} + \frac{1}{3} + \frac{1}{3} = 1$$

8.2 The Probability of (NOT A)

The event NOT A, represented $\bar{A}$, is the set of outcomes that are not equivalent to the event A.

For example, if event A = "It is raining"

then event $\bar{A}$ = "It is not raining."

The probability of event A = $\frac{1}{2}$

The probability of event Ā = $\frac{1}{2}$

The sum of the probabilities P(A) + P(Ā) = $\frac{1}{2} + \frac{1}{2} = 1$

Always P(A) + P(Ā) = 1 or P(A) = 1 - P(Ā)

8.3 Probability involving OR (Addition of Probability)

In probability problems involving two (or more) events, the event may or may not have outcomes that count as successful for both events. If events A and B have no successful outcomes in common and are independents events, then

$$P(A \vee B) = P(A) + P(B) \quad \text{or} \quad P(A \text{ or } B) = P(A) + P(B)$$

Example: In a toy box there are 30 balls: 10 red, 5 blue, and 15 white. What is the probability that a blue or a red ball will be taken out of a box? (Note that it is impossible to take both a blue and a red ball at once.)

Probability of red $P(R) = \frac{10}{30} = \frac{1}{3}$

Probability of blue $P(B) = \frac{5}{30} = \frac{1}{6}$

Probability of a red or a blue ball $P(A \text{ } or \text{ } B) = \frac{1}{3} + \frac{1}{6} = \frac{1}{2}$

8.4 Probability involving AND (Multiplication of Probability)

Multiplying the probability that event A will occur by the probability that event B will occur, results in the probability that events A and B will both occur, provided A and B are independent events.

$P(A \wedge B) = P(A) \cdot P(B)$ or $P(A \text{ and } B) = P(A) \cdot P(B)$

Example:

The probability of tossing a fair coin two times and getting two heads (H) is the product of the probability of obtaining a head on each of the two tosses.

$$P = (H \text{ and } H) = \frac{1}{2} \cdot \frac{1}{2} = \frac{1}{4}$$

8.5 A Rule for the Probability of (A or B)

If the events A and B have successful outcomes in common,

$P(A \text{ or } B) = P(A) + P(B) - P(A \text{ and } B)$

Example:

In your hand you hold five cards: the 5 of diamonds, the 2 of clubs, the 2 of diamonds, the 2 of spades, and the queen of spades. Your opponent will draw one card from your hand and needs either a 2 or any card from the diamonds suit. Find the probability of P (2 or diamonds).

Solution:

The probability that the opponent will draw a 2 is $P(2) = \frac{3}{5}$

The probability that the opponent will draw a diamond

$$\text{is P(diamond)} = \frac{2}{5}$$

But, one card, the fire cards: 2 of diamonds, is counted as a successful outcome in either case, and if we simply added the probabilities, we would be counting that card twice. In other words, this card satisfies the condition "2 and diamonds."

$$\text{So P(2 and diamonds)} = \frac{1}{5}$$

P(2 or diamonds) = P(2) + P(diamonds) - P(2 and diamonds) =

$$= \frac{3}{5} + \frac{2}{5} - \frac{1}{5} = \frac{4}{5}$$

If the events A and B have *no* successful outcomes in common,

P(A and B) = 0, and P(A or B) = P(A) + P(B).

8.6 Basic Formulas of Permutations

A permutation is an arrangement of a number of things in a definite order. The notation used for the number of possible permutations *P* of *r* things chosen from *n* things is: ${}_nP_r$

When the things are all different :

if $r = n$ $\quad {}_nP_n = n(n-1)(n-2)(n-3)....3\cdot2\cdot1$ or ${}_nP_n = n!$

Where n! ("n factorial") = $n...3\cdot2\cdot1$

Examples:

1. In how many ways can the letters A, B, and C be arranged if all letters are to be used each time and no letter is to be used more than once?

$_3P_3 = 3! = 3{\cdot}2{\cdot}1 = 6$ Answer: 6 ways

self –check ABC, ACB, BAC, BCA, CAB, CBA

if $r < n$ $_nP_r = n(n-1)(n-2)(n-3)....(n-r+1)$

2. The expansion of $_nP_r$ has exactly r factors. How many arrangements of two flags can be made from 6 flags of different colors?

n=6; r=2 $_6P_2 = 6 \cdot 5 = 30$ Answer: 30

When not all things are different:

In this case, the number of possible arrangements is reduced when the set of items includes a subset of identical items.
The number of ways to arrange *n* things in which

p things are alike is $\dfrac{n!}{p!}$

When *p* things are alike and *q* things are alike,

the formula is $\dfrac{n!}{p!q!}$

Example:

How many different arrangements are possible using all the letters of the word MARMALADE?

In all there are 9 letters.
Of identical items we have 3 A's and 2 M's.

In all there are 9 letters. Of alike letters there are 3 A's and 2 M's

$$\frac{9!}{3!2!} = 30{,}240$$

There are 30,240 arrangements possible.

8.7 Combinations

There are ten (n) different items in a box. We need to take two (r) items. How many different pairs can we take from the ten? This type of problem is a classic example of combinations.

For combinations, the arrangement of the items is not important. In general, for counting numbers *n* and *r*, where $r \leq n$, the number of combinations of n things, taken *r* at a time, is found by using the formula

$$_{n}C_{r} = \frac{_{n}P_{r}}{r!}$$

In our case, n=10; r=2 $\quad {}_{10}C_{2} = \frac{_{10}P_{2}}{2!} = \frac{10 \cdot 9}{1 \cdot 2} = 45$

Answer: 45 ways

For example, we have four letters : A,B,C, D. How many combinations can we make if n=4 and r=2?

$$_{4}C_{2} = \frac{_{4}P_{2}}{2!} = \frac{4 \cdot 3}{1 \cdot 2} = 6$$

<u>self-check</u> A,B A,C A,D B,C B,D C,D – 6 combinations

8.8 The Formula of Bernoulli

Let an independent trial be performed *n* times in which the probability of the event *A* is constant and equal to *p*. It follows that the probability of the failure of the event *A* to occur is also constant and equal to $q = 1 - p$.

The probability that the event A will occur exactly r times in n trials is given by the formula

$$P_n(r) = {}_nC_r p^r q^{n-r}$$

This formula is called the Bernoulli Formula.

Example:

The probability that the consumption of gasoline in a car in the course of a single day will not exceed the average consumption is equal to $p = 0.75$. Find the probability that, in the next six days, the car will not exceed the average consumption four days in a row.

Solution:

The probability of normal consumption of gasoline on each of the six days is constant and equal to $p = 0.75$. It follows that the possibility of exceeding average consumption on each day is also constant and equal to $q = 1 - 0.75 = 0.25$.

The desired probability can be calculated using the Bernoulli Formula:

$$P_6(4) = {}_6C_4 p^4 q^2 = \frac{6 \cdot 5}{1 \cdot 2}(0.75)^4 \cdot (0.25)^2 = 0.30$$

8.9 Probability Problems

Example 1: Mr. Fox dialed his sister's phone number. Since he forgot the last digit, he decided to dial at random. What is the probability that the last digit dialed was correct?

- Mr. Fox could dial any of the ten digits. Therefore, the number of possible outcomes is equal to 10.

Number of favorable outcomes is =1. $P(E)=\frac{1}{10}$

Example 2: Mr. Fox dialed a number forgetting what the last two digits were. He only knew that the last 2 digits were different and dialed it at random. What is the probability that the two digits dialed are correct?

- Mr. Fox could dial only so many digits as there are permutations for the 10 digits by 2.

  ${}_{10}P_2 = 10 \cdot 9 = 90$ therefore, the number of possible outcome is equal to 90. Number of favorable outcomes is equal to 1.
  $P(E)=\frac{1}{90}$

Example 3:

Mrs. Buckman has 7 tapes with rock and 5 tapes with classical music. What is the probability that the first tape is one with rock and the second one with classical music?

- The probability that the 1st tape is with rock is equal to $P(E_1)=\frac{7}{12}$

  The probability that the 2nd tape is with classical music is equal to $P(E_2)=\frac{5}{12}$

  The probability that the 1st tape is one with rock and the second one with classical music is:

$$P(E_1 \ and \ E_2) = P(E_1)\cdot P(E_2) = \left(\frac{7}{12}\right)\left(\frac{5}{12}\right) = \frac{35}{144} \approx 0.243$$

8.10 Commonly Asked Questions: Probability

1) **Q:** Are there any real life problems that involve probabilities of 0 and 1?

A: There are many situations that involve such probabilities.

For example, the chance that the sun will rise tomorrow or that the ball will always fall to the ground is equal to 1. Similarly, the probability of winning a lottery without buying a lottery ticket is 0. However, the main practical application of mathematical probability theory is in product safety planning.

2) **Q:** Why is combinatorics used in the theory of probability?

A: Permutations and combinatorics allows us to determine the number of combinations that can be made from elements of any nature. It is often necessary to determine the total number of possible outcomes, in order to determine probability.

3) **Q:** Can probability be measured in terms of percentage?

A: It is possible, but not recommended.

4) **Q:** What is the difference between $A \wedge B$ and $A \cap B$?

A: $A \wedge B$ belongs to logic and expresses the operation of conjunction. $A \cap B$ indicates the elements in the intersection of the two sets

APPENDIX 1: Table of Measures

	Metric Units	*Customary units*
LENGTH	1millimeter(mm)=0.001meters(mm)	1 foot (ft) = 12 inches (in)
	1centimeter (cm) = 0.01 meters	1 yard (yd) = 36 inches
	1decimeter (dm) = 0.1 meters	1 yard = 3 feet
	1decameter (dam)=10 meters	1 mile (mi) = 5,280 feet
	1hectometer (hm)=100 meters	
	1kilometer (km =1,000 meters	
MASS	1milligram (mg) = 0.001grams(g)	1 pound(lb) = 16 ounces(oz)
	1centigram (cg) = 0.01grams	1ton (T) = 2000 pounds
	1decigram (dg) = 0.1 grams	
	1decagram (dag) = 10 grams	
	1hectogram (hg) = 100 grams	
	1kilogram (kg) = 1,000 grams	
VOLUME	1milliliter (ml) = 0.001 liters (l)	1cup (c) = 8 fluid ounces (oz)
	1centiliter (cl) = 0.01 liters	1pint (pt) = 2 cups
	1deciliter (dl) = 0.1 liter	1quart (qt) = 2 pints
	1decaliter (dal) = 10 liters	1quart = 4 cups
	1hectoliter (hl) = 100 liters	1gallon (gal) = 4 quarts
	1kiloliter (kl) = 1,000 liters	
AREA	1square centimeter (cm^2) = =100 sq. millimeters (mm^2)	1square foot (ft^2)=144 sq .inches (in^2)
	1square meter (m^2) = =10,000 sq. centimeters	1square yard (yd^2) = 9 sq. feet
	1hectare (ha) = 10,000 sq. meters	1acre = 43,560 square feet
	square kilometer (km^2) = =1,000,000 sq. meters	1square mile (mi^2) = 460 acres
TIME		1 minute (min) = 60 seconds(s)
		1 hour (h) = 60 minutes
		1 day (d) = 24 hours
		1 week (wk) = 7 days
		1 year (y) = 12 months
		1 year = 365 days
		1 century (c) = 100 years

Conversion Factors from the English System to the Metric System

Length	1 inch = 2.54 centimeters
	1 foot = 0.305 meters
	1 yard = 0.914 meters
	1 mile = 1.61 kilometers
Liquid Measure	1 fluid ounce = 29.6 millimeters
	1 pint = 0.473 liters
	1 quart = 0.946 liters
	1 gallon = 3.78 liters
Mass	1 ounce = 22.4 grams
	1 pound = 454 grams
Area	1 square inch (sq. in.) = 6.45 sq. centimeters (cm^2)
	1 square foot (sq. ft.) = 929 sq. centimeters
	1 square yard (sq. yd.) = 0.836 sq. meters (m^2)
	1 square mile (sq. mi.) = 2.59 sq. kilometers (km^2)
Volume	1 cubic inch (cu. in.) = 16.4 cubic centimeters (cm^3)
	1 cubic foot (cu. ft.) = 0.0283 cubic meters (m^3)
	1 cubic yard (cu. in.) = 0.765 cubic meters

APPENDIX 2:

Greek Alphabet

Α α	alpha
Β β	beta
Γ γ	gamma
Δ δ	delta
Ε ε	epsilon
Ζ ζ	zeta
Η η	eta
Θ θ	theta
Ι ι	iota
Κ κ	kappa
Λ λ	lambda
Μ μ	mu
Νν	nu
Ξ ξ	xi
Οο	omicron
Ππ	pi
Ρρ	rho
Σσ	sigma
Ττ	tau
Υυ	upsilon
Φφ	phi
Χχ	chi
Ψψ	psi
Ωω	omega

Index

D

E